Dr. Brown speaks on behal~~~~~~~~~~~~~~~~~~~~~~~ ...~~ are not adequately trained to express in writing their own encounters with the supernatural power of God. With the skill of a surgeon, Dr. Brown takes the sword of the Spirit to the crippling cancer of cessationist doctrine that has, for so long, paralyzed the Body of Christ from walking in the fullness of the Holy Spirit's anointing. Along with personal, scriptural, and historical examples, Dr. Brown presents an impelling case for the reality of the Holy Spirit's activity in the Church today. May the message of this book be amplified a million fold and thereby drown out the voice of those, who like the spies of old, kept God's people from entering into all that He had promised them. Buy a copy for yourself, your friend and your pastor. They'll thank you for it!

- DAVID RAVENHILL
AUTHOR OF *How to Survive the Anointing*

I thank God for this biblically-robust, pastorally-sensitive, historically-informed, and graciously-articulated account of the work of the Holy Spirit in the church of Jesus Christ. Michael Brown is a model for us all of how one can be theologically rigorous and a fair-minded gentleman at the same time. His arguments are clear and, in my opinion, persuasive, and will contribute greatly not only to deeper clarity on this important topic but also to increased unity in the body of Christ.

- SAM STORMS, PH.D.,
BRIDGEWAY CHURCH, OKLAHOMA CITY, OK,
AUTHOR OF *Signs of the Spirit:
An Interpretation of Jonathan Edwards's
"Religious Affections"*

Dr. Michael Brown's Authentic Fire puts the brakes on John MacArthur's crusade against charismatics with irrefutable logic, extraordinary insight, Christ-like graciousness, and an undisputable handling of Scripture. This is the definitive book to give to anyone who asks, "Is John MacArthur's denunciation of charismatic Christians fair and accurate?"

- FRANK VIOLA,
AUTHOR OF *Pouring Holy Water on Strange Fire* AND
God's Favorite Place on Earth

Michael Brown writes with clarity and courtesy as he confronts one of the most explosive issues among all those who uphold the Bible as the plumb line of truth. Dr. Brown convincingly combines faithful exegesis, seasoned insight, and extensive research to show that the resurrected Christ continues to "present Himself alive...by many convincing proofs." He points us to a rock-solid faith in God's inerrant Word and invites us to a Christ-centered life that is animated by His life-giving Spirit.

- DAVID SHIBLEY,
FOUNDER AND WORLD REPRESENTATIVE FOR
Global Advance

Michael Brown demolishes the weak arguments outlined in John MacArthur's Strange Fire book and conference. He does so robustly but without resorting to divisive or schismatic language. Graciously Brown invites cessationists to understand the biblical reasons why charismatics believe what we do. Charismatics are also reminded that we do need to be more discerning as there are indeed unhelpful extremes in our movement. This book will help you think through these issues. It will fill charismatics with renewed confidence to boldly follow our convictions. It should also help cessationists to appreciate that the Charismatic movement does have something to teach the broader Church, even as we also have much to learn from others.

- DR. ADRIAN WARNOCK,
AUTHOR AND BLOGGER AT **adrianwarnock.com**

AUTHENTIC
FIRE

Michael L. Brown, PhD

**CREATION
HOUSE**

AUTHENTIC FIRE by Michael Brown
Published by Creation House
A Charisma Media Company
600 Rinehart Road
Lake Mary, Florida 32746
www.charismamedia.com

Unless otherwise noted, all Scripture quotations are from the Holy Bible, English Standard Version. Copyright © 2001 by Crossway Bibles, a division of Good News Publishers. Used by permission.

Scripture quotations marked AMP are from the Amplified Bible. Old Testament copyright © 1965, 1987 by the Zondervan Corporation. The Amplified New Testament copyright © 1954, 1958, 1987 by the Lockman Foundation. Used by permission.

Scripture quotations marked KJV are from the King James Version of the Bible.

Scripture quotations marked NAS are from the New American Standard Bible. Copyright © 1960, 1962, 1963, 1968, 1971, 1972, 1973, 1975, 1977, 1995 by The Lockman Foundation. Used by permission. (www.Lockman.org)

Scripture quotations marked NET are from the New English Translation, copyright © 1996-2006 by Biblical Studies Press, LLC. http://netbible.com. All rights reserved. This material is available in its entirety as a free download or online use at http://netbible.org/.

Scripture quotations marked NIV are from the Holy Bible, New International Version. Copyright © 1973, 1978, 1984, International Bible Society. Used by permission.

Scripture quotations marked NJV are from the New Jewish Version, copyright © 1985 by Jewish Publication Society. All rights reserved.

Scripture quotations marked NLT are from the Holy Bible, New Living Translation, copyright © 1996, 2004, 2007. Used by permission of Tyndale House Publishers, Inc., Wheaton, IL 60189. All rights reserved.

Scripture quotations marked THE MESSAGE are from *The Message: The Bible in Contemporary English*, copyright © 1993, 1994, 1995, 1996, 2000, 2001, 2002. Used by permission of NavPress Publishing Group.

Previously published by Excel Publishers, copyright © 2014, ISBN 978-1-62999-005-7

All emphasis in scripture citations is the author's.

Design Director: Justin Evans

Visit the author's website: www.AskDrBrown.org.

Library of Congress Cataloging-in-Publication Data: 2015938281
International Standard Book Number: 978-1-62998-455-1
E-book International Standard Book Number: 978-1-62998-456-8

20 21 22 23 24 — 12 11 10 9 8
Printed in the United States of America

Contents

PREFACE

F ive days a week, as I do my live, two-hour radio broad- cast, I hear the voice of John MacArthur in my ears, and it is a voice I enjoy hearing. As local radio stations are playing their own ads or announcements during the one-minute or two- minute breaks during the show, I hear a feed from the main satellite network, and it often repeats the same clips over and again, with Pastor MacArthur's one-minute mini-messages be- ing prominently featured.

I can tell you honestly that during the most intense moments of the Strange Fire controversy, or after reading what I consid- ered to be outlandish statements in the *Strange Fire* book, I have never been agitated in the least when hearing my elder brother's voice. And, when I am able to focus on what he is saying (since those short breaks during live radio are often quite busy), I have almost always enjoyed and affirmed his message.

So, this book is not written out of frustration, nor do I have an axe to grind, nor I am trying to win an argument, nor do I have an allegiance to a particular party or group that would color my sentiments. Instead, I have written this book with peo- ple like Jason in mind. He is in his mid-to-late thirties and has been seriously committed to the Lord the last few years. He posted this on Facebook in the immediate aftermath of the Strange Fire conference, shortly before my interview with Phil Johnson, John MacArthur's editor:

> I've been listening to [Pastor] MacArthur in the morn- ing on my way to work and Dr. Brown's radio show at

night for a while now. Please keep this in mind, both Dr. Brown and MacArthur have been the top two Christian leaders in helping me come to Christ and helping me to not fall away by reminding me to keep my focus on Jesus. Dr. Brown has helped me a great deal with apologetics as well and learning the balance between legalism and grace. This is a dicey topic that in the long run has potential to reveal a greater truth and hopefully help Christians to become even more unified. I'm more interested in that than any kind of one upsmanship, and I know for sure that Dr. Brown and I would assume that [Pastor] MacArthur are too.

A woman emailed me to let me know that she was a monthly supporter of my ministry and a member of Pastor MacArthur's church, encouraging me to keep addressing these issues while expressing love and respect for both of us. And, to be sure, every day as I go on the air and talk about relevant issues, I'm aware that Dr. MacArthur is heard on these same stations (plus many more), that he has been on the radio far longer than I, and that I have a responsibility to the larger listening audience, not wanting to tear down but to build up. It is in that spirit that this book has been written, and so it is invitation as much as it is exhortation.

Authentic Fire is not meant to be a rebuttal of *Strange Fire* at every point. Instead, while interacting at times with material from the book and conference, and while correcting what I believe to be serious errors and misstatements, the book is more of a positive response to *Strange Fire*. So it is my hope that *Authentic Fire* will serve a lasting, worthwhile purpose even for those who will never read *Strange Fire*.

But before you dive into *Authentic Fire*, allow me to explain the origins of this book. In June of this year (2013), callers began to ask me if I had heard about the Strange Fire conference, which I had not, and it was with some degree of shock that I watched the promotional material and read the pre-conference quotes. As a result, I felt prompted to write a series of articles that addressed the controversies head on, beginning June 20,[1] respectfully appealing to Pastor MacArthur to tone down his charges while appealing publicly and privately for a face to face meeting to discuss things together with other leaders. (That has not yet happened but I do hope it will in the not too distant future.)

Along the way, I learned that he would be releasing a book as well, but writing my own book in response to his was the last thing on my mind, given the major writing deadlines I was already under, not to mention a fairly intense ministry schedule. Interestingly, when I was sent an Advanced Reader's Copy of the book, Randy, one of my staff members who opens my packages, emailed me when it arrived on October 4th (I was out of state), saying, **"I suspect another *Real Kosher Jesus* miraculous writing assignment coming!"** He was referring to something that happened last year when my good friend and frequent debating partner, Rabbi Shmuley Boteach, was about to publish his book *Kosher Jesus* and I got burdened to write a full-length response (also a stand-alone, Jewish evangelism tool) called *The Real Kosher Jesus*. God gave me grace to write the bulk of the book in three weeks, and within ten weeks of writing the first words of the book, the published version was sitting on my desk, to me a publishing miracle.

Would the same thing happen with *Strange Fire*? In my mind, it couldn't, although I didn't dismiss the email out of hand, wondering if perhaps I would write a thirty-fifty page rebuttal, releasing it quickly as an e-book. But then something happened. The day before the Strange Fire conference began, I felt stirred to write one last article, which went viral (for details, see Chapter One). This only added to the fact that somehow, through my past articles and the radio show, I had emerged in the eyes of many as a leading voice challenging Strange Fire. (In fact, some of Pastor MacArthur's team had replied to my previous articles on his Grace to You website or elsewhere, and some of my concerns were respectfully addressed at the conference in one of Phil Johnson's sessions.)

The first day of the conference (one month ago today), I was flooded with questions via email and social media, asking if I was going to write a book in response, and a publisher contacted me as well, wanting to push out an e-book quickly if I could write one quickly. More importantly, I felt the Lord wanted me to do so, and virtually overnight, this book was born. (When I speak of feeling stirred or burdened to write or say that I felt the Lord wanted me to do something, I'm simply sharing my perspective, not claiming divine inspiration. I imagine that Pastor MacArthur felt the Lord wanted him to do what he did, feeling a burden to address things that deeply grieved him.)

Because I had to finish editing work on another manuscript first, I was not able to get to this book until October 24th, after which, by God's amazing grace, I was able to write the entire manuscript in roughly two weeks' time, doing the editing and annotating the third week. My great appreciation to the team at Charisma Media for helping to bring this to completion in such a short period of time. In a period of five-six weeks, this book went from being birthed in writing to being made available to the general public.

My deep appreciation to my colleague at FIRE School of Ministry, Prof. Steve Alt, who carefully proofread the manuscript as soon as it was finished. Whatever errors remain are entirely mine. He also contributed an appendix responding to Pastor Tom Pennington's presentation on cessationism at Strange Fire. My appreciation is also due to: Prof. Craig Keener for writing an appendix specifically for *Authentic Fire*; Dr. Sam Storms for allowing me to use his recent, full-length blog article on prophecy today; Rev. David Shibley, for providing a statement from a world missions perspective; John Lambert, one of our ministry school grads, now with the US Center for World Mission, for reviewing some of the relevant demographic surveys; Dr. Adrian Warnock, for allowing the generous use of his material in Chapter Nine of this book (see there for details) as well as for reading this manuscript carefully; Prof. Jon Ruthven, for pointing me to some key references; Frank Viola, for useful input on the manuscript and for making available to me his critique of *Charismatic Chaos* and *Strange Fire*; and Andrew Wilson, from the UK-based ThinkTheology blog, for encouraging the use of his material in Appendix 3. I also acknowledge with appreciation Zondervan Publishers for allowing me to use excerpts from my book *Israel's Divine Healer*, as well to Destiny Image for allowing me to quote extensively from a number of my books published with them. They greatly encouraged me as well to get this book out.

Let me finally make three brief notes about terminology and citations: First, when I speak of "charismatics" in general,

I'm referring to all professing Christians who believe in the ongoing manifestation of the New Testament charismatic gifts (such as prophecy, tongues, and healing), although not all believe in contemporary apostles and prophets. When I distinguish between Pentecostals and charismatics, the former refers to members of Pentecostal churches (such as the Assemblies of God or the Church of God in Christ), the latter to those outside of such churches (which would therefore include charismatic members of traditionally non-charismatic denominations, as well as other movements like the Vineyard). Second, in recent months, I have increased the call for teachers and preachers and professors and Bible translators to stop using the name "James" in place of "Jacob" (which is what the Greek says throughout the New Testament),[2] even encouraging the recovery of "Judah" for "Jude" as well (yes, this certainly makes a difference!). So, throughout the book, although hardly relevant to the larger issues at hand, I use "Jacob" with "James" in parentheses. Third, although I was tempted to provide massive documentation for all controversial points in the endnotes, both the nature of this book and the publishing schedule ruled against that, and so, except for a sections, the annotation is meant to be practical and representative. Also, for the benefit of e-book readers and to make things more accessible in today's digital age, whenever possible, I cited online versions of relevant texts (all of them were available as of the writing of this Preface).

From my heart, I thank our incredible ministry team for their faithful and loving support and encouragement, our prayer warriors for holding up my hands up during these very intense three weeks, and Nancy, my bride of thirty-seven years, for allowing me to focus on getting this project done. My prayer is that the Lord Jesus, John MacArthur's Savior as well as mine, would be glorified through this book, that His people would be built up and unified, and that together, we would touch a dying world in the life and power of the Spirit.

November 16, 2013 (en route to Shanghai, China)

Endnotes

[1]http://www.charismanews.com/opinion/in-the-line-of
-fire/39944-john-macarthur-strange-fire-and-blasphemy
-of-the-spirit; http://www.charismanews.com/opinion/in-the
-line-of-fire/40118-ap-appeal-to-john-macarthur-to-embrace
-god-s-true-fire; http://www.charismanews.com/opinion/in-the-
line-of-fire/40288-r-c-sproul-false-prophecies-and-the
-word-of-god; http://www.charismanews.com/opinion/in
-the-line-of-fire/40327-lack-of-fire-the-true-crisis-in-the
-contemporary-charismatic-church; http://www.charismanews
.com/opinion/in-the-line-of-fire/40415-time-to-talk-not
-fight-a-response-to-john-macarthur-s-ministry; http://www
.charismanews.com/opinion/in-the-line-of-fire/40503-is
-african-charismatic-christianity-a-counterfeit; http://www
.charismanews.com/opinion/in-the-line-of-fire/40758-why-we
-need-the-manifest-presence-of-god; http://www.charismanews
.com/opinion/in-the-line-of-fire/41371-a-final-appeal-to-pastor
-john-macarthur-on-the-eve-of-his-strange-fire-conference;
http://www.charismanews.com/opinion/in-the-line-of
-fire/41529-be-careful-about-what-you-call-a-different-gospel ;
http://www.charismanews.com/opinion/in-the-line-of
-fire/41494-let-s-not-bite-and-devour-one-another

[2]See http://www.charismanews.com/opinion/38591-recovering
-the-lost-letter-of-jacob.

CHAPTER ONE

A "COLLECTIVE WAR" AGAINST CHARISMATICS

It is with good reason that pastors and leaders who differ with Dr. John MacArthur on the issue of the Charismatic Movement do so with deference and respect, since his very substantial and beneficial contribution to the Church in this generation is undeniable. How many pastors have written an expository commentary on every book of the New Testament? How many have pointed so clearly to Jesus Christ, crucified, buried, risen, ascended, and Lord of all? How many have refused to concede even the tiniest point of biblical truth when pressed by the secular media? And how many have achieved the eminent status he has over so many years as a mega-church pastor without a credible report of a major scandal? As I wrote in my first article addressing the Strange Fire conference back in June, 2013, "if we had more leaders like John MacArthur, the Church and the world would be in much better shape."[1]

I stand by those words today, and it is with respect and honor to an elder brother in the Lord that I write this book.[2] In fact, it is because of the scope of his influence that I have written *Authentic Fire*, since the Strange Fire conference (which took place in October, 2013) and *Strange Fire* book (which is being released as I do the final edit of this book) have caused no small stir.[3]

In short, Pastor MacArthur's criticisms of the Charismatic Movement are inaccurate, unhelpful, often harshly judgmental, sometimes without scriptural support, and frequently divisive in the negative sense of the word. Where he rightly points out some of the most glaring and serious faults in the Charismatic Movement, I add my "Amen," having addressed these same abuses for many years myself. (See below, Chapter Two.) But when he damns millions of godly believers, demeans the real work of the Spirit, accuses true worshipers of blaspheming the Spirit, and calls for an all-out war against the Charismatic Movement, a strong corrective is needed, along with a positive statement of the truth of the matter. That is the purpose of this book.

Pastor MacArthur's Call for a "Collective War" against Charismatics

Even before the Strange Fire conference, Pastor MacArthur had stated that: "The Charismatic Movement is largely the reason the church is in the mess that it's in today. In virtually every area where church life is unbiblical, you can attribute it to the Charismatic Movement... bad theology, superficial worship, ego, prosperity gospel, personality elevation, all of that comes out of the Charismatic Movement."[4] He added, "...its theology is bad, it is unbiblical, it is aberrant, it is destructive to people because it promises them what it can't deliver. And then God gets blamed when it doesn't come. It is a very destructive movement, and has always been."[5]

He actually claimed that charismatics are blaspheming the Spirit and attributing "to the Holy Spirit even the work of Satan."

Yes, in his view, charismatics have "stolen the Holy Spirit and created a golden calf and they are dancing around the golden calf as if it is the Holy Spirit...The charismatic version of the Holy Spirit is that golden calf...around which they dance with their dishonoring exercises."[6] These are very serious charges, and they were hardly moderated at the conference or in the book.

Within a few short pages in *Strange Fire*, Pastor MacArthur states that the Charismatic Movement is "a farce and a scam" that "has not changed into something good," claiming that it represents "the explosive growth of a false church, as dangerous as any cult or heresy that has ever assaulted Christianity." Accordingly, he calls for a "collective war" against these alleged "pervasive abuses on the Spirit of God."[7]

He claims that "The 'Holy Spirit' found in the vast majority of charismatic teaching and practice bears no resemblance to the true Spirit of God as revealed in Scripture," again accusing the modern Charismatic Movement of "attributing the work of the devil to the Holy Spirit." And, he writes, "As a movement, they have persistently ignored the truth about the Holy Spirit and with reckless license set up an idol spirit in the house of God, dishonoring the third member of the Trinity in His own name."[8]

"In recent history," he writes, "no other movement has done more to damage the cause of the gospel, to distort the truth, and to smother the articulation of sound doctrine," going as far as to say that, "charismatic theology has made no contribution to true biblical theology or interpretation; rather, it represents a deviant mutation of truth."[9] And without nuancing his words in the least, he simply states that "Satan's false teachers,

marching to the beat of their own illicit desires, gladly propa-
gate his errors. They are spiritual swindlers, con men, crooks,
and charlatans."[10]

Yes, "By inventing a Holy Spirit of idolatrous imaginations,
the modern Charismatic Movement offers strange fire that has
done incalculable harm to the body of Christ. Claiming to focus
on the third member of the Trinity, it has in fact profaned His
name and denigrated His true work."[11]

This is just a representative sampling, but it is enough to
make clear that when Pastor MacArthur has called for a collective war against charismatics, he means just what he says,
believing that the vast majority of charismatics are not truly
saved, while those who are saved are involved in serious error
and some level of deception. It is with good reason that leaders
around the world have raised their concerns about these sweeping indictments.

Other Leaders Speak Up

On October 24, 2013, Mark Galli, editor of *Christianity Today*,
posted this on the magazine's website in "The Galli Report":

> I've already mentioned the Strange Fire Conference
> hosted by John MacArthur, which the well-known pas-
> tor used as a platform to continue his campaign against
> charismatics. This week, I found "A Final Appeal to Pastor
> John MacArthur on the Eve of His 'Strange Fire' Confer-
> ence" by charismatic author Michael Brown—with which
> I found myself in deep sympathy.[12]

In the article which Galli mentioned and which was posted the day before the Strange Fire conference began, I described Pastor MacArthur's position as "a tragic error, a decided step in the wrong direction and a rejection of both the testimony of the written Word and the work of the Spirit today," also saying that he used "divisive and destructive language based on misinformation and exaggeration."

And I closed the article with these words after offering five rebuttals to Pastor MacArthur's charges:

> And so, even though it seems futile at this point, once again, on the eve of the "Strange Fire" conference, I appeal to Pastor MacArthur to reconsider his ways, to reexamine what the Word really says about these issues, to travel to the nations and see firsthand what the Spirit is doing, and to sit with charismatic leaders to seek the Lord together for His best for the church and the world.
>
> It's not too late, sir, to humble yourself under God's mighty hand, and I humble myself before you as I write these words, reaching out to you once more in the name of Jesus and urging you to recognize and embrace the Spirit's true fire today.[13]

Despite the strength of these words and the force of this appeal, Mr. Galli, the senior editor of *Christianity Today*, found himself "in deep sympathy" with what I wrote, and he is certainly not alone in being troubled by the Strange Fire movement. Many other highly-respected, well-seasoned leaders have also raised their voices, including Dr. Timothy George, Dean of Beeson Divinity School of Samford University and general editor of the Reformation Commentary on Scripture.

In his November 4, 2013 article, "Strange Friendly Fire," he wrote:

> Within the worldwide charismatic movement, there are no doubt instances of weird, inappropriate, and outrageous phenomena, perhaps including some of the things MacArthur saw on TBN. Many Pentecostal leaders themselves acknowledge as much. But to discredit the entire charismatic movement as demon-inspired because of the frenzied excess into which some of its members have fallen is both myopic and irresponsible. It would be like condemning the entire Catholic Church because some of its priests are proven pedophiles, or like smearing all Baptist Christians because of the antics of the Westboro Baptist Church.
>
> When told that his all-charismatics-are-outside-the-pale approach was damaging the Body of Christ because he was attacking his brothers and sisters in the Lord, MacArthur responded that he "wished he could affirm that." This is a new version of *extra ecclesiam nulla salus*—except that the ecclesia here is not the one, holy, catholic, and apostolic church but rather an exclusively non-charismatic one.[14]

Focusing on the *Strange Fire* book, Baptist seminary professor and New Testament scholar Dr. Thomas Schreiner was troubled as well by Pastor MacArthur's broad-brushed tone, despite his many points of agreement with MacArthur's theology. He wrote:

We can be thankful for MacArthur's longtime passion for the truth of the gospel and for his unswerving commitment to the Word of God. He rightly reminds us that we must be bold and courageous in renouncing false teaching. At the same time, the charismatic movement is painted with too broad of a brush in Strange Fire. We can be thankful for the many good things that have occurred and are occurring in the charismatic movement as well.[15]

More bluntly, Ron Phillips, pastor of Abba's House (formerly Central Baptist Church), posted an article entitled, "Is Pastor John MacArthur Reading the Same Bible Pentecostals Are?," noting that "his stance on the gifts of the Spirit, support of cessationism, and his related and unrelenting attacks upon his brothers and sisters who believe and walk in the fullness of the Spirit are – quite simply – wrong."[16]

Even believers sympathetic to Pastor MacArthur's position were disappointed with the sweeping nature of his condemnations, as typified by a man named Johnathan who posted this on the AskDrBrown Facebook page: "Was a "Cautious but Open" sort of Southern Baptist... Though I was wanting to hear them out due to my "cautious" side giving consideration to the cessationist case, I was extremely underwhelmed by the argumentation from Strange Fire Conference, and disappointed in a lot of the broad brush rhetoric."[17]

Others were not as kind in their assessment of the Strange Fire camp, and one blogger had this to say:

There's lots of fraud in the ranks of Pentecostalism, especially among the televangelists. Exposing that is a good thing.

However, when attacking dishonesty in charismatic circles, critics need to guard against dishonesty, too. Otherwise, critics are just as bad as the charlatans they (rightly) deride.

The problem I have is that, at least in my admittedly limited observation, some members or follow[er]s of the MacArthur circle suffer from Richard Dawkins syndrome. Dawkins has such contempt for Christianity that he can't bring himself to take Christianity seriously even for the sake of argument.

And some members/followers of the MacArthur circle reflect the same mindset. They exhibit such unbridled contempt for charismatic theology that they can't take it seriously even for the sake of argument. They demand evidence, yet they don't make a good faith effort to be informed. So the objection is circular, given their studied ignorance.

There's a word for that: prejudice.

This also results in a distressing display of spiritual pride. Consider [a particular leader's] endless stream of smug, back-patting tweets–which receive self-congratulatory kudos from his fawning fans.

Don't become the thing you hate.[18]

What then is the truth about the charismatic movement? Where has Pastor MacArthur spoken accurately and where has he misspoken? And what do the Scriptures have to say about these critically important issues? We'll take these questions up in the rest of the book.

Endnotes

[1] http://news.charismanews.com/opinion/in-the-line-of-fire/39944-john-macarthur-strange-fire-and-blasphemy-of-the-spirit

[2] At the time of writing, he is seventy-four and I am fifty-eight, and his publications and radio broadcast have had far more circulation than mine (and many stations that air his show air mine as well).

[3] John MacArthur, *Strange Fire: The Danger of Offending the Holy Spirit with Counterfeit Worship* (Nashville: Nelson Books, 2013).

[4] From an interview with Phil Johnson, his editor, on the Grace to You website, January 16, 2011; http://www.gty.org/resources/sermons/GTY133/Theology-and-Ministry-An-Interview-with-John-MacArthur

[5] Ibid. See also his message "The Modern Blasphemy of the Spirit," http://www.gty.org/resources/sermons/90-415/the-modern-blasphemy-of-the-holy-spirit, October 23, 2011.

[6] https://www.youtube.com/watch?v=f09vfUgenYQ

[7] *Strange Fire*, xvii.

[8] Ibid., xiv. Interestingly, in the Advanced Reader's Copy of *Strange Fire* that Thomas Nelson was kind enough to send me, this sentence read, "blaspheming the third member of the Trinity in His own name," something to which I had taken strong exception in my articles and radio broadcast; see above, n. 1. Note, however, that charges of "blasphemy of the Spirit" are still brought against charismatics throughout *Strange Fire*, perhaps as many as two dozen times, despite the change of wording here. Phil Johnson, Pastor MacArthur's editor, in one of his sessions at the Strange Fire conference, sought to clarify what Pastor MacArthur meant when he brought the charge of "blaspheming the Spirit" against charismatics, since I claimed that this meant that many charismatics, including fine leaders, had committed the unpardonable sin (see Mark 3:28-30), an utterly outrageous charge. Mr. Johnson explained that there is a specific sin called "the blasphemy of the Spirit," marked by the definite article in Matthew 12:31, and no one was accusing charismatics of committing *that* sin. See http://www.youtube.com/watch?v=F2JAoNoCVDY. In response, it can be stated that: 1) there is no such distinction made in Mark 3:28-30, which is

the text many are familiar with; and 2) Pastor MacArthur has failed to make such nuanced distinctions in some of the strong charges he has leveled (see also above, n. 4). To the contrary, in *Strange Fire*, x-xi, he claims that some charismatic "antics" are sometimes *worse than* the strange fire brought by Nadab and Abihu in Leviticus 10 – remember that the Lord killed them for their irreverence – after which he proceeds to speak about the unforgivable nature of blasphemy of the Spirit. Phil Johnson was gracious enough to join me on the air after the Strange Fire conference, and I told him plainly that I felt that Dr. MacArthur was swinging with a baseball bat and he was coming along afterwards with a toothpick, saying, "That's not what he really meant." I would therefore urge everyone involved in all sides of the current debate to be more careful and precise in their speech, regardless of how deeply they care about the issues (which I assume we all do). For my interview with Mr. Johnson, go here: http://www.youtube.com/watch?v=R7aQjsDYbcQ.

[9] *Strange Fire*, xv.

[10] Ibid.

[11] Ibid.

[12] http://www.christianitytoday.com/lyris/gallireport/archives/10-25-2013.html; my article was posted on October 15, 2013 and enjoyed wide circulation; see
http://www.charismanews.com/opinion/in-the-line-of-fire/41371-a-final-appeal-to-pastor-john-macarthur-on-the-eve-of-his-strange-fire-conference.

[13] http://www.charismanews.com/opinion/in-the-line-of-fire/41371-a-final-appeal-to-pastor-john-macarthur-on-the-eve-of-his-strange-fire-conference

[14] http://www.firstthings.com/onthesquare/2013/11/strange-friendly-fire/timothy-george

[15] http://thegospelcoalition.org/book-reviews/review/strange_fire

[16] http://www.charismanews.com/opinion/41579-is-pastor-john-macarthur-reading-the-same-bible-pentecostals-are

[17] For Pastor MacArthur's post-conference defense of the broad-brushed rhetoric, see
http://www.challies.com/interviews/john-macarthur-answers-his-critics.

[18] http://triablogue.blogspot.com/2013/08/strange-fire-conference.html; the leader they mentioned was Pastor Dan Phillips, a close co-worker of

AUTHENTIC FIRE 11

some of John MacArthur's team; see http://www2.blogger.com/profile/16471042180904855578

CHAPTER TWO

REJECTING THE STRANGE FIRE, EMBRACING THE AUTHENTIC FIRE

The other day a caller to my radio show criticized me for not addressing charismatic abuses more frequently. In response, I asked him, "How long have you been listening to my show?" He replied, "One day." How interesting!

I then asked him how many of my books and articles he had read. The answer, as expected, was zero. What then was the basis for his criticism? He obviously heard others level this same charge against me and he repeated it without bothering to see if it was true. But this charge has not only been brought against me. It is claimed that, as a movement, we Pentecostals and charismatics have not done a good job of policing our own house. Is this true?

Before addressing this larger question, let me say that while I am absolutely unashamed to be called a Pentecostal-Charismatic believer, I am terribly ashamed at many things that are done in the name of the Holy Spirit today, especially by leaders on "Christian" TV. Without a doubt, if this represented the true core of the Charismatic Movement, the heart and soul of who we are, I would never want to be called a charismatic again. It would be similar to how Baptists would feel if Fred Phelps, the notorious leader of Westboro Baptist Church, was the poster

boy for the Baptist Church in America. (Phelps and his followers are famous for their "God Hates Fags" campaigns and their
celebrations at the funerals of Americans killed in battle.)

The fact is that I have worked with Pentecostal and charismatic leaders throughout America and around the world and I
have found the great majority of them to be men and women
of integrity, lovers of Jesus and the Word, with a heart to touch
the world. (More importantly, I'm convinced that based on the
Scriptures, the cessationist position is completely untenable; see
below, Chapter Six.) That being said, there is absolutely no excuse for the many doctrinal errors, financial abuses, moral scandals, and personality cults that are all too common in our movement, and I can hardly blame other believers for judging us by
much of the nonsense broadly associated with the charismatic
Church. We have made ourselves an easy target.

Setting Our Own (Charismatic) House in Order

But it would be wrong to think that we have been silent about
these issues. Pastor David Wilkerson, founder of Teen Challenge, author of *The Cross and the Switchblade*, and co-founder
of Times Square Church in New York City was one of the most
prominent Pentecostal leaders of the last fifty years. (He died in
a car crash at the age of seventy-nine in 2011.) He often thun-
dered against these abuses, speaking out often against the carnal prosperity gospel and even weeping as he preached against
weirdness carried out in the name of the Spirit.[1]

His printed sermons, sent out roughly every three weeks to as
many as 900,000 recipients, after which they were often copied
and given away, with some churches even handing them out

with their church bulletins on Sundays, had a powerful influence in America and beyond for several decades. I would encourage everyone to read his message "A Christless Pentecost," containing some amazingly prescient quotes from Frank Bartleman, one of the early Pentecostal leaders, and pointing to the centrality of Jesus.[2]

Professor Gordon Fee, one of the greatest Pentecostal biblical scholars (see below, Chapter Three), wrote an entire book strongly critiquing the "health and wealth gospel," while most of the major Pentecostal denominations rejected these extremes in internal statements to their pastors and leaders. Regarding the prosperity gospel (which Fee rightly noted was in a different class than the Pentecostal belief in divine healing), he wrote:

> American Christianity is rapidly being infected by an insidious disease, the so called wealth and health Gospel—although it has very little of the character of Gospel in it...
>
> The cult of prosperity thus flies full in the face of the whole New Testament. It is not biblical in *any* sense...besides being non-biblical, the theology that lies behind this perversion of the Gospel is sub-Christian at several crucial points.
>
> ...despite all protests to the contrary, at its base the cult of prosperity offers a man-centered, rather than a God-centered, theology.[3]

He could not have been any more clear.

Other prominent leaders, like Jim Cymbala, pastor of Brooklyn Tabernacle and author of books like *Fresh Wind, Fresh Fire:*

What Happens When God's Spirit Invades the Hearts of His People and *Spirit Rising: Tapping into the Power of the Holy Spirit*, have dealt with abuses primarily by emphasizing biblical truths, steering in the middle of the stream of the Spirit's moving rather than pursuing the extremes, thereby majoring on the majors. And at a recent conference hosted by Pastor Cymbala at Brooklyn Tabernacle, David Jeremiah, a conservative evangelical pastor and author, was one of the speakers, even mentioning how, when he had cancer, he contacted Pastor Cymbala's church for prayer support because the people there knew how to pray.

Many other Pentecostal and charismatic pastors have followed this same course, and the reason they don't feel the need to address the latest abusive service on Christian TV is because it is not part of their world or the world of most (or all) of their congregants. The truth be told, the majority of Pentecostal and charismatic churches in America are hardly caught up in some kind of charismania. Instead, they could use a fresh touch of the Spirit, some having gone the way of "seeker sensitive Christianity," becoming more concerned with drawing a crowd than facilitating an encounter with God, while others have the form but not the power, being more charismatic in appearance than in reality (as in the largely empty saying, "We have a charismatic form of worship").[4]

And it is interesting that John Wimber, founder of the Vineyard Movement, and one of Pastor MacArthur's most frequent targets in his *Charismatic Chaos* book, had much to say about charismatic abuses. In one of his most important books, *Power Healing*, Wimber wrote:

> I also visited several healing meetings [he wanted his readers to know he was *not* speaking about Kathryn

Kuhlman]...and became angry with what appeared to be the manipulation of people for the material gains of the faith healer...Dressing like sideshow barkers. Pushing people over and calling it the power of God. And money, they were always asking for more, leading people to believe that if they gave they would be healed...[5]

I have also seen groups where the expected behavior of the ones being prayed for was that they fall over. This was nothing more than learned behavior, religion at its worst.[6]

I have made it a matter of policy never to accept gifts for healing. Greed and materialism are perhaps the most common cause of the undoing of many men and women with a healing ministry...When I pray over people for God to release the healing ministry, I always instruct them never to accept money for healing.[7]

With regard to the alleged emotionalism and unbridled fanaticism found in charismatic meetings, Wimber had a totally different approach:

During the time of prayer for healing I encourage people to 'dial down', that is, to relax and resist becoming emotionally worked up. Stirred up emotions rarely aid the healing process, and usually impede learning about how to pray for the sick. So I try to create an atmosphere that is clinical and rational...while at the same time it is powerful and spiritually sensitive. Of course, emotional expression is a natural by-product of divine healing and not a bad response. My point is that artificially creating an emotionally charged atmosphere militates against divine healing and especially undermines training others to pray for the sick.[8]

In a 1997 interview with *Christianity Today*, Wimber shared his views on the unusual phenomena that often took place in his meetings as people said they were touched by the Spirit:

> I don't have any objection to phenomena, per se. I think Jonathan Edwards has adequately addressed the issues of phenomena in revival...However, *I think if it's fleshly and brought out by some sort of display, or promoted by somebody on stage, that's abysmal.* But if God does something to somebody, that's between that person and God.[9]

And in a 1996 interview with *Christianity Today*, Wimber dispelled any illusions about a superficial, health and wealth gospel:

> Some Christians believe we should never struggle with doubt, fear, anxiety, disillusionment, depression, sorrow, or agony. And when Christians do, it is because they're not exercising the quality of faith they ought to; periods of disillusionment and despair are sin. If those ideas are true, then I'm not a good Christian. Not only have I suffered physically with health problems, but I also spent a great deal of time struggling with depression during my battle with cancer.[10]

Reading *Strange Fire* and *Charismatic Chaos*, you would hardly imagine that major charismatic leaders spoke in terms like this.

I should also mention leaders like Lee Grady, for years editor of *Charisma* magazine and the author of many articles speaking out loudly and clearly against many charismatic abuses, some of which were promoted in the very pages of the magazine he edited, an issue he and his team sought to address. The blurb for his 2010 book *The Holy Spirit Is Not for Sale: Rekindling the Power of God in an Age of Compromise*, states,

> For more than sixteen years, veteran journalist J. Lee Grady has kept a finger on the pulse of the charismatic and Pentecostal renewal, which restored the power of the Holy Spirit to the church, but which now suffers from abuse. Since many Spirit-empowered believers have lost their original focus and purity, Grady delves into some of the problems that plague churches and ministries: financial scandal, faulty theology, moral failure, and more.[11]

During the "Lakeland Revival," which ended suddenly with the moral failure of its leader, Grady wrote an article including these warnings, without denying the fact that people were being touched by the Spirit. He wrote that we should: "1) Beware of strange fire. . . . 2) Beware of bizarre manifestations. . . . 3) Beware of hype and exaggeration . . . ."[12] Shades of the warnings at the Strange Fire conference, and this from a leading charismatic. And note that Grady's most recent article, at the time of this writing, is, "Five Ways the Prosperity Gospel Is Hurting America."[13]

And let's not forget Pentecostal statesmen like Jack Hayford, pastor of the Church on the Way in Van Nuys, California, a man of exemplary integrity, a devoted teacher of the Word, a humble leader to leaders, editor of the *Spirit-filled Life Bible*, and founder of *The King's University*. He too has helped encourage the vitality of the Spirit while rejecting extremes, and he has done so as a spiritual father and mentor to many.

Derek Prince, who died in 2003, was another leading fig-
ure in the charismatic movement, having studied at Cambridge
as a Greek and Latin scholar, specializing in logic and writing his Master's thesis on "The Evolution of Plato's Method of
Definition." And while I have taken strong exception to Pastor
MacArthur's wide-ranging charges of charismatic "blasphemy
of the Spirit" (see above, Chapter One), he is hardly the first
leader to raise concerns about these issues. As Prince once wrote
in more nuanced but very strong terms:

> We are warned by Jesus Himself to be very, very careful
> how we speak about the Holy Spirit, how we represent
> the Holy Spirit. Jesus uses the word blasphemy, and I de-
> cided to look it up in my big Greek lexicon. The primary
> meaning of "to blaspheme" is given in the lexicon as this:
> "to speak lightly or amiss of sacred things." So when you
> speak lightly or amiss concerning the Holy Spirit, or mis-
> represent the character of the Holy Spirit, by definition
> you are close to blaspheming.
>
> If you have ever done that, or been prone to do it, or
> been associated with those who do it, I want to offer you
> some sincere advice: You need to repent. You need to set-
> tle that matter once and for all with God and never again
> be guilty of misrepresenting God's Holy Spirit. For the
> Holy Spirit is holy and He is God.[14]

Reformed pastor John Carpenter is quite right in saying that

> the suggestion that "charismatics" simply never police
> their own is false. David Wilkerson was out-spoken and
> just as severe in his appraisal of the prosperity "gospel"
> as is John MacArthur…The Assemblies of God famously

tried to discipline Jimmy Swaggart and eventually de-
frocked him when he wouldn't submit. Yes, there should
be more of such correction but people are only responsible to discipline what is under their authority. Should we
hold all Baptists responsible for the Westboro Baptists?
Should we accuse everyone who believes in the inspiration of scripture (like me) for being as irrational as the
King James Onlyists?[15]

Again, this is just a sampling, but it is a reminder that we
have hardly turned a blind eye to the many abuses and errors in
our movement, and pastors in Africa and India (among other
countries) have shared with me how they are now addressing
the unfortunate invasion of these abuses via American preachers and leaders.

My Own Words of Correction as a Charismatic Insider

On a personal level, I have preached and taught and written
about these issues for decades, and to give context to much of
the rest of this book, especially for those who don't know me, it
would be helpful to share some examples. In my 1989 book *The
End of the American Gospel Enterprise*, which was a call for repentance in the Church with the hope and promise of national
revival, I often focused on my fellow charismatics, since these
were the circles in which I primarily traveled. (Leonard Ravenhill, the close friend of A. W. Tozer and the author of *Why Revival Tarries*, wrote the Foreword to this book.)

Speaking in general of the American evangelical church,
but speaking primarily to my own major audience, which was
charismatic, I wrote:

The Lord has called us to be holy and set apart from sin, just as He is holy. But are we really much different than the unsaved? We have been greedy, covetous, divisive, and slanderous. We have been undisciplined in our spending, family life has become a burden, and we have made celebrities out of our leaders. Instead of producing self-effacing ministries that exalt the Lord, we have created man-centered, flesh-exalting, personality cults. Adultery and sexual sin are everywhere, and so many of us are ruled by bodily lusts. Is this the "glorious church"?[16]

Then, more specifically addressing my fellow-charismatics:

This is the great indictment against our "Spirit-filled" congregations: we have had the fanfare without the fire, the hype without the happening. *With all our boasts, with all our noise, with all our big talk, we are a generation that has experienced precious little of the fullness of God.*

We must be honest with ourselves: Have we ever seen someone who was born totally blind healed in front of our eyes? Have we witnessed the instantaneous restoration of a quadriplegic? When is the last time we saw a whole community repent and be saved? Was our congregational building ever literally shaken? But that is what "Bible days" were about!

Can't we acknowledge that something is lacking when our so-called "miracle services" are anything but miraculous? Can we continue to watch the deformed cripples wheeled in and out of our meetings while people with backaches and headaches are healed? Doesn't this scene remind us of Nazareth, where Jesus could not do any miracles, "except lay His hands on a few sick people and heal them. *And He was amazed at their lack of faith*" (Mark 6:5-6)? Isn't it time that we admit to our unbelief? If we were really in faith, things would be different![17]

And this, for the American Church:

Look at our American scene today. The reproach we suffer is not for the Messiah's sake; we are not scorned because of our militant stand. No. We are mocked because of our leaders' sins, because of our failure to be holy and clean. Gospel and greed seem to go hand in hand, and our society equates evangelist with exploiter. Yet Jesus is the Head of the Body! How can this be?[18]

What kind of fruit has this "salvation without sacrifice" message produced? It has brought about a whole generation of double-minded "believers," a multitude of worldly "children of God." It has filled our church buildings without changing men's hearts. But a great shaking is coming to the Body. And while the "no-cross gospel" has drawn the big crowds, the numbers will not stand when the shaking arrives.[19]

Then this, with special charismatic application:

Our funds have been spent on our own edification and our energies devoted to build up our lives. We are stuffed with new revelation and gorged with the hottest new truth. Yet instead of getting healthy, we're fat; instead of getting stronger, we're stale!

We are specialists in praise and worship, and experts on interpretive dance. Apostles and prophets are again in our midst, and Word-teachers fill our whole land. But the "old-time power" is missing and divine visitation is rare. The blessing of God is departing and we are left with a great big game.

Our ship has set sail, its decks are all full, but the wind of the Spirit has waned.[20]

In my 1990 book *How Saved Are We?*, I devoted an entire chapter to "The Prosperity Trap," stating there:

But the American church not only lives among thorns, we now preach a "thorny" gospel! We tell worldly minded people that following Jesus is the path to success. "If you walk with the Lord," we say, He will make you wealthy!" *But that is not the gospel.* "Take up your cross" does not mean "become rich and famous." "Leave everything and follow Me" is not the same as "get everything by following Me." We are catering our gospel to carnality!

...Oh yes – God can and will supply all our needs, and there is nothing shabby about His provision. He is not glorified through our poverty and lack. He gains nothing by us groveling in debt. He is a God of infinite wealth. He can afford to share it with us. *All* that we need is found in Him. As we seek His kingdom first, it will *all* be provided for us. But God "will not aid men in their selfish striving after personal gain. He will not help men to attain ends which, when attained, usurp the place He by every right should hold in their interest and affection" (A. W. Tozer). Material wealth is never to be our goal.

...This is what has happened to our modern day prosperity gospel: *it has run aground on the shallow shores of*

greed and ambition; it has capsized in the turbulent wa-
ters of selfishness; it has sunk under the weight of covetous
hearts. May it never sail again![21]

The next year, 1991, I wrote *Whatever Happened to the Power*
of God: Is the Charismatic Church Slain in the Spirit or Down for
the Count? Based on the title of this book alone, not to mention its content, you can understand why I find it amusing when
people say I have failed to address abuses in my own backyard.
Really? Pastor MacArthur even quotes approvingly a passage
from this book in his *Strange Fire*, where I talk about sick people
falling to the ground and shaking without getting healed.[22]

Since I can't very well quote the contents of that entire book
here – and note that the book has chapters focusing on the exaltation of Jesus, the call to holiness, and the need for repentance
– I'll just provide a small sampling of quotes.

In the chapter entitled "God Must Show Himself Holy," I
spoke of the consequences of Nadab and Abihu offering up
strange fire to the Lord (yes, more than twenty years before the
"Strange Fire" conference!), writing:

> The fire fell twice that day—all in a matter of minutes!
> First the flames from Heaven consumed Aaron's sac-
> rifices; then the flames from Heaven consumed Aaron's
> sons. First there was joy; then there was judgment. First
> there was exhilaration; then there was agony. In an in-
> stant the mood of the nation had turned. The people of
> Israel—and Aaron—were getting to know their God. He
> was an all-consuming Fire.
>
> *Moses then said to Aaron, "This is what the Lord spoke of*
> *when He said: 'Among those who approach Me I will show*

Myself holy; in the sight of all the people I will be honored'"
(Leviticus 10:3).

Either by sanctioning our specific obedience or by condemning our presumptuous disobedience, God will show
Himself holy before the world. He will; He shall; He must.
What an awesome responsibility it is to be in the service
of the Lord. He will get Himself honor *through us!*[23]

I also asked:

Does Jesus approve when He is presented with game-
show hype and Hollywood irreverence? Does the Lord
endorse a Gospel that leaves out the Cross and treats sacrifice as a dirty word? Is He pleased when His servants
plead for money and beg for bigger offerings in His name
as if *He* were making them do it? What does Jesus think
of such things?[24]

In the chapter, "Is Christianity a Fraud?", I wrote,

...do angels long to look into what we now experience?
The thought is almost ludicrous. They are probably bored
too!

Are we glowing brightly in the Lord? Do the unsaved
see the light of our good deeds and praise our Father in
Heaven? It doesn't take much consideration to come to
a simple conclusion: What we are presently experiencing
is *not* what the Word of God describes. *It simply is not
happening in most of our lives.*[25]

In the chapter, "The Spirit Does the Work," after talking
about past revival and how the crowds thronged to hear the
gospel, I asked,

Then why aren't the crowds knocking down our doors for the bread of life? (It may be happening in other parts of the world, but it is certainly not the norm in the United States.) Why aren't they flocking to us for the only real antidote? It's because we don't have the goods! On top of that, we haven't convinced the world that it is sick, starving, and on the verge of eternal death.[26]

Other chapters in the book included, "Has the Gift of Healing Hit a Brick Wall?", "Leaving the Land of Make Believe" (where I talk about superficial and even fantasy-based spiritual warfare), and "Hi-Tech Believers and a Push-Button God" (in which I decry our "microwave ministry" mentality), but just a few more quotes will suffice. In the chapter, "How Painful Are Honest Words," I wrote,

> There has been so much disobedience and defilement, so much carnality and corruption, that we have greatly driven the presence of God away. It is possible for believers to continue praying, having family devotions, witnessing, singing choruses, tithing, and attending services, *and not even know that the Spirit of the Lord has become distant.* We have become so accustomed to the superficial that we hardly miss the supernatural. We are more "Spirit-frilled" than Spirit-filled. We are so used to the "outer fringe of His works" that we often forget the inner essence of His ways (Job 26:14).
>
> …What a shame! We believe in our exaggerated reports. We have been duped by our fabulous words. Dozens of ministries throughout the land claim to have either outstanding, overwhelming, or sensational signs,

wonders, and miracles. They commonly report spectacular acts of God. To hear them talk, you would almost
think that compared to them, the apostles were spiritual
novices. (Don't laugh. Some teachers claim that if Paul
had had *our* revelation, he wouldn't have had his thorn
in the flesh, and if Stephen had known his full authority,
he wouldn't have been martyred. Rather than laugh, we
should weep.) Maybe the apostles will admire the contemporary saints one day—but that day is certainly not
today.[27]

And in the chapter, "Leaving the Land of Make Believe," I wrote:

There are many who claim to have great faith. They rebuke demons by the thousands and dispatch angels by
the millions. They decree supernatural blessings and im-
part incredible anointings. But talk is cheap. If so much
is happening in the spiritual realm, where is the proof in
the natural realm? Where are the overwhelming victories?
Which American cities are being overturned for the Lord?
Where is the divine visitation?[28]

And after all this, the strongest chapter of in the book might
have been "The Samson Cycle," in which I compared the story
of Samson to much of the charismatic Church of America.

Now, if I had never addressed the failings of the American
charismatic church after writing these books, no one could have
accused me of turning a blind eye to these errors. The fact is,
though, I have steadily drawn attention to these issues in the
years since. In 1993, in *It's Time to Rock the Boat: A Call to God's*

People to Rise Up and Preach a Confrontational Gospel,[29] I addressed more issues of gospel compromise, many of which per-
tained to charismatics, and in 1995, in *From Holy Laughter to
Holy Fire: America on the Edge of Revival,*[30] I spoke of the need
to go beyond the "refreshing" movements that were current in
that day and to seek God for a repentance-based, outpouring of
the Spirit.

In the *Holy Fire* book, I even published a sarcastic poem
called, "We All Fall Down," which spoke about our fascination
with people being "slain in the Spirit" while the world around
us was falling apart.[31] I wrote another sarcastic poem in 1995
called "Slobbering in the Spirit" which addressed some of the
bizarre things that I had heard about that were taking place in
the name of revival (although I did not witness most of them
firsthand.) It included these lines:

> We're getting drunk on God's new wine
> And everything is mighty fine.
>
> So come along, relax, don't fear it;
> Now we're slobbering in the Spirit!
>
> Growling, roaring, barking too,
> It's all part of the Holy Ghost Zoo![32]

During this same season, I also emphasized in my preaching
and teaching that the Great Commission was to make disciples,
not drunkards.

Although the next fifteen years of writing were primarily
devoted to producing a five-volume Jewish apologetics series,
working on a commentary on Jeremiah and a 700-page study
on the effects of homosexual activism on America, I continued

to address charismatic abuses, writing this in 2009 in the Preface to the reprint of *Whatever Happened to the Power of God* in 2009.

> I believe the needs in the Church of America are more urgent now than when the books were first written. Simply stated, we've "been there and done it" time and time again—whether the "it" be the latest apostolic or prophetic fad, the latest special anointing, the latest heavenly revelation, or the latest move of the Spirit destined to usher in the return of Jesus. After having their hope deferred over and over again, many believers have grown cynical (and/or adjusted their doctrinal beliefs), others have lost hope, and others have become flakier and increasingly unbiblical.
>
> We have, of course, learned some lessons. Power without holiness is fatal; dynamic experience without the Word is dangerous; hype and crowds and excitement can't raise the dead—just to name a few. And, tragically, we've seen more scandals and falls and abuses of authority than most of us could have ever imagined.[33]

In February, 2013, long before the Strange Fire conference was announced, I wrote an article that was shared (not read) more than 74,000 times on one website alone. It was entitled "Sex Symbols Who Speak in Tongues," and it began with these words:

> I was at the grocery store the other day when I was unexpectedly confronted with an adult-oriented magazine located right next to the vitamin section. I immediately had

to look away from the front cover, which featured a scantily clad, seductively posed, sex symbol. Yet it was only a few weeks ago that I read an article about how this same sex symbol loves to speak in tongues and has to restrain herself from outbursts in tongues while attending church services. What?

This is actually a perfect illustration of American charismatic Christianity, where you can say you love Jesus (like the rapper "The Game" claims to do) and still frequent strip clubs (as "The Game" still does), or where you can flow in the gifts of the Spirit and become a made-for-TV preaching sensation, only to announce that God told you that you married the wrong woman, leading to a quick divorce and remarriage.

Yes, this is the "gospel" of the 21st century, "Spirit-filled" church of America, where the cross is bypassed, denial of the flesh is scorned, purity is called legalism, and anything goes if it feels good.

It is the "gospel" of self, in which Jesus dies to make you into a bigger and better you, a "gospel" in which God is here to serve you and help you fulfill your dreams, and where the measure of all things is not how God feels about it but how you feel about it (or how it makes you feel).[34]

The article closed with this: "It's time to say goodbye to this watered-down, sin-excusing, so-called gospel that offers everything and calls for nothing. It's time to get back to the cross and back to the truth. Otherwise, as America collapses in a heap of amoral ruin, the soft preachers of America will be largely to blame."

There were other articles before and after this,[35] but enough has been said to demolish the idea that I haven't been addressing issues and abuses within our movement. In fact, over the last twenty-four years, I believe I have addressed this even more frequently than Pastor MacArthur has, and I have done so as an insider. (I should also mention that my newest book, released one month after this one and entitled *Hyper-Grace: Exposing the Dangers of the Modern Grace Message*, focuses primarily on charismatic teachers.)[36]

Should We Always Name Names?

Have I named names? For the most part no, since there is so much immaturity in the Body and we are so prone to division that the moment someone's name is mentioned, even in the context of a minor correction, that person is instantly demonized by some, as if their whole message is suspect. (I recognize that in some cases, the whole message *is* suspect, but not in most cases.) It's also important to note that while Paul did name names at times (see, for example, 1 Timothy 1:20; 2 Timothy 1:15; 2:17-18; 4:10, 14; in 1 Timothy 1:3 and Titus 1:10-11 Paul avoids naming names), for the most part he addressed issues, exposing what was wrong and pointing to what was right.

With regard to the state of the Church today, if I say, "Pastor Charles Stanley teaches once saved always saved, and I disagree with that doctrine," some people will immediately look at this fine pastor with suspicion, questioning everything he has to say, while others will look at me with suspicion! And in short articles and general sermons, where it is not always possible to lay out full documentation in a nuanced way, I generally avoid naming names. Also, having been on the receiving end of all kinds of false attacks and slander (as are most public figures), I have not wanted the same abuse heaped on others if it could be avoided.

You see, it is one thing to address serious errors and abuses, as I and others have done. It is another thing to fail to recognize and, worse still, mock the contemporary work of the Spirit, to vilify godly leaders, and to damn to hell countless millions of brothers and sisters in Jesus. And it was *because of the extremely divisive nature of the Strange Fire conference and book*, I have spoken and written, not to add to the division but rather to call for spiritual sanity, biblical clarity, and godly unity in the midst of the accusations and attacks.[37]

Embracing the Authentic Fire

In short, it is one thing to reject a false move of the Spirit; it is another thing to embrace a true move of the Spirit, and it is all too easy to miss the true move because it is not perfect. (Is there any spiritual movement in Church history that has been perfect? See also below, Chapter Four.) And it is well documented that leading pastors in past generations, right up to our own day, have rejected bona fide revival movements because they came in different packaging or through different vessels than was expected.

The glorious Welsh Revival of 1904-1905 was rejected by Peter Price, one of the most respected leaders of his day. He called it, "A sham . . . a mockery, a blasphemous travesty of the real thing."[38] When D. L. Moody and Ira Sankey came to Sunderland, England in 1874, pamphlets posted on public buildings by leading ministers warned against their meetings of Moody and

Sankey: "Kindly reflections on the present religious movement: Part one, questionable procedure. Part two, probable evil results." As for Sankey's music ministry, some protested that "Solo singing is not worship. It's a parade of human conceit. It's distracting, irreverent."[39] Looking back today, Moody's ministry in England and Scotland in 1874-75 is considered to be one of the greatest, most far reaching spiritual events of the century.

Theologian Robert McAfee Brown wisely observed,

> Very often the man who first appears as a heretic turns out to be the one who was recalling Christendom to a long-neglected truth. He may have shouted a little too loudly as the only way of getting a hearing, but had he not shouted, had he not rocked the boat, his fellow-Christians might not have become aware that they were heading for dangerous shoals. Protestantism has an obligation to "suffer fools gladly" lest it stifle the message of one who is "a fool for Christ."[40]

It is with good reason that James Robe asked many years ago, "Can you find in your hearts to be like [those] Jews, who prayed and longed for the coming of the Messiah, and when He came, rejected and crucified Him, because He came not in the way their prejudices led them to look for Him?" As Simeon prophesied in Luke 2:34-35 about the infant Jesus, "This child is destined to cause the falling and rising of many in Israel, and to be a sign that will be spoken against, so that the thoughts of many hearts will be revealed" (NIV). That is the common pattern of revival, just as it happened at Pentecost in Acts 2: Some mocked, others praised God.

Jonathan Edwards had to deal with this during the Great Awakening, as one of his chief critics was the rationalist pastor Charles Chauncey who had a problem with the emotional displays and unusual physical responses so common in the revival. (Really, they are common in most revivals, due to the intensely deep work of the Spirit in people's lives.) In response, Edwards wrote,

> Persons are very ready to be suspicious of what they have not felt themselves. It is to be feared that many good men have been guilty of this error... These persons that thus make their own experience their rule of judgment, instead of bowing to the wisdom of God, and yielding to His Word as an infallible rule, are guilty of casting a great reflection upon the understanding of the Most High.[41]

The fact is, while the Word does tell us to judge doctrine and conduct, it does not tell us to judge *styles* of worship (slow songs; fast songs; choirs; hymns; contemporary tunes; spontaneous singing; dancing; clapping; shouting; raising hands; liturgy; silence; etc.) or *responses* to the Spirit (weeping in sorrow; laughing for joy; shaking; trembling; falling; going into trances; etc.).

And so, while the charismatic movement often *has* been guilty of abusing the Scriptures rather than using them properly, and while it *has* had an inexcusable number of scandals, it has also been used by God to reap a massive harvest of souls worldwide – people who have turned from darkness to light and from Satan to God – as well as create a fresh hunger for the Word, set many captives free from longtime bondages and addictions, produce a renewed interest in worship and intimacy with Jesus, and recover some of the gifts and power of the Spirit that much of the Church had neglected or rejected. Tragically, rather than embrace a God-birthed forest because of quite a few bad trees, the Strange Fire movement has followed the error of Lutheran leaders in Germany who, more than 100 years ago, decided that the incipient Pentecostal movement was, "Not from above, but from below."

A Contemporary Revival

I was an eyewitness to and participant in a contemporary revival movement known as the Brownsville Revival (also called the Pensacola Outpouring), serving as a leader in roughly 800 revival services as well as more than 1,500 classes and teaching sessions.[42] And I have been an eyewitness to the lasting fruit of that revival, resulting in a missions movement that today has full-time workers in more than twenty nations, not to mention the salvation of many thousands of lost sinners and the renewal of even more thousands of backslidden or lukewarm believers.[43]

To give one, typical example, consider the testimony of A. W. Jones, one of our ministry school graduates. He had been a drug addict and alcoholic for twenty-four years when he enrolled in the Teen Challenge program to get help. With others in the program, he attended an Awake America event in which the Brownsville leaders traveled as a team to different parts of the country to minister. At the meeting, he responded to the call to surrender his life to Jesus and was instantly and permanently set free from these addictions, subsequently coming to our ministry school. Today, he and his wife are serving as missionaries in Mexico, where they have labored for more than ten years. This is just one story of one life touched through the Brownsville

Revival, and it could easily be multiplied by the thousands during the revival, as night after night, lost sinners, backsliders, and compromised believers responded to the strong altar calls to turn to Jesus and leave their sins behind.

Pastor MacArthur, however, had a very different assessment of the Brownsville Revival. He wrote:

> I was down in Florida and people are being rocked down there by this Pensacola craziness that's going on in the name of revival and people flipping and flopping and diving on the floor and gyrating and speaking in bizarre and unintelligible fashion and all of this kind of wild thing is going on. And they keep saying this is God, this is of God.
>
> Can I be very straightforward with you? It is an offense to our rational, truth-revealing God, it is an offense to the true work of His Son, it is an offense to the true work of the Holy Spirit to use the names of God or of Christ or of the Holy Spirit in any mindless, emotional orgy marked by irrational, sensual and fleshly behavior produced by altered states of consciousness, peer pressure, heightened expectation or suggestibility.[44]

So, because we spoke in tongues in the revival (after all, we were Pentecostals), because people were overcome by the Spirit's power and often fell to the ground during the prayer time at the end of the service (for the most part, this took place only after the Word was preached and the altar call was given and people were ministered to individually by a counselor), because some people shook and trembled when they testified before being baptized, a Jesus-exalting, Word-based, Spirit-empowered, life-changing move of God was rejected and scorned in the strongest of terms.

May I remind you that the one who is testifying to this is the same person who has consistently rebuked charismatic excesses and errors? The same one who wrote *Whatever Happened to the Power of God: Is the Charismatic Church "Slain in the Spirit" or Down for the Count?* in 1991 and "Sex Symbols Who Speak in Tongues" in 2013? The same one who wrote the sarcastic poems entitled "We All Fall Down" and "Slobbering in the Spirit"? Yet when the real thing arrived – something I had prayed for and fasted for and longed for years – I embraced it with tears of joy while others mocked it. And that's the great concern I have today.

Separating the Real Problems from the Fringe Issues

Please allow me to make myself perfectly clear. For the most part, I avoid Christian TV (although there are more and more good networks coming to the fore and many fine individual programs), finding some of it downright embarrassing if not outright despicable, especially some of the manipulative fund raising which I find absolutely sickening. *Virtually all of these TV abuses take place in charismatic circles.* How tragic and how inexcusable.

In the days of what was called the Lakeland Revival, I noted in my journal that it was an accident waiting to happen, sharing my concerns with my colleagues and co-workers. Although I never attended any of the meetings and watched only two services online, one of them absolutely horrified me, as some of the most respected charismatic leaders in the nation gathered to lay hands on the main leader, Todd Bentley, in what seemed to be kind of a coronation service.

Some of these men were friends of mine, and I was so grieved over what was taking place that I had to turn the meeting off, unable to watch what seemed to be almost an act of self-mockery. (My precious wife Nancy urged me to sit down with her some days later and watch the entire ceremony recorded online, and it was even worse the second time around.) Discussing that meeting with a charismatic leader from England a few months later, we both felt as if it signified some level of divine discipline on the charismatic Church of America, exposing our lack of discernment.[45] Again, I say this to reiterate that I am the last person to minimize some of the problems we are facing.

I was also mortified to see some YouTube videos of meetings with young people "tokin' the Ghost," as they made believe they were smoking or snorting drugs – except the drug of choice was "Jehovauana" (as in, Jehovah + marijuana) – acting the part of drunken fools.[46] It was so abominable to me that I devoted an entire radio broadcast to it, despite the fact that it probably represents the tiniest, absolutely fractional percent of charismatics worldwide, perhaps amounting to a few thousand (or hundred?) people out of half a billion. (Do the math.) Yet John MacArthur mentions things like this in his *Strange Fire* book, speaking of "people 'tokin' the Ghost" and referencing Todd Bentley's meetings,[47] as if this somehow was indicative of charismatic meetings worldwide. (Students in my ministry school, which is absolutely charismatic, were shocked to hear that things like this had taken place.)

If I had a dollar for every person who has recently asked me why I don't renounce "people barking like dogs" in meetings,

I would be rich (well, not quite rich, but well on my way). The fact is that in all my years in the Lord, most of that time spent in charismatic circles, and with more than 130 ministry trips overseas, I have never seen this phenomenon once. (When I heard about it in 1995, I disparaged it in the poem I cited, above.)

Of course I do renounce "barking in the Spirit," but why in the world should I spend my time rebuking a chimera? Why even bring attention to it? It would be like asking me why I'm not renouncing snake handling services – except that those services are far more common than services in which people bark like dogs. In cessationist circles, that would be like me asking the speakers at the Strange Fire conference, "Why didn't you renounce Fred Phelps in every session?" Or, "Why didn't you renounce First Baptist Church in Crystal Springs, Mississipi for refusing to marry a black couple in their church building last year?"[48]

While working on this book one night I stopped for a moment to look at a Christian book catalogue and noticed a blurb advertising *Strange Fire*, part of which said, "Here he speaks out against 'false worship practices' such as barking, laughing, and extrabiblical revelation." In response, I posted this on Facebook and Twitter: "I am quite confident that there are more people sleeping in cessationist services than there are people barking in charismatic services."[49] (That is actually an extreme understatement, given the fact that quite a few church attenders get drowsy during Sunday morning services while "barking in the Spirit" is rarer than chupacabra sightings.)

In fact, if you want to know how "barking in the Spirit" is viewed in the larger charismatic world (for those who ever heard of it) consider this quote from 1997 by one of the charismatic leaders most commonly attacked in the Strange Fire camp, namely Benny Hinn (and it was on Christian TV, at that):

> Some of what is happening today, some of these manifestations where people are barking, making sounds of animals - I can tell you, that is not the Holy Spirit. It is purely demonic. The Holy Ghost does not bark. Only a devil barks. If somebody barks in my meeting, I'll cast the devil out of that man...
>
> Much of what happens is pure emotionalism - contagious laughter. What does it do except make you look stupid? I am not interested in some emotional up. All I want is the power of Almighty God that will transform your life...
>
> I've never known Jesus to bark. Have you? Can you imagine Peter the apostle barking in the book of Acts? But you know why some have accepted such nonsense? Because they're not grounded. They are not grounded. Don't you dare experiment with anything. If it's not in the Bible, don't do it!...
>
> I asked Dr. [Lester] Sumrall before he died. I said, "Dr. Sumrall, what do you think of all these things happening, people barking and doing all these things?" "Devils, devils," he said. "Devils."[50]

The truth is that the Strange Fire movement has missed the Authentic Fire – the fire of revival, the fire of Pentecost, the fire of the Charismatic Movement – wrongly judging the whole by its worst parts, building on a faulty exegesis of Scripture (see below, Chapter Six) and a flawed pneumatology (theology of the Spirit; see also below, Chapter Nine), so scandalized by the abuses that it cannot see, let alone embrace, the good. And you can be assured that there is much, much good taking place around the world and throughout America in the dynamic life and power of the Spirit (see below, Chapter Ten).

The truth is that there are massive needs in cessationist circles in America today too. If we focus just on Southern Baptists, the denomination has had more than its share of leadership scandals, not to mention a massive defection of young people, the lack of growth by conversion in most churches for many years, and even the challenges of liberalism in some of their schools of higher learning. (See Chapter Five).

And as one man posted on my YouTube channel: "I have talked to too many cessationists who complain that their children are leaving the church and many are becoming atheists. It's not surprising since so much doubt is sown in them as children. When they grow up and go to college, they just take that next step and doubt ALL miracles, including those in the Bible."

In Luke 19, Jesus wept over Jerusalem and His Jewish people because they missed the time of their visitation (see Luke 19:41-44). We cannot afford to miss God's visitation again today at such a critical moment in the world's history.

Endnotes

[1] http://www.youtube.com/watch?v=dvoAGEZf-nI

[2] http://www.tscpulpitseries.org/english/1980s/ts820001.html

[3] Gordon D. Fee, *The Disease of the Health and Wealth Gospels* (repr. Vancouver, BC: Regent College Publishing, 2006), Kindle Locations 30-31, 167-173.

[4] http://www.charismanews.com/opinion/in- the- line- of- fire/ 40327- lack- of- fire- the- true- crisis- in- the- contemporary- charismatic-church

[5] John Wimber and Kevin Springer, *Power Healing* (San Francisco: HarperSanFrancisco, 1987), 21.

[6] Ibid., 214.

[7] Ibid., 136.

[8] Ibid., 174.

[9] http://www.christianitytoday.com/ct/1997/july14/7t8046.html?start=2, my emphasis.

[10] http://www.christianitytoday.com/ct/1996/october7/ 6tb049.html; I found these quotes all listed at http://en. wikipedia.org/wiki/John_Wimber, but some were cited from a British edition of *Power Healing*, whereas all citations here are from the American edition.

[11] Minneapolis, MN: Chosen Books, 2010.

[12] http://www.charismamag.com/fireinmybones/Columns/051408.html

[13] http://www.charismanews.com/opinion/41754-5-ways-the- prosperity-gospel-is-hurting-africa

[14] From his book *Protection from Deception*, available online at http://www.sermonindex.net/modules/newbb/viewtopic.php?topic_ id=18887&forum=34

[15] http://www.christianpost.com/news/recovering-from- strange-and-friendly-fire-107976/; he also notes (more controversially to some), "Jack Deere, with others, imposed church discipline on Paul Cain for moral failures. John Wimber distanced his Vineyard churches from 'The Toronto Blessing' and rebuked the 'Kansas City Prophets.'"

[16] *The End of the American Gospel Enterprise* (rev. ed.; Shippensburg, PA: Destiny Image, 1993), 5.

[17] Ibid., 10-11.

[18] Ibid., 20.

[19] Ibid., 24.

[20] Ibid., 79. Although I do believe that apostles and prophets were not limited to the first century (meaning, "small a" apostles as opposed to the twelve apostles), I was being somewhat sarcastic in this quote, saying, "With all our so-called apostles and prophets, why are we such a mess?"

[21] *How Saved Are We?* (Shippensburg, PA: Destiny Image, 1990), 61-63.

[22] *Strange Fire*, 202, quoting Michael L. Brown, *Whatever Happened to the Power of God? Is the Charismatic Church Slain in the Spirit or Down for the Count* (Shippensburg, PA: Destiny Image, 1991), 69. In the book, I'm placed by Pastor MacArthur in the category of "thinking charismatics," while Phil Johnson at Strange Fire referred to me as a "thoughtful charismatic." I'm sure this was meant to be taken positively, so I certainly want to acknowledge that. For the record, though, while Pastor MacArthur stated in his book that I had serious concerns with people being "slain in the Spirit" in services with "faith healers," my main point was that something is obviously missing when the sick person appears to be touched powerfully – to the point of being overcome and falling to the ground – without being healed. I am not troubled by the concept of being "slain in the Spirit" itself.

[23] *Whatever Happened to the Power of God*, 17 (emphasis in the original).

[24] Ibid., 20

[25] Ibid., 24-25.

[26] Ibid., 38.

[27] Ibid., 59-60, emphasis in the original.

[28] Ibid., 76.

[29] Shippensburg, PA: Destiny Image, 1993.

[30] Second edition; Shippensburg, PA: Destiny Image, 1996; the original title of the book (which I was not pleased with at all), first released in slightly abridged form by Huntington House, was *High Voltage Christianity: Sparking the Spirit in the Church*. Ironically, that first publisher insisted that "revival" was not a hot topic at that time and they would not allow me to put the word "revival" in the title or the subtitle of the book. The third edition is entitled, *A Time for Holy Fire: Preparing the Way for Divine Visitation* (Concord, NC: FIRE Publishing, 2008).

[31] *From Holy Laughter to Holy Fire*, 22-23. The book contains an abbreviated form of the full poem.

[32] I posted the entire poem online June 18, 2013 at http://askdrbrown.org/slobbering- the- spirit/.

[33] Shippensburg, PA: Destiny Image, 2007; 1.

[34] http://www.charismanews.com/opinion/38090-sex-symbols-who-speak-in-tongues. As of October 29, 2013, it was shared 74,200 times just on this website; interestingly, my next most shared article was, "A Final Appeal to Pastor John MacArthur on the Eve of His 'Strange Fire' Conference," shared on this same website 71,600 as of this same date. See http://news.charismanews.com/opinion/in- the- line-of-fire/41371-a-final-appeal-to-pastor-john-macarthur-on-the-eve-of-his-strange-fire-conference.

[35] See http://www.charismanews.com/opinion/in- the- line- of- fire for a good number of relevant articles.

[36] Lake Mary, FL: Charisma Media, 2014.

[37] See   again   http://www.charismanews.com/opinion/in-the-line-of-fire for the articles relevant to Strange Fire.

[38] Cited in Brown, *From Holy Laughter to Holy Fire*, 26.

[39] Cited in ibid., 52.

[40] Robert McAfee Brown, *The Spirit of Protestantism* (London: Oxford University Press, 1965), 8.

[41] There are many editions of Edwards' works. This citation is taken from Jonathan Edwards, *A Narrative of the Revival of Religion New England; with Thoughts on That Revival* (Glasgow: William Collins, 1829), 127.

[42] For a print version of some of the Brownsville messages from Steve Hill, the evangelist and principle speaking in the revival for almost five years, see Stephen Hill, *White Cane Religion: And Other Messages from the Brownsville Revival* (Shippensburg, PA: Destiny Image, 1997). Logos Bible Software is in the process of preparing to release a digital, transcribed version of approximately 250 of my day sessions (and select messages) from the Brownsville Revival, so interested readers will be able to see at a glance what was taught to leaders and visitors for a period of four years, with the database fully searchable.

[43] For the missionaries that our own organization oversees and helps support, the great majority of them being grads from our ministry school,

see http://www.fire- international.org/. This is all to the Lord's glory and is
posted here to honor Him. Many other grads have served or are serving on
the foreign mission's field, but they are working with other organizations and
so are not listed here.

[44]http://www.gty.org/resources/print/sermons/80- 180; it is unclear to
me whether Pastor MacArthur actually attended any of the services. In one
of his sessions at the Strange Fire conference, Phil Johnson cited claimed
that the real legacy of the Brownsville Revival was a split and an eleven
million dollar debt; see http://www.youtube.com/watch?v=F2JAoNoCVDY.
(This was partially based on an article by Lee Grady which was widely circulated on anti-charismatic websites, see http://www.cbn.com/spirituallife/
churchandministry/charisma_grady_brownsville.aspx. Although I hesi-
tate even to address these charges, since it gives them unnecessary attention,
because some people have asked about them, I'll take a moment to give the
rest of the story. First, the church was in substantial debt before the revival
began (because of its church building program) and then, after erecting another large building to accommodate the overflow crowds that attended the
meetings for several years, the debt increased by several million more. This
was due to financial decisions that were made and obviously is no reflection
on whether the Holy Spirit was being poured out on the lost and backslidden.
Would anyone judge the quality of a church or ministry today primarily on
whether it had building-related debt? Second, as for the split, which arose
largely over a conflict regarding some denominational issues, after working together for four years (sometimes with ministry schedules of up to 100
hours a week), there was a separation between the leaders of the church and
school. (Actually, given our different backgrounds and histories, it's remarkable that we worked so closely together for so long, especially in light of the
intense pressure that revival can bring.) Note also that the church itself did
not begin to experience real decline until a few years *after* the split when the
pastor and worship leader resigned to move on to other ministry. I should
also mention that the split itself came in the waning months of the revival
(although the church and ministry school were very healthy themselves),
which, miraculously, had continued strong for more than four years (in comparison with many other significant, historic revivals which barely lasted a
year, let alone five years). Finally, within two years of the split, the major
parties involved had reconciled (for my reflections on the reconciliation, see
Chapter Ten, below). But if we are to judge a ministry or church by whether
it ever experienced a split, we would have to discredit Paul (who had a split
with Barnabas in Acts 15) as well as countless thousands of other churches,

ministries, and individuals. Not only so, but with this same methodology, we could discredit Jonathan Edwards and the Great Awakening, since, subsequent to the awakening, he was dismissed from his church in Northhampton because of a dispute regarding who could partake of the Lord's supper, yet this was the very church where God moved so powerfully in that time of revival. Finally, there were other missing elements in the aforementioned article (in particular regarding the history of Brownsville Revival School of Ministry, which continues with the same primary leadership team and faculty to this day, now sixteen years later, as FIRE School of Ministry), but the reality is that the wonderful, Jesus-exalting fruit of the revival continues to grow worldwide, as disciples are reproducing disciples. See also immediately above, n. 43.

[45] Although I don't agree with everything in Andrew Strom's book, *Kundalini Warning: Are False Spirits Invading the Church?* (n.p.: RevivalSchool, 2010), specifically the degree to which some of the major error in some charismatic circles is directly traceable to a "kundalini" spirit (something also claimed at Strange Fire), I absolutely concur with many of his incisive criticisms throughout the book, in particular his section devoted to Lakeland, regardless of whether the Spirit genuinely touched people during the meetings, especially during the times of worship.

[46] I have been told that John Crowder, a main leader in this abusive practice, stepped away from this in recent years, while one of his colleagues, Benjamin Dunn, has asked that he not be judged by these videos which he now finds immature. My point in writing this is not to express endorsement of their ministries (I express other, strong differences with them in my *Hyper-Grace* book) but rather to say that even though this is the extreme fringe of the extreme fringe, the leaders who were most widely associated with it have renounced the practice.

[47] *Strange Fire*, 6-7.

[48] http://religion.blogs.cnn.com/2012/08/06/church-that-refused-to-marry-black-couple-releases-apology/

[49] Posted 11:56 PM, November 3, 2013.

[50] Cited in Strom, *Kundalini Warning*, 15-16.

CHAPTER THREE

A GREAT BIG BLIND SPOT

According to a popular blog,[1] Pastor John MacArthur spends thirty-two hours putting together a single sermon, meaning eight hours a day for four days.[2] That speaks of precision, care, detail, focus, and preparation, of devoting oneself carefully to a subject before addressing it.

How then can a man of this caliber make such patently false statements about charismatics, statements that even common sense would preclude? One answer would be willful ignorance, meaning he knows what he is saying is false and yet he says it anyway, but my esteem for Pastor MacArthur and my commitment to walk in love towards him does not allow me to consider this possibility.

What then is the problem? If it is not willful ignorance, then it must a blind spot – a great, big blind spot – one that is so large that it does not allow him (or those who follow in his footsteps) to see clearly. The purpose of this chapter is to make this blind spot so conspicuous that the only way it can remain is through willful ignorance.

"No Other Movement Has Done More Damage to the Gospel"

Here are some statements made by our esteemed brother at the Strange Fire conference or in his *Strange Fire* book:

**1) "In recent history, no other movement has done
more to damage the cause of the gospel, to distort the
truth, and to smother the articulation of sound doctrine... The Charismatic Movement *as such* has made
no contribution to biblical clarity, no contribution to
interpretation, no contribution to sound doctrine."[3]**

Of course, one could immediately challenge the idea that
the positive contributions of Charismatic scholars and theologians *as Charismatics* can somehow be separated from the positive contribution of Charismatic scholars and theologians in
general.[4] This would be like discounting most (or all) of the
positive contributions of cessationist scholars and theologians
since, it could be argued, they did not primarily make those contributions *as cessationists*. Not only so, but this line of thinking
actually produces a false dichotomy, as if you can easily separate
one's theology and spiritual experience from the whole of one's
life – be it in biblical interpretation, theology, worship, or acts
of service or worship.

Yet as flawed as Pastor MacArthur's premise is, his claims are,
quite candidly, so utterly false that they can be easily refuted,
even on his own terms.

Oswald Chambers and A. W. Tozer

Let's start with Oswald Chambers, author of the most widely
read daily devotional of the last 100 years, *My Utmost for His
Highest*. Chambers was known for his extraordinary spiritual
penetration, and all of his books (which were compiled after
his untimely death by his wife who had taken notes from his

teachings and messages) cut to the core of fleshly efforts and manmade religion. And how his writings exalt Jesus!

Among his hundreds of piercing and powerful quotes are gems like these: "The dearest friend on earth is a mere shadow compared to Jesus Christ." And, "Character in a saint means the disposition of Jesus Christ persistently manifested." And, "Prayer does not fit us for the greater work; prayer is the greater work."

You say, "But what does this have to do with charismatic theology? Chambers was hardly a Pentecostal."

Actually, the turning point in his life *as a believer* came when he was baptized in the Spirit (he also referred to it as receiving "the gift of the Spirit") after a severe, four year test marked by desperate spiritual hunger. In describing this intense trial of his of his faith, he recounted,

God used me during those years for the conversion of souls, but I had no conscious communion with Him. The Bible was the dullest, most uninteresting book in existence, and the sense of depravity, the vileness and bad-motivedness of my nature was terrific. I see now that God was taking me by the light of the Holy Spirit and His Word through every ramification of my being.

The last three months of those years things reached a climax. I was getting very desperate. I knew no one who had what I wanted. *In fact, I did not know what I wanted. But I knew that if what I had was all the Christianity there was, the thing was a fraud.*[5]

When the breakthrough finally came, it was dramatic: "I claimed the gift of the Holy Spirit in dogged committal on Luke 11:13. I had no vision of Heaven or of angels. I had nothing. I was as dry and empty as ever, no power or realization of God, no witness of the Holy Spirit."

But something supernatural had taken place. God had taken hold of his life. Four years later Chambers said, "If the previous years had been Hell on earth, these four years have truly been Heaven on earth. Glory be to God, the last aching abyss of the human heart is filled to overflowing with the love of God. Love is the beginning, love is the middle, and love is the end. After He comes in, all you see is "Jesus only, Jesus ever.""[6]

Looking back, Oswald Chambers could say, "The baptism of the Holy Ghost does not make you think of time or eternity; it is one amazing, glorious now.... It is no wonder that I talk so much about an altered disposition: God altered mine; I was there when He did it, and I have been there ever since.""[7]

According to the official, My Utmost for His Highest website (www.utmost.org), Chambers worked with the Pentecostal League of Prayer, serving as "traveling speaker and representative of the League of Prayer, 1907-10,"[8] although he opposed division over speaking in tongues. And let's remember that according to Pastor MacArthur, the Charismatic Movement, which he and other historians trace back to the Azusa Street Revival (which began in 1906), "was a farce and a scam from the outset; it has not changed into something good."[9] Yet Oswald Chambers was involved with this very movement from its earliest days.

So, Chambers experienced a life-changing baptism of the Spirit *subsequent* to salvation – a Pentecostal distinctive, whether or not he spoke in tongues – and he worked closely with Pentecostals, even as a speaker and representative for the

Pentecostal League. It is likely that it is this aspect of his background which explains quotes like this, among many others: "If in preaching the gospel you substitute your knowledge of the way of salvation for confidence in the power of the gospel, you hinder people from getting to reality."[10]

How about A. W. Tozer, one of the leading spiritual lights in the middle of the twentieth century? He was the longtime pastor of Southside Alliance Church in Chicago, a leader in the Christian Missionary Alliance denomination, and the author of many classic works, including *The Knowledge of the Holy* and *The Pursuit of God*.[11] To be perfectly honest, I have a real problem reading Tozer, since I find myself highlighting almost every line of every page! This speaks of the incredible quality of what he wrote.

From 1989-1994, I had the wonderful privilege of becoming a close friend of Leonard Ravenhill, most famous for his book *Why Revival Tarries*, a book for which Ravenhill's close friend A. W. Tozer wrote the Foreword, a mini-classic in itself.[12] And "Bro. Len," as this saintly old man was known to me, related how the most memorable thing he ever heard Tozer say was this: "There are occasions when for hours I lay prostrate before God without saying a word of prayer or a word of worship – I just gaze on Him and worship."[13]

What most people do not know about Tozer was that one of his principal mentors was F. F. Bosworth, a balanced Pentecostal pioneer known for his healing ministry and his book *Christ the Healer*, widely considered to be one of the best books written on the subject. According to Tozer biographer Lyle W. Dorsett, Bosworth "introduced [Tozer] to a biblical and fruitful healing ministry, as well as to a balanced and sober view of all the sign gifts, including tongues."[14] And, he writes, "If Tozer did not stress Christ as Healer, he conducted meetings in tandem with Bosworth where hundreds and even thousands experienced genuine physical healing."[15] Dorsett also notes that Tozer learned from his mother-in-law about "the baptism and power of the Holy Spirit."[16]

Are you surprised to read this? Perhaps it is even more surprising, especially if you are a cessationist, to realize that it was Tozer's experiences in the Spirit that helped to shape him as a man of God. Now, pick up one of his classic books and read it again, and realize that this was someone who believed in the baptism of the Spirit subsequent to salvation as well as the ongoing operation of the sign gifts.

Against this background, Tozer's comments now make more sense. He wrote:

> Satan knows that Spiritless evangelicalism is as deadly as Modernism or heresy, and he has done everything in his power to prevent us from enjoying our true Christian heritage.
>
> A church without the Spirit is as helpless as Israel might have been in the wilderness if the fiery cloud had deserted them. The Holy Spirit is our cloud by day and our fire by night. Without him we only wander aimlessly about the desert.[17]

We can also better understand this classic Tozer comment: "If the Holy Spirit was withdrawn from the church today, 95 percent of what we do would go on and no one would know the difference. If the Holy Spirit had been withdrawn from the New

Testament church, 95 percent of what they did would stop, and everybody would know the difference."[18]

As for Bosworth, he visited the Azusa Street Revival, so reviled by Pastor MacArthur, and he is seen in a famous picture together with William J. Seymour at this early time in the modern Pentecostal movement. Based on what I call the genetic fallacy (see below, Chapter Four), that would mean that A. W. Tozer should be rejected because he was mentored by a Pentecostal leader, F. F. Bosworth, who drank from the (allegedly) polluted well of Azusa Street. (The reality is that God birthed something glorious at Azusa Street, albeit coming through imperfect people, and this is part of Tozer's positive spiritual heritage.)

So, two of the most spiritually-deep, Christ-centered authors of the last century, Oswald Chambers and A. W. Tozer, both read far more today than in their lifetimes, were involved in the Pentecostal movement and were heavily impacted by the gifts and power of the Spirit.

Was Pastor MacArthur unaware of this? And were these spiritually discerning men too blind to see that they were involved in a supposedly counterfeit movement? And can anyone say with a straight face that their experiences in the Spirit and their collaboration with Pentecostals can somehow be separated from the whole of their lives?[19]

Charismatic Bible Scholars, Theologians, and Philosophers

Turning to the realm of biblical scholarship, there are quite a few Pentecostal-charismatic scholars who have made

tremendous contributions to biblical theology and biblical interpretation today, and this despite the fact that the early Pentecostal movement often downplayed seminary training and
higher education, using Acts 4:13 as their motto. There we read
that when the Jewish leadership "saw the boldness of Peter and
John, and perceived that they were uneducated, common men,
they were astonished. And they recognized that they had been
with Jesus." The King James reads, "they were unlearned and ig-
norant men," and for some Pentecostals, especially in the early
days, that was almost the goal: "If it was good enough for the
apostles, it's good enough for us."

Now, the fact is that being with Jesus is far more important
than seminary training (the Greek in Acts 4:13 speaks of formal
religious training), and Mark 3:14 tells us that Jesus "appointed
twelve (whom he also named apostles) so that they might *be
with him* and he might send them out to preach." And when Paul
brought the gospel, he relied on the power of the Spirit more
than on his own brilliance or great education (see 1 Corinthians
2:1-5, and below, Chapter Six). At the same time, it is possible to
be with Jesus and be well-educated, and so, over the years, it is
not surprising that more and more Pentecostal and charismatic
biblical scholars and theologians have emerged.

A small sampling would include Dr. Gordon D. Fee, one of
the greatest New Testament textual scholars of this generation,
and general editor of the prestigious New International Commentary on the New Testament, to which Fee contributed a
highly-praised commentary on 1 Corinthians, a commentary
for which he was ideally suited to write as a Pentecostal. (He is
an ordained minister with the Assemblies of God, the largest

Pentecostal denomination in the world.) Outside of his commentary on 1 Corinthians, his magnum opus is *God's Empowering Presence: The Holy Spirit in the Letters of Paul,* a work of almost 1,000 pages. Speaking of this volume, the New Testament professor and commentator Andrew T. Lincoln wrote,

Students of Paul's letters and theology have long been in need of a major scholarly investigation of his treatment of the Spirit. By providing such an investigation with the same high standards of scholarship and skills of communication exhibited in his outstanding commentary on 1 Corinthians, and by doing so with an eye on the present renewed interest in the work of the Spirit in the church, Gordon Fee has put us doubly in his debt. His effective combination of thorough and robust exegesis with invigorating theological reflection that views Paul's experience of and concern with the Spirit from an eschatological and Trinitarian perspective drives home what we should have known that the Spirit is far more central to Paul's thought than most of his interpreters have recognized. Fee's comprehensive and challenging new study will be appreciated not only by professional interpreters of Paul but by all who have a serious interest in the biblical resources for spiritual renewal.[20]

So, Fee is not only a Pentecostal scholar who has made a great contribution to biblical scholarship and theology, but he has done so *as a Pentecostal*, opening up important new vistas for the rest of the church, especially in academic circles. This is the precise opposite of what Pastor MacArthur said. And note that Fee, as a Pentecostal minister who believed in divine healing, actually wrote a book entitled, *The Disease of the Health and Wealth Gospels.*[21]

As for the importance of the ongoing work of the Spirit, he wrote:

> My colleagues in New Testament scholarship may disagree with me here, but I am convinced that the dynamic, empowering dimension of life in the Spirit was the "norm" in the early church, and that they simply would not have understood the less-than-dynamic quality of life in the Spirit (without the Spirit?) that has been the "norm" of so much of the later church. Precisely because it was "normal" in this sense, it was the *presupposition* of life in the Spirit for them; thus they felt no compulsion to talk about it at every turn.
>
> Precisely because I understand this dimension of life in the Spirit to be the norm, I think it is repeatable, and should be so, as the norm of the later church.[22]

Other top New Testament scholars who are charismatic or Pentecostal include:

- Craig S. Keener, professor of New Testament at Asbury Theological Seminary, author of the widely used *IVP Bible Background Commentary: New Testament*, as well as some of the best commentaries on books like Matthew and John. In fact, four of his books have won awards in *Christianity Today*. His most recent commentary, on the Book of Acts, runs to roughly *6,000 pages* and is one of the most massive works of scholarship on any New Testament book. Keener has also written a highly-praised, seminal, 1,200 page study called *Miracles: The Credibility of the New Testament Accounts*. Without a doubt, Keener's charismatic background contributes to his work on Acts as well as his study on Miracles, not to mention informing his popular study on the Holy Spirit, *Gift and Giver: The Holy Spirit for Today*. (For Dr. Keener's contribution to this volume, see Appendix A, below.)

- Ben Witherington is a colleague of Dr. Keener who currently serves as Jean R. Amos Professor of New Testament for Doctoral Studies at Asbury Theological Seminary. "Witherington has written over forty books, including *The Jesus Quest* and *The Paul Quest*, both of which were selected as top biblical studies works by *Christianity Today*."[23] Witherington speaks of "the day I was at a healing and exorcism service in Tremont Temple in Boston and the next thing I knew, I was speaking in tongues. I need to tell you while of course there are always counterfeits when it comes to spiritual gifts, the genuine experience is simply one that comes unbidden and sweeps over you...And why should this surprise us. The Holy Spirit is so much more powerful than we are and our little wills, and the Spirit does not want to be quenched by us as Paul reminds the Thessalonians in 1 Thess. 5."[24]

- N. T. Wright is probably the most influential and prolific New Testament scholar of this generation, author of dozens of books and also an Anglican bishop until 2010. In his non-technical commentary on 1 Corinthians, he wrote, "'Tongues' refers to the gift of speech which, through making sounds, and using apparent or even actual languages, somehow bypasses the speaker's conscious mind. Such speech is experienced as a stream

of praise in which, though the speaker may not be able to
articulate what precisely is being said, a sense of love for
God, of adoration and gratitude, wells up and overflows.
It is like a private language of love."[25] Well said! While
Prof. Wright is certainly not a classic Pentecostal, he is
certainly a continuationist, writing, "I am *not* saying that
healings and 'tongues' do not happen, or do not matter.
They do, and they do."[26]

- Peter H. Davids is the author of significant commentaries
  on James, 1 Peter, 2 Peter, and Jude, as well as a contribu-
  tor to the *Hard Sayings of the Bible* series. In his commentary to 1 Peter in the New International Commentary series, he wrote, "The need today is to recapture the biblical
  tension. It is the need to meet illness with prayer... and to
  meet persecution with endurance."[27]

- Max Turner was Professor of New Testament at London
  School of Theology. His charismatic roots contributed to
  his theological interest in the Holy Spirit, leading to *The
  Holy Spirit and Spiritual Gifts: Then and Now* (1996) and
  *Power from on High: The Spirit in Israel's Restoration and
  Witness in Luke-Acts* (1996)

- Graham Twelftree earned his master's degree from Oxford University and then "went on to study under world
  renowned New Testament scholar James D. G. Dunn
  at the University of Nottingham. After completing his
  doctoral dissertation, *Jesus, the Exorcist: A Contribution to the Study of the Historical Jesus*, he went on to
  author dozens of books and journal articles including
  perhaps his most noted work *Jesus the Miracle Worker*:

A *Historical & Theological Study* (Grand Rapids: IVP, 1999)."[28] Obviously, his charismatic background contributed to his writings, which in turn have contributed to New Testament theology and interpretation. His most recent book is *Paul and the Miraculous: A Historical Reconstruction.*[29]

- Jeffrey Niehaus holds a Ph.D. from Harvard University in English Literature and is a highly respected Old Testament and Semitic scholar, serving as Professor of Old Testament at Gordon Conwell Theological Seminary. His bio on the school's faculty page states, "He brings to the study of the Old Testament a broad background in literary studies and extensive research in Ancient Near Eastern milieus. In addition to teaching, *Dr. Niehaus ministers and lectures in various churches on such topics as spiritual warfare and gifts of the Holy Spirit,* and is a member of the Academy of American Poets.[30] His academic and spiritual life are obviously closely intertwined.

There are also a good number of Pentecostal and charismatic theologians and philosophers, including:

- J. P. Moreland, widely considered to be one of the premier evangelical philosophers and apologists, serving as Distinguished Professor of Philosophy, Talbot School of Theology.[31] He writes that, "My fundamental life-commitment, the very reality that drives me on a daily basis, is increasingly to fall in love with the Triune God, to bring honor to Jesus Christ and make him famous among the nations, and to become like him in attitude and action. Under the power of the Spirit, I want to lead a victorious Christian life and experience a Christ-honoring, vibrant death." This includes, "*Attending to the supernatural life of a disciple of Jesus*, empowered by the Holy Spirit and the Kingdom of God, in which I learn to grow in seeing answers to prayer, the sick healed, the demonic addressed appropriately, and words of knowledge, prophecy, and wisdom flowing through me for the edification of others."[32] According to Moreland, "Fewer and fewer Christian scholars hold to cessationism, and it may fairly be called an increasingly marginalized viewpoint."[33]

- Wayne Grudem, currently Professor of Theology and Biblical Studies at Phoenix Seminary and formerly a professor at Trinity Evangelical Divinity School. He was the General Editor of the *ESV Study Bible*, widely used in Reformed theological circles, and author of the 1,291 page *Systematic Theology*, considered one of the best works of its kind in this generation. He has also written popular books on charismatic issues.[34]

- R. T. Kendall, served as pastor of Westminster Chapel in London, England for twenty-five years, the same congregation previously pastored by none other than D. Martyn Lloyd-Jones, who is held in the highest esteem by John MacArthur. Dr. Kendall, a strong Calvinist and a committed charismatic, earned his D. Phil. at Oxford University, and has written more than forty-five books, most recently *Holy Fire: A Balanced, Biblical Look at the Holy Spirit's Work in Our Lives*.[35] A blurb to the book asks,

"Are you charismatic? He is bigger than your signs-and-wonders events. Are you Reformed? He will not be limited by your theology. As Jesus said of the Holy Spirit, 'He blows where He will.'"[36]

- J. Rodman Williams, who earned a Ph.D. in philosophy of Religion and Ethics at Columbia University and Union Seminary. He was the author of the groundbreaking three-volume work *Renewal Theology* (Vol. 1, *God, the World, and Redemption*, Vol. 2, *Salvation, the Holy Spirit, and Christian Living*, and Vol. 3, *The Church, the Kingdom, and Last Things*, now published in one large volume by Zondervan).[37]

- Sam Storms, who earned a Th.M. in Historical Theology from Dallas Theological Seminary and received his Ph.D. in Intellectual History from the University of Texas at Dallas, writing his dissertation on the topic of "Jonathan Edwards and John Taylor on Human Nature: A Study of the Encounter between New England Puritanism and the Enlightenment." He served as an associate professor of theology at Wheaton College and was on the pastoral staff with Mike Bickle in Kansas City. (Bickle has frequently been targeted by the Strange Fire camp.) There is a clear charismatic influence in many of his twenty-two books.[38]

My own academic and theological work has also been shaped by my Pentecostal-charismatic heritage, leading to my doctoral dissertation at New York University, "I Am the Lord Your Healer: A Philological Study of the Root *Rapa'* in the Hebrew Bible and the Ancient Near East," along with articles on that

same Hebrew root for both the *Theologische Wörterbuch zum
alten Testament* (in English, the *Theological Dictionary of the
Old Testament*) and the *New International Dictionary of Old
Testament Theology and Exegesis*, along with a detailed monograph entitled *Israel's Divine Healer*, part of Zondervan's Studies
in Old Testament Biblical Theology Series. My spiritual background also contributes to my understanding of prophetic ministry, reflected in my commentary on Jeremiah in the revised
edition of the *Expositor's Bible Commentary*.[39] In fact, a leading cessationist scholar who encouraged me to write the commentary felt I was uniquely suited to do so because of my background.

This is just a representative sampling, but it exposes the glar-
ingly false nature of Pastor MacArthur's statement that "charismatic theology has made no contribution to true biblical theology or interpretation; rather, it represents a deviant mutation
of truth."

"Where's the Charismatic Hospital?"

**2) "People who have any connection to Judaism and Chris-
tianity have a connection to philanthropy. It is a striking
anomaly, however, that there is essentially zero social benefit to the world from the Charismatic Movement. Where's
the charismatic hospital? Social services? Poverty relief? This
is a scam."[40]**

This was spoken by Pastor MacArthur in a Q & A session
at Strange Fire, and when Phil Johnson, his editor appeared on
my radio show, rather than repudiate the quote and apologize
for it, he expressed his agreement with it.[41] Talk about a massive

blind spot! How many hundreds of books could be written just refuting this one terribly misguided statement?

In keeping with the Strange Fire line of thinking, Mr. Johnson made the claim that if there were, in fact, any Charismatics involved in acts of philanthropy or compassion or the like, this could not be attributed to the fact that they were Charismatics, a false dichotomy I addressed earlier in this chapter. (Again, would Pastor MacArthur actually argue that cessationists engage in acts of compassion *because* they are cessationists, or would he agree that it is because they are Christians?)

Still, even Phil Johnson's false caveat is easily refuted, since many of the Charismatic ministries of compassion were birthed out of an encounter with the Spirit, or they were part of the holistic theology of the leaders, who believed in ministering healing through the gospel to spirit, soul, and body (which obviously includes social and humanitarian work), or they were the result of a specific leading of the Lord. In fact, if not for being touched dramatically by the Spirit in the past, the majority of the missionaries and native leaders we serve with around the globe would not be in the ministry at all.

To give you just the tiniest sampling, consider Teen Challenge, founded by Pastor David Wilkerson and without a doubt, Spirit-birthed and Spirit-empowered. Teen Challenge centers feature an intensive, twelve-month in-house, discipleship program "offering hope and healing for those with life-controlling problems since 1958."[42] There are currently more than 1,000 programs and centers in almost 100 countries, with countless tens of thousands of addicts and other troubled young people having gone through the program. Studies have consistently demonstrated that those who complete the Teen Challenge program have a far higher, long-term success rate than those completing secular programs.[43]

Or consider the work of Drs. Mark and Huldah Buntain, longtime missionaries to India with the Assemblies of God. Their website notes that:

The story begins in 1954 when Dr. Mark and Dr. Huldah Buntain, with their baby daughter, Bonnie, sailed to Calcutta for a one-year service opportunity. Observing first-hand the growing plight of India's poor, they began to launch a series of compassionate ministries. Their one-year stay suddenly turned into 55 as their efforts grew into a large holistic network of programs...

Today, Calcutta Mercy Hospital provides quality healthcare at an affordable price with 173 beds and 30 multi-specialty centers. Serving over 100,000 patients a year, 40 percent are treated free of charge irrespective of their caste, creed, or religion. Its breadth of care continues to expand as new medical services and facilities are added each year and Mercy Clinics are planted in surrounding villages. Dedicated to the complete health and happiness of Calcutta's poor, Calcutta Mercy Ministries supports a larger holistic network of programs that includes a blind school, daily feeding stations for 25,000, leadership training centers, and a Hope House for disadvantaged children.[44]

If you're still looking for "the charismatic hospital," Pastor MacArthur, look no further. (And to Mr. Johnson, I repeat: You cannot separate the Buntains and their ministry from their Pentecostal faith.) But this, of course, is barely the tiny tip of a massive (and beautiful) iceberg.

And while we're speaking of the Assemblies of God, numbering almost seventy million worldwide, consider another one of their ministries of compassion, Latin America Child Care, which is "dedicated to transforming the lives of needy children with the Good News of Jesus Christ through education and ministries of compassion."[45] The website states that, "Over the years, God has perfected the first plan into a proven, effective formula of evangelism and education that gives needy children hope. Today, LACC serves nearly 100,000 children in 300 schools and projects in 21 countries throughout Latin America and the Caribbean."[46]

Or how about Love-N-Care Ministries, based in Visakhapatnam, India and founded by P. Yesupadam, with whom I have had the privilege of working annually since 1993. Yesupadam was an untouchable who almost died of malnutrition as a boy, rescued by a Canadian missionary who found him lying on the side of the road and brought him to a hospital to recover. But rather than turning to the Lord, he despised the very thought of God (his father, who had become a Christian, had given him the name Yesupadam, which meant Jesus Foot, which he despised all the more) and at the age of eleven, he joined the Naxalites, violent Maoist Communists, signing his pledge with his own blood.

As the years went on, he became a violent, heavy drinking atheist, until he attended a church service with his wife. During that service, he had a vision of Jesus with His arms stretched out, saying, "This is how much I loved you." He was transformed from that day on, receiving a tremendous burden to reach his people with the gospel and to help the needy and suffering. He was once stoned for preaching in a militant Hindu village in

Tuni, but the elders who stoned him subsequently came to faith and became the pastors of the church. I had dinner in one of their homes in 1995.

Overcoming all odds, with very little funding, and relying heavily on the Holy Spirit, his ministry has now outstripped the work of many megachurches in America, including:

- Children's homes, where orphans and other needy children are housed, fed, clothed and discipled. The children "are cared for spiritually through daily training in the Scriptures, waking every morning at 5:00 for prayer and worship and maintaining a disciplined and well-balanced daily schedule. They are being raised up as a mighty army to establish a new generation to reach India and the ends of the earth with the gospel."[47]

- Public schools, which "were established to uphold the vision of training well-disciplined, godly children in a loving environment," serving both the kids in the children's homes as well as children from the surrounding area, including non-believing Hindu children who are hearing the gospel for the first time. The school at their home base is one of the top schools in the city.

- Disabled Vocational Training Programs: "Shunned by society but desperately in need of hope and a future, disabled young men and women are being trained by Love-n-Care Ministries in the Printing Press, Computer Center, and Tailoring Center in a 1 year program. The Indian government provides a certificate for each graduate, enabling them to begin their own business or find employment which helps them support their families. A Baptist church in Utah provides each graduate of the Tailoring program with their own treadle style sewing machine."[48] One of the greatest privileges of my life has been handing certificates to crippled and deformed men and women who have completed the program and beam with joy as they are honored publicly for their accomplishments.

- Yesupadam's ministry has also built one hospital and dental clinic so far (they are praying for funds to build a larger hospital on the side of a mountain they purchased from the government) along with an old age home and a government-recognized nursing school to train registered nurses and midwives.[49]

- The graduates from their discipleship training centers have planted 6,000 churches in unreached tribal regions, and the pastors can be fully supported for just thirty dollars a month.[50] Some of their workers have been severely beaten, others have endured severe living conditions, and some have been martyred.[51] I can assure you that for Yesupadam and his team, their devotion to Jesus, their empowerment by the Spirit, their burden for the lost, and their heart of compassion for the poor all go hand in hand.[52]

- On average, they provide 5,000 meals a day (can you imagine the weight of that responsibility), and I assure you if you tried to separate Yesupadam's ministry of compassion from his overall walk with Jesus, empowered and helped by the Spirit, he would have no idea what were you talking about.

Similar stories from around the world could easily be told, with
countless Charismatic ministries involved in works of compassion and mercy, resulting in social services, hospitals, programs
feeding the poor, and so much more. Honestly, it boggles my
mind that Pastor MacArthur could have such a skewed view
of Charismatics – both in America and the nations – and I'm
sure that right within his home state of California there are numerous, outstanding, Charismatically-based and operated ministries of mercy.[53]

Immediately after the Strange Fire conference, I played the
quote, cited above, for some of our FIRE School of Ministry
graduates working in the Philippines, where our team consists
of fifty people (including children) in this one country alone. I
asked the three single women who joined me on the radio to
explain the work they were involved with there, and while all
of our grads are involved in some kind of gospel outreach to
the lost, they are often active in humanitarian work as well. In
response, these godly ladies explained that their ministry work
focused on: 1) feeding the poor; 2) housing orphans; 3) combat-
ing abortion; 4) rescuing children sold into sex slavery (human
trafficking) – and this was just one part of one ministry of one
group of grads from one small school. And the women assured
me that it was because of a powerful encounter with the Holy
Spirit that they were on the mission field and that they relied
heavily on the Spirit in their humanitarian work.[54]

To repeat: There are countless other examples of ministries
just like this, many that are far larger and more established
than some of the ones I have mentioned, including the Convoy
of Hope, Operation Blessing (founded by the much maligned

Pat Robertson), and LIFE Outreach International (founded by James Robison).[55]

Pastor MacArthur asked, "Where is the charismatic hospital? Where are the charismatic social services? Where are the people coming together to relieve poverty?" Over here, sir, and over there, sir, and as far as the eye can see around the world, sir. I do hope you will be glad to hear this!

"The Movement Itself Has Brought Nothing That Enriches True Worship"

3) "...the movement itself has brought nothing that enriches true worship."[56] I know that many of you reading these words are shaking your heads with incredulity, since plenty of cessationists recognize what passionate worshipers charismatics are – and I don't just mean boisterous. I mean passionate in the best sense of the word: fervent, focused, devoted, given over to, and absorbed. That's why it's not uncommon for charismatic worship services to go an hour or more before the Word is preached (with the preaching often lasting for an hour as well), and that's why we sometimes have whole days (or nights) of worship where we come together just to adore the Lord in song and prayer and praise.

On countless occasions, I have been in services where Jesus was so exalted in our midst that we could only fall to our knees or on our faces, glorifying the King of Kings. I have often seen God's Spirit poured out so mightily in worship that suddenly, people began to repent of their sins, convicted by the holy presence of a holy God. And how wonderful it is to see young people with tears of joy celebrating the power of the blood of Jesus and the resurrection of our Lord.

As for "enriching true worship," who can begin to list the songs produced by Charismatic worship leaders? How many churches sing songs written by Darlene Zschech and her colleagues at Hillsong? Or by Matt Redman? Or by Michael W. Smith? Or what of the veritable flood of wonderful worship songs that have come directly out of the Vineyard Movement, including "Isn't He?", written by John Wimber himself.

In the Messianic Jewish world, I think of worship leaders and psalmists like Paul Wilbur and Marty Goetz, or in the contemporary, black gospel tradition, men like Israel Houghton, Eddie James, and Donnie McClurkin. And there are the many fine, contemporary Christian, charismatic songwriters like Andrae Crouch, author of many beloved classics. Truly, the list goes on and on.

That's why blogger and author Dr. Adrian Warnock wrote in response to Pastor MacArthur's comment,

It is astonishing to me that the great modern choruses and hymns written by charismatics could be rejected so wholeheartedly. What of such popular songs as "In Christ Alone" written by a team including Stuart Townend, part of the same family of charismatic church's [sic] as myself? Has that song not been a blessing? Has it not, dare I suggest it, added to biblical understanding for many? Does he really reject Hillsong music like this, not to mention Jesus Culture, and a host of others? The Charismatic Movement has contributed masses towards worship! Not just the songs, but a renewed passion for God, and dare I say it a more biblical approach to using our whole bodies to worship God at times noisily.[57]

Take a few minutes to watch a powerful moment of charismatic worship on YouTube – say Kari Jobe, singing the Revelation Song, where even the children are engaged in heartfelt adoration,[58] or Lindell Cooley and the choir at Brownsville Assembly singing Lord Have Mercy,[59] or the Brooklyn Tabernacle Choir singing Worthy Is the Lamb,[60] or young people at The Ramp singing Beautiful the Blood[61] – and then tell me that this is just mindless, empty babble.[62] The fact that the same lyrics are sometimes sung repeatedly during worship is hardly something to ridicule (as was done at the Strange Fire conference, to the enjoyment of the attendees),[63] as if this was the only thing done in charismatic worship services, and as if it is always wrong to repeat the same phrase for emphasis (see Psalm 136, for example).

And if you've ever offered powerful worship to the Lord while singing "Majesty," one of the most widely-sung contemporary worship songs, remember that this too was written by a charismatic – actually, a Pentecostal statesman, Pastor Jack Hayford. And he wrote this song because the Spirit glorifies and exalts King Jesus:

Majesty, worship His majesty

Unto Jesus be all glory, power and praise
Majesty, kingdom authority flow from His throne
Unto His own His anthem raise
So exalt lift up on high the name of Jesus
Magnify, come glorify Christ Jesus the King
Majesty, worship His majesty
Jesus who died now glorified
King of all kings.

The reality is that there is a massive, glorious, God-glorifying, holy river overflowing with powerful Charismatic worship, and to anyone with an open heart and mind, it is impossible to miss.

Charismatic Leaders Don't Look Like Jesus

4) "I'll start believing the truth prevails in the Charismatic Movement when its leaders start looking more like Jesus Christ."[64]

On a certain level, this statement, which was actually tweeted out on the Strange Fire account, is the most insulting, as well as the most easily refuted, of Pastor MacArthur's unfortunate comments, since there are so many godly charismatic and Pentecostal believers. And the failings of some prominent leaders (see below, Chapter Four) does not detract in the least from the godliness of these every day, non-superstar believers, nor does it detract from the godliness of the many devoted charismatic leaders. Since so many cessationist readers have charismatic friends or family members who are exceptional Christians, there's no need to belabor this point, and I'll just mention two individuals here, one quite famous and the other hardly known. (Also, while I don't personally know all the charismatics mentioned earlier in this chapter, those I do know are exemplary people as well.)

The first is none other than Corrie Ten Boom, the heroine of "The Hiding Place" of book and movie fame. She was one of the most beloved Christians of the twentieth century, coming to prominence when she shared her testimony at Billy Graham evangelistic outreaches. A woman who learned to forgive her

Nazi tormentors, she explained, "When He tells us to love our enemies, He gives along with the command, the love itself." Perhaps her most famous quote is, "There is no pit so deep, that God's love is not deeper still." Listening to her speak and seeing her smile was to see and hear Jesus, yet Corrie Ten Boom was a charismatic, and a committed one at that.

> People who remember her primarily for *The Hiding Place* may not realize that she was very involved in the Charismatic Movement, networking internationally with Christian groups who were pursuing miraculous healing, speaking in tongues, and prophetic words. She was very committed to that charismatic expression of her Christian faith. But during those decades when, at least in America, the extremely charismatic people were building their own separate relational networks, getting odd television shows, emphasizing what set them apart from everybody else, and often embarrassing their non-charismatic brothers and sisters, Corrie Ten Boom projected a calm, centered kind of evangelical Christianity. She was a kind of itinerant elder statesman for the charismatics, and made the rest of us feel that after all, if Corrie Ten Boom was one of them, they must not be as weird as their television representatives made them seem.[65]

How true!

Pastor MacArthur has claimed that charismatics have "polluted prayer with private gibberish" (meaning tongues), claiming that all modern tongue-speaking is either demonic, learned behavior, or psychologically induced, referring to tongues as "mumbling in nonsensical prayer languages."[66] Corrie Ten

Boom would have strongly demurred, agreeing with Prof. N. T. Wright that the tongues in which she spoke were a "private language of love" to the Lord.

The second saintly charismatic I'll focus on is one known to a far smaller circle of people but whose life of less than thirty years made a tremendous impact on those he touched. I can speak about him personally since I knew him personally, but I cannot even mention his name because it could endanger his co-workers who continue to reach out in the country in which he was killed.

In his mid-twenties, he went as a missionary to a dangerous Islamic country and served there with his wife and young children, teaching English and practical skills to impoverished Muslims, fully knowing the risks involved. Because he and his co-workers could not publicly teach about Jesus, they did so first by the quality of their lives, setting a living example of Jesus for these Muslims to see as they built relationships with them in private. One day, to illustrate how Jesus washed His disciples' feet, they told a parable about a king who washed his servants' feet and then, to the shock of their students, this young man and his coworkers got on their knees and washed the dirty feet of these students, who sobbed and wept at this act.

A few days later, he was killed by Al-Qaeda terrorists, sparking days of peaceful protests as many of the Muslims who knew him (including women in burqas) risked their own lives by marching in the streets, speaking out against his death and commending him as a saintly Christian man who came to serve the poor and the needy. (I literally had to stop writing this section while I paused to sob, especially in light of the glowing testimony of his widow which I heard just one week before writing this chapter.)

I will never forget attending his funeral and watching his four-year-old son, the older of two boys, after his father's casket was lowered into the ground saying, "Bye bye, Daddy! I love you!" One day, his name will be known along with martyrs like Jim Elliot, and the stories of his commitment to Jesus and to the lost will not be exaggerated. Be assured that he was a passionate charismatic and that his life had been transformed by the Spirit of God.

It has been my privilege over the last forty-two years to work with many godly charismatics, people whose personal piety and devotion to Jesus puts most of us to shame, making Pastor MacArthur's comment all the more deplorable. The good news is that these godly charismatics will certainly forgive him from the heart and pray God's richest blessing on him.

I too join in that prayer, asking the Lord to help Pastor MacArthur recognize this massive blind spot in his life to the point that in this next season of his life and ministry, he will be deeply appreciative and greatly enriched by the theological, charitable, worshipful, and individual contributions of the charismatic part of the Body of Christ.

Endnotes

[1] http://www.pastoralized.com/2013/09/26/the-number-of-hours-keller-piper-driscoll-and-5-others-spend-on-sermon-prep/

[2] http://unashamedworkman.wordpress.com/2007/03/21/macarthurs-sermon-preparation/

[3] The first part of this quote is from *Strange Fire*, xv; the second part came from Pastor MacArthur's opening message at the Strange Fire conference; see http://www.christianpost.com/news/strange-fire-conference-john-macarthur-calls-out-charismatic-movement-as-unfaithful-106849/, my emphasis.

[4] Remarkably, Mike Riccardi, in an attempt to defend Pastor MacArthur against painting with too broad of a brush, actually digs the hole deeper by clarifying exactly what MacArthur was saying: "It's plain that MacArthur has not claimed that *absolutely nothing* good exists throughout the entire Charismatic Movement. Rather, he is saying that the good that *does* exist—which would include the fact that he believes that people *have* been truly saved through the evangelistic efforts of the movement, among other things like Grudem's *Systematic Theology* and Piper's preaching—all that good that *has* come from the movement has come *in spite of it*, and not *because of it*" http://thecripplegate.com/myths- about- the- strange- fire- conference/

[5] See, conveniently, http://earthenvessels- donbiro.blogspot.com/2007/12/oswald- chambers- testimony- of- exchanged.html. Emphasis in my original copy but not here.

[6] Ibid.

[7] http://utmost.org/classic/the- life- that- lives- classic/ and http://www.sermonindex.net/modules/newbb/viewtopic.php?topic_id=42667&forum=40

[8] http://utmost.org/oswald- chambers- bio/

[9] *Strange Fire*, xvii.

[10] I'm not saying that cessationists would not affirm this quote but rather that Chambers' experience with the Spirit colored this theology.

[11] Pastor MacArthur cites Tozer's *The Knowledge of the Holy* on 180 of *Strange Fire*, referring to it as a "classic work."

[12] For its first publication, see Leonard Ravenhill, *Why Revival Tarries* (Minneapolis: Bethany House,1959).

[13] Leonard Ravenhill also shared this quote in his Foreword to James Snyder, *The Life of A. W. Tozer: In Pursuit of God* (Ventura, CA: Regal, 2009), 6.

14See Lyle Dorsett, *A Passion for God: The Spiritual Journey of A. W. Tozer* (Chicago: Moody, 2008), 80.

15Ibid., 78

16Ibid., 80

17A. W. Tozer, *Keys to the Deeper Life* (repr., Grand Rapids: Zondervan, 1988), 50; see also http://www.sermonindex.net/modules/newbb/viewtopic. php?topic_id=22632&forum=34&4

18This is widely quoted, without original attribution.

19As a born debater, I automatically anticipate potential objections to my material as I write or speak, so I'm quite aware that many will say, "We're not talking about people like Chambers and Tozer, and we certainly don't consider them charismatic like some of those TBN frauds." The problem, however, is that the sweeping statements and broad generalizations made by Pastor MacArthur do not allow for such nuanced statements, notwithstanding the fact that I would be the first to agree that Chambers and Tozer lived in a different spiritual universe than today's carnal prosperity preachers. The fact is that both of these spiritual luminaries were deeply impacted by the Pentecostal moving of the Spirit and ministered widely in Pentecostal circles, and their writings cannot be fully understood or appreciated outside of this context.

20Gordon D. Fee, *God's Empowering Presence: The Holy Spirit in the Letters of Paul* (repr., Grand Rapids: Baker Academic, 2009). Lincoln's comments are cited on Amazon.com website advertising the book.

21Cited above, Chapter Two

22Gordon D. Fee, *Gospel and Spirit: Issues in New Testament Hermeneutics* (Grand Rapids: Baker Academic, 1991), 102-03.

23http://www.benwitherington.com/

24http://benwitherington.blogspot.com/2007/01/here- come- pentecostals.html

25Tom Wright, *Paul for Everyone: 1 Corinthians* (London: SPCK, 2003), 181-182.

26http://www.fulcrum- anglican.org.uk/events/2005/inthechurch.cfm

27Peter H. Davids, *The First Epistle of Peter* (New International Commentary on the New Testament: Grand Rapids: Eerdmans, 1989), 43-44

[28] http://en.wikipedia.org/wiki/Graham_Twelftree

[29] Grand Rapids: Baker Academic, 2013.

[30] http://www.gordonconwell.edu/academics/view-faculty-member.cfm?faculty_id=15885&grp_id=8946, my emphasis.

[31] http://www.jpmoreland.com/about/professional- achievements/

[32] http://www.jpmoreland.com/jps- heart/encouraging- kingdom- living/, his emphasis.

[33] J. P. Moreland, *Kingdom Triangle* (Grand Rapids: Zondervan, 2007), 175.

[34] http://www.waynegrudem.com/

[35] Lake Mary, FL: Charisma House, 2014.

[36] This book, in part, is also a response to Pastor MacArthur's anti-charismatic theology.

[37] http://renewaltheology.net/

[38] http://www.samstorms.com/about- dr- storms

[39] http://askdrbrown.org/about/academic- c- v/

[40] http://thecripplegate.com/strange-fire-panel-qa-2-mac=arthur-mbewe-johnson-busenitz/

[41] This is the transcript of a relevant portion of our radio interaction on October 21, 2013. For the full exchange, go here: http://www.lineoffireradio.com/2013/10/21/dividing-over-truth-or-just-plain-divisive-dr-brown-interviews-chris- tian-leaders-regarding-the-strange-fire-conference/

MLB: "Phil I want to be totally candid with you. Pastor McArthur needs to apologize to charismatics around the world for one of the ugliest statements and misinformed statements I've ever heard." (I then played the clip from the Strange Fire conference, quoted immediately above.)

PJ: "Well I strongly agree with him actually. I've done quite a bit of work in other parts of the world as well, and it seems to me that American televangelists who are involved worldwide as a group, and there're, yeah, there're exceptions alright, but as a group, the televangelists, the best known charismatics who have exported their theology from America, to India, to Africa, to third world countries as a whole, as a group. What they do is for their own self-aggrandizement, to (illegible) people out of money."

PJ: "...I'm saying American televangelists are the example that set the example. There are many examples, there are many African Pentecostal leaders who do the same thing. And in fact I wish I could take you to Africa and take a tour of some of this, I would show you first hand, more even in India. I know you have been there right?"

MLB: "...Can't you at least say he spoke to broadly there, that he painted with to broad a brush?"

PJ: "Can't you say that you look at this broad movement, which is a broad movement? With rose colored glasses."

[42] http://teenchallengeusa.com/

[43] See, e.g., http://www.acadc.org/page/page/2495014.htm For a moving presentation on the anniversary of the 20th anniversary of Bombay Teen Challenge, go here: https://www.facebook.com/BombayTeenChallenge/posts/123248857738829

[44] http://www.buntain.org/who- we- are/our- history

[45] http://lacc4hope.org/our- mission

[46] http://lacc4hope.org/about- us

[47] http://lncministries.org/ministries- childrens.php

[48] http://lncministries.org/ministries- educational.php

[49] http://lncministries.org/ministries- medical.php

[50] http://lncministries.org/support.php

[51] http://www.lineoffireradio.com/2010/12/06/washing-the-feet-of-a-martyrs-widow-in-india-live-from-mumbai/. This was one of the most moving, difficult radio shows of my life, broadcast live from India in December, 2010.

[52] See Terri Whittaker, *Yesupadam: Reaching India's Untouched* (Washington, DC: Believe Books Real Life Stories, 2007).

[53] See, for example, http://www.dreamcenter.org/.

[54] For the broadcast, see http://www.lineoffireradio.com/ 2013/10/22/authentic-fire-and-strange-fire-and-sorting-out-the-issues/. While finishing

the writing of this book, Typhoon Haiyan, an absolutely devastating storm, ripped through the Philippines, killing thousands and leaving hundreds of thousands homeless. Within a day, our FIRE missionaries were on the move, devising a plan to bring aid to them. It is in their blood to serve the hurting and the poor, and all the senior leaders there had their lives dramatically changed during the Brownsville Revival.

[55] The featured project, as of this writing (November, 2013) is this: "This Fall, Mission Feeding has committed to feed 420,000 children in Africa and, in light of a severe drought, even more in some of the hardest hit areas of Angola and South Sudan. Together we can share food to save lives and also share the life-giving gospel of Jesus Christ." http://lifetoday.org/outreaches/mission- feeding/

[56] http://www.challies.com/liveblogging/strange-fire-conference-john-macarthurs-opening-address

[57] http://www.patheos.com/blogs/adrianwarnock/2013/10/strange-fire-john-macarthur-claims-no-good-has-come-out-of-the-charismatic-movement/

[58] http://www.youtube.com/watch?v=bL0nDrEYDnk

[59] http://www.youtube.com/watch?v=V7d2GFbp- pc

[60] http://www.youtube.com/watch?v=4Gae- n0Pb7Q

[61] http://www.youtube.com/watch?v=Z2- 7cYPLXGE

[62] For a typical example of this charge, see *Strange Fire*, 72. Similar examples could be easily multiplied.

[63] https://www.youtube.com/watch?v=S3{_}vli3t7Ds; the relevant section starts about fifty-one minutes into the video. For my own thoughts on this, see below, Chapter Nine, n. 16.

[64] https://www.facebook.com/JohnMacArthur.GracetoYou/posts/740211222660681

[65] http://www.patheos.com/blogs/scriptorium/2009/04/corrie- ten- boom- was- born- and- died- today/

[66] *Strange Fire*, 16. The word "nonsensical" occurs twelve times in the book, and it is just one of the many derogatory ways that Pastor MacArthur describes charismatic praying and worshiping

CHAPTER FOUR

THE GENETIC FALLACY AND THE ERROR OF GUILT BY ASSOCIATION

One of the primary arguments presented in *Strange Fire* is that the modern Pentecostal-Charismatic movement has been corrupt from the start. Pastor MacArthur states that, "When the Pentecostal Movement started in the early 1900s, it was largely considered a cult by theological conservatives."[1] Perhaps this was simply a matter of the religious establishment of the day rejecting something fresh and new that the Spirit was doing?

According to *Strange Fire*, that was hardly the case. Rather, it is alleged that, from the beginning, the movement was marked by aberrant practices and scandals (as noted, Dr. MacArthur brands it "a farce and a scam from the outset"),[1] such as people falsely claiming to speak in foreign languages; followers of one of the pioneer leaders, Charles Parham, beating a disabled woman to death while trying to drive rheumatism out of her; Parham himself being arrested on charges of sodomy; Parham also being a sympathizer with the Ku Klux Klan and holding to strange theological views, like Anglo-Israelism, just to name a few of the charges brought.[3] "All this," we are told, "raises significant questions about the claims of the modern Pentecostal Movement, given the dubious nature of its initial beginnings..."[4]

In response, it should be first be noted that, despite the modern Pentecostal Movement generally being traced back to Charles Parham and the subsequent Azusa Street Revival, historians have documented numerous instances of modern glossolalia – speaking in tongues – prior to the twentieth century. For example, Alan Heaton Anderson, in his 2013 book *To the Ends of the Earth: Pentecostalism and the Transformation of World Christianity*, published by Oxford University Press and part of the prestigious Oxford Studies in World Christianity, cites detailed examples of speaking in tongues, revelatory dreams, and prophetic utterances in revivals dating back to 1860 in India (with examples even before that in other parts of the world). Anderson notes that, "The main characteristics of this revival movement were confessions of sin and an emphasis on holiness," along with the conversion of many souls.[5]

The primary leader involved in this revival was John Christian Arulappan (1810–67), part of the Church Missionary Society. He refused to receive any salary for his missionary work to his Indian people, not wanting anyone to be able to claim he was hired to do this as a job. (He was hardly a prosperity preacher!) Hearing of the revivals that had broken out in America and Britain in the late 1850's, he gave himself to prayer for revival in his own country, which was followed by the outpouring that began in 1860.

After preaching on Sunday night, the Spirit began to convict the lost:

> The next day morning two of the females went to the next village and spoke about Christ and they read and searched the Scriptures with one of my sons-in-law. The next morning after prayer was over, they came into the

house and wanted me to pray for them, and cried with groans and tears, and told me that they were sinners, and that they should pray for the Holy Spirit. ... I could not stop their crying until I had prayed thrice with them, and shewed them several passages.[6]

In the months that followed, the Spirit began to work in unusual ways, although quite common in revivals through the centuries:

From the 4th May to the 7th instant [August] the Holy Ghost was poured out openly and wonderfully. Some prophesied and rebuked the people: some beat themselves on their breasts severely, and trembled and fell down through the shaking of their bodies and souls. They wept bitterly, and confessed their sins. I was obliged to pray without ceasing for the consolation of everyone.[7]

But there was more:

In the month of June some of our people praised the Lord by unknown tongues, with their interpretations...Then my son and a daughter and three others went in to visit their own relations, in three villages, who are under the Church Missionary Society, they also received the Holy Ghost. Some prophesy, some speak by unknown tongues with their interpretations. Some Missionaries admit the truth of the gifts of the Holy Ghost. The Lord meets everywhere one after another, though some tried to quench the Spirit.[8]

This is just one of the accounts cited by Henderson, and it predates the Pentecostal outpouring associated with Parham by

forty years, being marked by confession of sin, holiness, and salvation of the lost.[9] So, even if some of the events surrounding
the early twentieth century Pentecostal outpouring *were* suspect
– I say this for argument's sake, whether true or not – that would
not speak to the ultimate roots of the modern movement, since
the modern tongues movement predates the twentieth century.

The Holy, Jesus-Centered Roots of the Pentecostal Movement

Moreover, if you take the time to read the writings of some of
the early Pentecostal leaders, like Frank Bartleman, the journalist whose writings about Azusa Street helped spread the news
worldwide, you will see immediately that this was a strong holiness, repentance movement. In fact, it was birthed directly out
of Wesleyan Holiness roots, and many of the early adherents believed that you could not receive the baptism of the Spirit and
the gift of tongues *until* you had been thoroughly sanctified. It
was Bartleman who wrote, the depth of any revival will be determined exactly by the spirit of repentance that is obtained. In
fact, this is the key to every true revival born of God."[10] He also
wrote, "No sacrifice on the altar means no fire. The fire of God
never falls on an empty altar. The greater the sacrifice, the more
the fire."[11]

As for the place of humility in ministry, he said, "The fact is
when a man gets to the place where he really loves obscurity,
where he does not care to preach, and where he would rather sit
in the back [pew] than on the platform, then God can lift him
up and use him, and not very much before."[12] When I first read
Bartleman's writings from the days of the Azusa Street outpouring many years ago, I was cut to the heart with holy conviction,

sometimes driven to my knees in repentance with a hunger for a real move of God in my own day.

And note how Bartleman's warnings more than 100 years ago echo the same concerns that the Strange Fire movement raises, meaning that the early Pentecostals had their eyes fixed clearly on Jesus. Reading Bartleman's words, you will immediately see how wrongly Azusa Street has been characterized:

> We may not hold a doctrine, or seek an experience, except in Christ. Many are willing to seek power in order to perform miracles, draw attention and adoration of the people to themselves, thus robbing Christ of His glory, and making a fair showing in the flesh. The greatest need would seem to be for true followers of the meek and lowly Jesus. Religious enthusiasm easily goes to seed. The human spirit so predominates the show-off, religious spirit. But we must stick to our text - Christ.[13]

And:

> Any work that exalts the Holy Ghost or 'gifts' above Jesus will finally end up in fanaticism. Whatever causes us to exalt and love Jesus is well and safe. The reverse will ruin all. The Holy Ghost is a great light, but focused on Jesus always for His revealing...Where the Holy Ghost is actually in control, Jesus is proclaimed the Head - the Holy Ghost, His executive.[14]

Bartleman also warned:

> The temptation seems to be toward empty manifestations. This does not require any particular cross, or death to the self-life. Hence it is always popular.

We may not put power, gifts, the Holy Ghost, or in fact anything ahead of Jesus. Any mission that exalts even the Holy Ghost above the Lord Jesus Christ is bound for the rocks of error and fanaticism.[15]

The main leader during the Azusa Street revival was William J. Seymour, a black preacher who was blind in one eye and who was also blind to the racial barriers that existed in so many fundamentalist churches in that day (including the very ones that Pastor MacArthur referred to as "theological conservatives," above). In fact, it was the racial unity in Jesus that so upset Charles Parham, who had been a teacher of Seymour's a few years earlier. Seymour, who was a strong holiness preacher, said, "There are many wells today, but they are dry. There are many hungry souls today that are empty. But let us come to Jesus and take Him at His Word and we will find wells of salvation, and be able to draw waters out of the well of salvation, for Jesus is that well."[16]

It was Jesus, not tongues or manifestations, that was central to Seymour, who also said, "The Pentecostal power, when you sum it all up, is just more of God's love. If it does not bring more love, it is simply a counterfeit."[17] As for his basic theology, he noted that, "Justification and regeneration are simultaneous. The pardoned sinner becomes a child of God in justification."[18] And, in clear gospel terms, he explained, "Justification deals with our actual sins. When we go to Him and repent, God washes all the guilt and pollution out of our hearts, and we stand justified like a new babe that never committed sin. We have no condemnation. We can walk with Jesus and live a holy life before the Lord, if we walk in the Spirit."[19]

So, the picture painted by Pastor MacArthur, focusing on Charles Parham, is both misleading and inaccurate, since there were documented instances of tongues and prophecy well before the early 1900s, while the early Pentecostal movement itself was marked by holy living (not to mention evangelism) far more than it was marked by scandal. As noted in very strong language by one Pentecostal leader, and with reference to the Strange Fire conference as a whole,

> While the speakers had set themselves up as experts on the subject, they were all remarkably ignorant about the many complexities, history and theological positions of Pentecostals. It seems to me, that if you are going to produce a book and begin a world-wide attack on something, you would at least have made a study of Pentecostals and Charismatics. If their education is so superior (they love flashing their PhD's), how come they never learnt that you cannot study a subject, as complex as Pentecostalism, by watching TBN a few times? (MacArthur freely admits that this goes back to a time he had surgery and had nothing else to do but watch TBN.)
>
> Every presentation was filled with inaccuracies, exaggerations and plain old lies. They had drawn a caricature, based on what they saw on TBN, and proceeded to convince themselves that all Pentecostals looked just like the caricature.[20]

The Genetic Fallacy Error

Yet there's more: The attempt to discredit a major movement by tracing it back to its alleged (and often disputed) roots is often misguided, especially when it is done with a critical spirit.

It is one thing to trace Mormonism back to Joseph Smith or Islam back to Muhammad, since that is exactly what Mormons and Muslims do, and they would gladly say if the founders of their respective religions did not receive new revelation from God, then their whole religion is false. It is another thing to look for alleged spiritual roots, as if a godly pastor in China who speaks in tongues today can be traced back to Charles Parham (and his alleged scandals). Or, as if a group of spiritually hungry Baptist women praying together in the 1970's, who suddenly began to speak in tongues (although they had no idea what was happening and had never heard about tongues) can be immediately discredited because the roots of the modern Pentecostal Movement were allegedly flawed.[21]

One of the most amusing (albeit pathetic) criticisms of the Brownsville Revival, of which I served as a leader from 1996-2000, went as follows: Steve Hill, the evangelist whom God used to spark the revival, was prayed for by someone who had been prayed for in Toronto (in what was called the Toronto Blessing, which began in 1994), and the Toronto movement was ignited by Randy Clark, who in turn was prayed for by Rodney Howard-Browne (of "holy laughter" fame), and Rodney has Word of Faith roots, which go back to E. W. Kenyon, who had roots in mind science – so Brownsville was not of God because its roots went back to mind science.[22] I kid you not! People even showed me charts that demonstrated this alleged chain.

The reality is that Steve Hill didn't have a Word of Faith bone in his body, let alone a connection to science of the mind, having been discipled by men like Leonard Ravenhill and David Wilkerson. In fact, by and large, those in the Word of Faith camp were not attracted to Steve's message because of his hardcore repentance preaching, while a daily devotional he compiled, based on Robert Murray M'Cheyne's Bible reading plan, was laced with quotes from the Puritans and others of their ilk. That's where Steve cut his teeth.

As for John Kilpatrick, the pastor of the church where the revival broke out, he was (and still is) ordained with the Assemblies of God, and I'm not aware of any of his teaching that would be classified as Word of Faith, let alone mind science. As for my own spiritual perspective, I point readers to Chapter Two, above, as well as to my body of published work over the last twenty-four years.

It was absolutely ludicrous, then, to discount Brownsville based on the alleged roots of the revival. Rather, the right way to judge it was based on the messages that were preached and the lives of those affected by the revival over a period of years. As Steve used to say week after week in the meetings, "The true test of an evangelist's ministry is ten years down the line," meaning, today's excitement doesn't matter. What matters is how you are living ten years from now as a result of these meetings. For my part, I repeatedly said during the services, "It doesn't matter if you shake or fall. The only thing that matters is how you're living when you leave this building."[23] Yet the alleged connection between Brownsville and mind science is still found on some web pages dating back to the 1990s.

The reality is that this kind of spiritual witch hunt cuts both ways, and had Pastor MacArthur not been a Calvinist and a dispensationalist (believing in a pre-tribulation rapture of the Church), it would have been interesting to see what he would have written. Let's start with the question of dispensationalism.

Some Church historians trace the modern Pentecostal movement back to the controversial, Scottish Presbyterian leader Edward Irving (1792-1834), who "came to believe in premillennialism— that the Lord's coming was imminent and that charismatic gifts including prophecy, healing, and speaking in tongues, and the fivefold offices of apostles, prophets, evangelists, pastors, and teachers were being restored to the church."[24] And according to Rev. Stephen Sizer, one of the most strident critics of Christian Zionism today, dispensational beliefs, formulated into a system by J. N. Darby, were built on the theology of Edward Irving, the proto-Charismatic. "Darby is rightly regarded as the first to espouse dispensationalism as a discrete theological system. However, William Kelly and Edward Irving played no small part in the restoration of premillennial speculations out of which Darby's dispensationalism arose."[25] Following the same logic that connected Brownsville with mind science, John MacArthur has charismatic roots!

As if this wasn't enough, some websites claim that, "Dispensationalism is the theological mother of non-Lordship teaching," meaning the teaching that a person can have Jesus as Savior without having Him as Lord.[26] Now, Pastor MacArthur forcefully opposes this non-lordship message (as do I),[27] yet it is alleged that in modern times, it is the dispensational system (which Dr. MacArthur espouses) that has birthed the non-lordship message (which he passionately rejects). What?

And there's more still. Dr. John Gerstner, a respected Calvin-istic theologian, claimed that dispensationalism "is in constant deviation from essential historical Christianity."[28] For Gerstner dispensationalism is an outright heresy, "a theology of persons holding to a deviation from the Christian religion."[29] Yet Pastor MacArthur is a dispensationalist, which means he is a heretic – and one with charismatic roots, no less. Who knew?

In all seriousness, regardless of the alleged origins of dispen-sationalism and regardless of the charges of heresy, there's only one way to evaluate its truthfulness: It must be examined care-fully by the testimony of the Scriptures, and there and there alone can it be found wanting or worthy. Again, I can only won-der what kind of elaborate attack against dispensationalism Dr. MacArthur would have written had he been disparaging that system rather than charismatics, both in terms of origins as well as fruit. (For the record, a large percentage of charismatics are dispensational; I have not been for more than thirty-five years, based on my reading of the Scriptures.)

Guilt by Association Cuts Both Ways

Before considering the question of the roots of Calvinism and the Reformed faith, let me say a word about the "guilt by associ-ation" charges that are commonly hurled by critics – and I don't just mean cessationist critics here. I'm referring to the common charge that, "So-and-so is suspect because he (or she) associates with so-and-so," or, "He can't be trusted because he spoke at that questionable conference," or, "He is obviously way off because he endorsed a book by a pastor who in turn endorsed a book by a teacher whose theology is highly questionable." And on and on it goes, as if any association with someone outside your own small camp makes one utterly suspect, or as if participating in a meeting with someone who subsequently had a moral failure makes your own morality questionable.

For example, in my radio interview with Phil Johnson, John MacArthur's longtime editor and one of the Strange Fire speakers, when I pressed him to repudiate some of the unconscionable statements made at the conference, actually playing audio clips for him (see Chapter Three, above), one of his primary responses (paraphrased here) was, "Well, your discernment can't be trusted because you are friends with people like Cindy Jacobs."[30]

Of course, that was hardly germane to the questions I was raising, nor was it germane to my life and ministry. Specifically, in response to a question I was asked by an individual on *Facebook* – not in a radio show or in a nationally televised sermon or a book – I stated that Cindy Jacobs was a friend whom I believed to be a godly woman. That was it! We have been in joint prayer meetings for the repentance of the American Church and for God's mercy on our nation, and she has been courageous enough to have me on her TV show to talk about the effects of homosexual activism on our country, a subject most Christian leaders are afraid to address. I applaud her for that. (At the same time, her heart has been filled with compassion for individuals with unwanted same-sex attractions.)[31]

"But wait," you say, "Cindy is part of the New Apostolic Reformation led by C. Peter Wagner, whom John MacArthur excoriates in his book, and Wagner even wrote the Foreword for Jacobs' book *The Reformation Manifesto*."

True enough, but I am not part of that movement nor have I followed Cindy's ministry in detail over the years so as to critique or commend all of her prophetic words. (I believe she would say the same about me and my ministry, and I seriously doubt she has listened to my last thousand messages and broadcasts!) I simply posted a response on Facebook, and I make no apologies for it.[32]

But once again, the sword cuts both ways, coming right back to Pastor MacArthur's door. Specifically, the most celebrated theologian who spoke at the Strange Fire conference was R. C. Sproul, who was mentored by – you guessed it – Dr. John Gerstner, the one who called dispensationalism a heresy. In fact, it was Dr. Sproul who wrote the Foreword to Gerstner's book! So then, should we judge John MacArthur as being guilty of giving a platform to the man who wrote the Foreword to the book that branded MacArthur's theology heretical? What a ridiculous mess.

One would have to think that Dr. Sproul repudiated this Foreword (which I'm not aware of), in which case his discernment back then would be questioned today, or else Pastor MacArthur didn't feel this past disagreement was sufficient to divide them over their present attack on charismatics, which illustrates the very point I'm making.

Recognizing Our Unity in the Midst of Our Diversity

We can have differences with one another on some issues and yet work together on other issues, and we all do that to some extent, unless we're in virtual isolation from everyone outside our group. And isn't it sometimes good strategy to accept an invitation to speak at a conference where your views would normally not be heard, hopefully bringing a new perspective (or even corrective) to those attending?

Over the years, I have taught at or been affiliated with a wide range of seminaries and ministry schools, and some of those schools are cessationist in their theology while others are strongly charismatic. In fact, I once taught a two-hour class at a charismatic ministry school on the subject of the Church and social transformation, then, a month later, I taught a one-week class on the book of Jeremiah at a cessationist seminary. When the subject of false prophets came up, one of the seminary students asked me, "What about false prophets today?," naming specific individuals, one of whom was the founder of the school I had taught at one month earlier!

I simply answered his question in principle – as accurately and scripturally as possible – without dealing with the individuals he named. As for the specific beliefs of a given seminary, I am always interviewed by the faculty of the schools that invite me to teach on a regular basis, and in only one case was the question of my charismatic beliefs an issue. (I subsequently taught for them as well.) As for my personal policy, it is simple: If I can honor the convictions of the group in question without compromising my own convictions and my schedule allows me to serve them, I will do so.

This would mean that if The Master's Seminary asked me to teach an intensive class on Jewish apologetics or advanced Hebrew exegesis (wouldn't that be sweet!), but they made clear that my charismatic beliefs were not to come up in or out of class, I would honor that and take it as a privilege to serve their fine student body. In the same way, because Pastor Kilpatrick and Steve Hill held to a pre-trib rapture (Pastor Kilpatrick was very strong in his beliefs about this), I never raised the issue in our ministry school, instructing our faculty to present the different views on the subject and explain what Brownsville Assembly believed. Even when students would press me, I would say, "These are the different beliefs, based on these verses," despite the fact that I was absolutely not pre-trib myself. Working together in this extraordinary spiritual outpouring, reaching the lost, making disciples, and raising up leaders and missionaries was far more important to me than dividing over our end-time theology, as vital an issue as that is.

But if you want to take the "guilt by association" mindset seriously, that would mean you would have to pull out your indelible ink, black marker and write off: Trinity Evangelical Divinity School, since I served there as a Visiting Professor and am good friends with some of their Old Testament and Semitics professors (I also preached at a special meeting for their students interested in revival); Denver Theological Seminary, since I serve as an Adjunct Professor there and am also friends with some of their main professors; Gordon Conwell Theological Seminary, Charlotte (same story); Southern Evangelical Seminary (co-founded by the revered theologian and apologist Dr. Norman Geisler, with whom I have shared meals and warm fellowship, and who invited me to speak at a chapel service there when he was president; I'm also an Adjunct Professor there, have done debates there, spoken at their annual apologetics conferences, and am good friends with a number of their professors) – and remember, I'm friends with Cindy Jacobs, which makes all these schools all the more suspect. (Yes, I'm being sarcastic, and I could add more schools to this list to drive home my point.)

Moreover, I have worked closely on a number of occasions with Dr. Darrell Bock, one of the preeminent New Testament scholars today and a professor at Dallas Theological Seminary, a leading dispensationalist, cessationist school. (In endnote 1, above, when Pastor MacArthur mentioned how theological conservatives rejected Azusa Street as cultlike more than one century ago, he cited Dallas Seminary back then as a case in point.) Professor Bock has joined me on my radio show, I have joined him on his podcast, we have joined forces in debates and recorded TV programs together, not to mention enjoyed some good laughs and some fine fellowship. So, should he then be discounted because I am his friend (and Cindy Jacobs is my friend, and Peter Wagner wrote the Foreword to one of her books)? Does this mean that Dallas Theological Seminary supports the New Apostolic Reformation? As exaggerated, ridiculous, and preposterous as this sounds, I have been the subject of similar witch hunts, and again, if the tables were turned, one can only wonder where this would go.

I recently spoke at a conference organized by Chosen People Ministries (they are non-charismatic) and hosted by the historic Calvary Baptist Church in Manhattan (note carefully: Calvary *Baptist* Church, not Calvary *Pentecostal* Church). And for all I know, I was the only non-cessationist speaker at the event. As reported by the *Christian Post*, the conference "featured renowned scholars and speakers including Darrell Bock, Craig Blaising, Mike Wilkins, John Feinberg, Craig Evans, Michael Brown, and was designed 'to help Christians develop a deeper understanding of current and future events in the Middle East through the lens of Scripture.'"[33]

Should Calvary Baptist Church now be considered suspect because I spoke for them – and I was a leader in the Brownsville Revival, which Pastor MacArthur called "craziness" and which Phil Johnson more recently called a "fiasco," not to mention that I said on Facebook that I was a friend of Cindy Jacobs, who is a friend of Peter Wagner, who is the leader of the New Apostolic Reformation? Perhaps the discernment of all the speakers should be questioned for working with a tongues-speaker like me? Or maybe *my* discernment should be questioned, since most (or all) of the speakers were *not* tongues-speakers and many (most?) were dispensationalists?

To the contrary, there was nothing exceptional to what we did at all. We honored one another as fellow-laborers in the Lord, we united for a very serious, common goal, and I believe those who attended were blessed and enriched by the varied (and harmonious) tapestry of biblical truth that came together. It would be one thing if one of the speakers had written a book called, "Why God wants us to kill the Arabs," and I wrote the Foreword for that book. Then you could call both of us to account. But to work together with other leaders for the purposes of righteousness (like combatting human trafficking) or to stand together for God's purposes for the salvation of the Jewish people or simply to recognize one another as brothers and sisters in the Lord is commendable, not contemptible.

Or consider Talbot Theological Seminary, part of Biola University, and recently rated the number one apologetics school in America (with Southern Evangelical Seminary rated number two). William Lane Craig, probably the most celebrated

Christian apologist today, is a member of the Talbot faculty, along with J. P. Moreland, who was mentioned above in Chapter Three. Yet Prof. Moreland is an unashamed charismatic who has even been involved in the Vineyard movement, which was birthed by John Wimber. And both Wimber and the Vineyard were harshly criticized by Pastor MacArthur in *Charismatic Chaos*.[34] Not only, then, should the entire seminary be considered suspect for having Prof. Moreland on the faculty, but, based on the "guilt by association" principle, Biola University as a whole should now be connected to John Wimber and the Vineyard movement. This is just another illustration of why this particular aspect of heresy hunting must be rejected as unreliable, unhelpful, and even unchristian.

The Genetic Fallacy and the Protestant Reformation

Returning to the genetic fallacy, let's consider how this works out for the Reformation, the fountainhead for Reformed theology (and, on a certain level, for Protestantism as a whole), with the principal luminaries being John Calvin and Martin Luther. Roman Catholic apologists have a field day with these men (Luther in particular) and with this period of history, arguing, "If this is the beginning of your movement, you are obviously in big trouble!"[35] Again, one can only wonder what Pastor MacArthur would conclude about Reformed theology had he been a Catholic apologist critically tracing the movement back to its origins more than 500 years ago.

What would he say of Luther's profanity and vulgarity? (It is commonly known that Luther's translators sometimes put his German vulgarities into Latin so as to make the translations less offensive.) For example, Luther claimed to chase the devil away with a fart: "Almost every night when I wake up the devil is there and wants to dispute with me. I have come to this conclusion: When the argument that the Christian is without the law and above the law doesn't help, I instantly chase him away with a fart."[36] Can you imagine what Pastor MacArthur would say if some charismatic televangelist had made such a crude remark?

And what would he say of Luther's statement that "even if we were to kill or commit adultery thousands of times each day," that would not separate us from Jesus?[37] Where would this fit in with "lordship salvation"? Or would Pastor MacArthur say that some of Luther's teaching resembled the "little gods" theology of some Word of Faith preachers? Luther claimed that "…every Christian is by faith so exalted above all things that, by virtue of a spiritual power, he is lord of all things without exception, so that nothing can do him any harm. As a matter of fact, all things are made subject to him and are compelled to serve him in obtaining salvation."[38]

And what of Luther's pronouncements against the peasants? "Like the mules who will not move unless you perpetually whip them with rods," he wrote, "so the civil powers must drive the common people, whip, choke, hang, burn, behead and torture them, that they may learn to fear the powers that be." And, "A peasant is a hog, for when a hog is slaughtered it is dead, and in the same way the peasant does not think about the next life, for otherwise he would behave very differently."[39]

These German peasants felt terribly betrayed by Luther, who earlier had supported their cause, making his calls for their deaths all the more disturbing. He wrote, "On the obstinate, hardened, blinded peasants, let no one have mercy, but let everyone, as he is able, hew, stab, slay, lay about him as though among mad dogs, ...so that peace and safety may be maintained... etc."[40]

According to William McGrath,

When he was in later years reproached for such violent language, and for inciting territorial lords to merciless slaughter (they killed over 100,000 peasants), he answered defiantly: "It was I, Martin Luther, who slew all the peasants in the insurrection, for I commanded them to be slaughtered. All their blood is upon my shoulders. But I cast it on our Lord God who commanded me to speak in this way."[41]

What? Not only was he unrepentant, but he claimed that God commanded him to speak these horrifically violent words.

Martin Luther and the Jews

Luther heaped vulgarities on the Jews as well, writing,

Well, now, I don't know in detail where they got it from, but I can guess approximately. Here at Wittenberg, in our parish church, there is a sow carved into the stone under which lie young pigs and Jews who are sucking; behind the sow stands a rabbi who is lifting up the right leg of the sow, raises the behind of the sow, bows down and looks with great effort into the Talmud [the most sacred books of traditional Judaism] under the sow, as if he wanted to read and see something most difficult and exceptional...For among the Germans it is said of someone who pretends to great wisdom without good cause: "Where did he read that? On the behind of the sow [crudely expressed]."[42]

And did I mention Luther's notorious 1543 book, *Concerning the Jews and Their Lies*, the strategies of which Hitler and the Nazis implemented with zeal? For Luther, the Jews were the worst enemy of all, "devils and nothing more":

> Verily, a hopeless, wicked, venomous and devilish thing is the existence of these Jews, who for fourteen hundred years have been, and still are, our pest, torment and misfortune. They are just devils and nothing more.
>
> Know, Christian, that next to the devil thou hast no enemy more cruel, more venomous and violent than a true Jew.[43]

What then was his counsel to the local German princes for dealing with the Jews?

> First, their synagogues or churches should be set on fire, and whatever does not burn up should be covered or spread over with dirt so that no one may ever be able to see a cinder or stone of it. And this ought to be done for the honor of God and of Christianity...
>
> Secondly, their homes should likewise be broken down and destroyed. For they perpetrate the same things there that they do in their synagogues. For this reason they ought to be put under one roof or in a stable, like gypsies...
>
> Thirdly, they should be deprived of their prayerbooks and Talmuds in which such idolatry, lies, cursing and blasphemy are taught.

Fourthly, their rabbis must be forbidden under threat of death to teach any more...

Fifthly, passport and traveling privileges should be absolutely forbidden to the Jews...

Sixthly, they ought to be stopped from usury. All their cash and valuables of silver and gold ought to be taken from them and put aside for safekeeping.

Seventhly, let the young Jews and Jewesses be given the flail, the ax, the hoe, the spade, the distaff and spindle, and let them earn their bread by the sweat of their noses...

In brief, dear princes and lords, those of you who have Jews under your rule – if my counsel does not please you, find better advice, so that you and we all can be rid of the unbearable, devilish burden of the Jews, lest we become guilty sharers before God in the lies, blasphemy, the defamation, and the curses which the mad Jews indulge in so freely and wantonly against the person of our Lord Jesus Christ, this dear mother, all Christians, all authority, and ourselves. Do not grant them protection, safe-conduct, or communion with us... With this faithful counsel and warning I wish to cleanse and exonerate my conscience.[44]

If reading all this were not terrifying enough, consider that many historians believe that the Holocaust officially began on what is known as "Kristallnacht," the Night of Broken Glass, November 9-10, 1938. During this ominous two-day period, Nazi soldiers followed Luther's counsel to a tee, setting the synagogues on fire and smashing the windows of Jewish places of business, among other humiliating and even murderous acts. I had no good answer for the rabbi who first pointed out to me that the Nazis carried this out in conjunction with the anniversary of Luther's birth. (He was born November 10, 1483).

In his important recent study, *Hitler's Willing Executioners,* Daniel Jonah Goldhagen points out that

> One leading Protestant churchman, Bishop Martin Sasse published a compendium of Martin Luther's antisemitic vitriol shortly after *Kristallnacht's* orgy of anti-Jewish violence. In the foreword to the volume, he applauded the burning of the synagogues and the coincidence of the day: "On November 10, 1938, on Luther's birthday, the synagogues are burning in Germany." The German people, he urged, ought to heed these words "of the greatest antisemite of his time, the warner of his people against the Jews."[45]

Not surprisingly, "Julius Streicher (one of Hitler's top henchmen and publisher of the anti-Semitic *Der Sturmer*) was asked during the Nuremberg trials [for war criminals] if there were any other publications in Germany which treated the Jewish question in an anti-Semitic way." Streicher put it well: "Dr. Martin Luther would very probably sit in my place in the defendants' dock today, if this book had been taken into consideration by the Prosecution. In the book "The Jews and Their Lies," Dr. Martin Luther writes that the Jews are a serpent's brood and one should burn down their synagogues and destroy them…"[46] So, according to Streicher, the Nazis were only doing what Luther urged them to do![47]

Now, if you own *Strange Fire*, go back and read the chapter outlining the various scandals associated with Pentecostal and charismatic leaders, from Charles Parham to Ted Haggard, and see if all of them combined come anywhere near the scandals associated with Luther, the father of the Protestant Reformation. What, then, does this say of Protestantism as a whole if the genetic fallacy were actually true?

And I haven't mentioned some of Luther's statements about *books of the Bible*, like James (Jacob), of which he said, "...the epistle of St. James is an epistle full of straw, because it contains nothing evangelical." And, "If nonsense is spoken anywhere, this is the very place. I pass over the fact that many have maintained, with much probability, that this epistle was not written by the apostle James, and is not worthy of the spirit of the apostle."[48]

As for Esther, a strongly pro-Jewish book, he wrote, "I am so great an enemy to the second book of the Maccabees [part of the Apocrypha], and to Esther, that I wish they had not come to us at all, for they have too many heathen unnaturalities."[49] Luther said this about the Book of Esther, part of the Word of God! Is there any statement by any contemporary charismatic leader that is comparable to this? (As for polygamy, Luther remarked, "I cannot forbid a person to marry several wives, for it does not contradict Scripture.")[50]

The Critics of John Calvin

As for John Calvin, while he cannot be criticized for vulgarities and profanities, and while the worst of the charges brought against him pale before Luther's failings, he too is an easy target based on his sometimes extreme theological statements coupled with his leadership style in the city of Geneva. A Catholic website had this to say about Calvin's authoritarian ways:

Death was the penalty for high treason against religion as well as for high treason against the city, and for the son who would strike or curse his father, and for the adulterer and the heretic. Children were whipped or hanged for calling their mother a devil. A mason wearily exclaimed "to the devil with the work and the master," and was denounced and condemned to three days in prison. Magicians and sorcerers were hunted down. They always confessed, of course. According to the city register, in 60 years, some 150 were burnt at the stake.

The years went by; Calvin's obsession gripped the Genevans. The number of dishes that could be served at table was regulated, as well as the shape of shoes, and the ladies' hair styles. In the registers are to be found condemnations such as these: "Three journeymen tanners were sentenced to three days on bread and water in prison for having eaten at lunch three dozen pates, which is a great immorality."

That was in 1558. Drunkenness, taverns and card games were punished by fines. The city's coffers filled up and served to pay new informers. For there were ears everywhere in the republic of evangelical liberty, and the failure to inform was itself a misdemeanor. "They are to be stationed in every quarter of the city, so that nothing can escape their eyes," wrote Calvin. Sermons were given on Thursdays and Sundays. Attendance was obligatory under pain of fine or flogging. Not even children were excused. The spies would verify that the streets and

houses were empty. Every year, the controllers of orthodoxy went house-to-house to have everyone sign the pro-
fession of faith voted that year. The last Catholics disappeared by death or exile. None spoke of changing religion,
for Calvin had had a law voted punishing by death anyone who would dare question the reforms of the "servant
of Geneva."[51]

I assume that supporters of Calvin have responses to all of
this, but again, I'm simply pointing out that if you want to look
through a critical, unsympathetic lens, and if you follow the
genetic fallacy, then both Calvinism and Calvinists must be
viewed with the greatest of suspicion. Yet at the Strange Fire
conference, Calvin often had pride of place, to the disappointment of some attendees, one of whom wrote on his blog (speaking of one of the talks given by Pastor Steve Lawson, who was
given the specific task of addressing what he believed Calvin
would say to Calvinistic charismatics):

> Lawson never opened the Scriptures once, but preached
> from the gospel according to Calvin. His whole presenta-
> tion was a presentation of what Calvin had to say about
> the miraculous (so-called by the Roman church) and the
> Pentecostal phenomena as displayed by some Anabaptist
> and Libertine groups.
>
>   He opened by extolling the glories of Lord Calvin. I
> had never heard so much unreserved praise and glory
> heaped on one man as I heard in this session. Not even the
> Charismatics with their personality cults go as far as Law-
> son did. Interesting how you perpetuate the very thing
> you so despise in others![52]

And if Pastor MacArthur had been a critic of Calvin rather than a follower, what would he have done with famous quotes like these?

> "...individuals are born, who are doomed from the womb to certain death, and are to glorify him by their destruction." (*Institutes of Christian Religion*, Book 3, Chapter 23, Paragraph 6)

> "The devil, and the whole train of the ungodly, are in all directions, held in by the hand of God as with a bridle, so that they can neither conceive any mischief, nor plan what they have conceived, nor how muchsoever they may have planned, move a single finger to perpetrate, unless in so far as he permits, nay unless in so far as he commands, that they are not only bound by his fetters but are even forced to do him service" (*Institutes of Christian Religion*, Book 1, Chapter 17, Paragraph 11)

> "I admit that in this miserable condition wherein men are now bound, all of Adam's children have fallen by God's will." (*Institutes of Christian Religion*, Book 3, Chapter 23, Paragraph 4)

And, of course Calvin held to "double predestination," meaning that some are predestined to heaven and others predestined to hell, a doctrine that I personally find more offensive than the doctrine that God wants His people to prosper financially. Thus Calvin wrote, "Many professing a desire to defend the Deity from an individual charge admit the doctrine of election, but deny that any one is reprobated. This they do ignorantly and childishly, since there could be no election without its opposite, reprobation." (*Institutes of Christian Religion*, Book 3, Chapter 23, Paragraph 1).[53]

Faulty Reasoning and Unfair Judgment

My point is not to excuse the sloppy theology and bogus biblical interpretation that is all too common in some charismatic circles, nor is it to minimize the seriousness of the scandals that have taken place in our midst over the years. Rather, it is to point out that: 1) Based on the genetic fallacy, the faith of all of Protestants (which includes all evangelicals) should be suspect, based on the life and teachings of Luther (whose failings we have barely sampled) and Calvin (whose theology is as hated as it is revered).[54] 2) Strange Fire critics use unequal weights and measures, attacking charismatics with one standard while defending the Reformers (and those in their own camp) with another standard.[55]

At the Strange Fire conference, Pastor MacArthur said:

There is a stream of sound teaching, sound doctrine, sound theology, that runs all the way back to the Apostles. It runs through Athanasius and Augustine, through Luther and Calvin, the great Reformation and Reformers, and the Puritans, and everything seems so clear to them. Through the Westminster divines and the pathway of Spurgeon and David Martyn Lloyd-Jones, and S. Lewis Johnson, and Jim Boice, and to R. C. Sproul. That's the stream of sound doctrine. The heroes of this generation are people in that stream...

But you have to understand, this other stream of evangelicalism goes back to about 1966, when the hippies came out of San Francisco, joined Calvary Chapel, and we had the launch of an informal, barefoot, beach, drug-induced kind of young people that told the church how we should act. Hymns went out. Suits went out. For the first time in the history of the church, the conduct of the church was conformed in a subculture that was formed on LSD in San Francisco and migrated to Southern California.

That launches the self-focused church that winds up in the seeker-friendly church, that splinters in the Vineyard movement, which develops into the charismatic stream. I don't go back to Lonnie Frisbee, who led the Jesus movement and died of AIDS as a homosexual. That's not my stream. But that's the stream that has produced the culturally-bound, seeker-driven church movement. And while there are good and bad and better and worse elements of it, that's where it comes from. We are very different.[56]

Putting aside the idea that suits are good and casual dress is bad,[57] note how Dr. MacArthur glorifies men and movements like Augustine (whom many connect to Catholicism –which John MacArthur vehemently rejects as non-Christian – more than to Protestantism), Luther and Calvin (whose shortcomings we have mentioned in brief), the Reformation (see also below, Chapter Six), and the Puritans (didn't they burn witches at the stake in Salem, Massachusetts?), claiming that a glorious stream – the stream of the New Testament itself – passes through these men and movements, while singling out Lonnie Frisbee, whose failings are also well known, as proof that the modern Jesus Movement. (For the record, I find great spiritual riches among the Puritans and have read and enjoyed their writings for years. I'm simply pointing out again how Pastor MacArthur uses unequal weights and measures. It's also interesting that he refers to D. Martyn Lloyd-Jones, who, while not a Pentecostal, spoke strongly of the need to experience God in the power of the Spirit, quite contrary to many of the sentiments expressed in the conference. See further below, Chapter Nine.)

A Realistic Assessment

Turning back to Martin Luther, I personally believe that it took a man of iron will with a forehead of granite to challenge the fifteenth century religious establishment, and Luther was that man, raised up by God for such a purpose. And yet, with so many serious flaws that were never transformed through the cross, he did a tremendous amount of harm as well as good, leaving a tarnished legacy. Yet that doesn't mean that all Protestants are tarnished, nor does it mean that we should all convert to Roman Catholicism, which might be the case if the genetic fallacy were true. Instead, fundamental doctrines and beliefs must be evaluated by the Scriptures, and, when judging others, we should remember this principle: "*Don't compare the best things about your religion [ideology] to the worst things about someone else's.*"[58] (I say we all commit this principle to memory and do our best not to violate it.)

So yes, it is true that there have been all too many scandals among charismatic leaders, as repeated in *Strange Fire*, yet for every charismatic TV preacher who has fallen, there are ten (or 100, or more) who have not. On the flip side, there is a website devoted exclusively to exposing Southern Baptist ministers and church workers who are alleged sexual predators (with claims of collusion and cover-up brought against some of the highest Southern Baptist leaders in the country),[59] and a December 11, 2008 report on ABP News relates, "The secrecy of Southern Baptist Convention officials about a financial scandal at their International Mission Board wasn't anything unusual. It's the sort of thing we've seen over and over again."

The report, by Christina Brown, claims,

> The secrecy of Southern Baptist Convention officials about a financial scandal at their International Mission Board wasn't anything unusual. It's the sort of thing we've seen over and over again.
>
> Southern Baptists need to begin seeing the pattern rather than merely viewing these things as isolated cases.
>
> It's a very common pattern: Without accountability, power corrupts. Religious organizations are no exception.
>
> The corruption manifests itself not only in the cover-up of financial wrongdoing, but also in the cover-up of clergy sex abuse. For both types of corruption, the root of the problem is a systemic lack of accountability.[60]

The fact is that charismatic leaders hardly have a monopoly on scandals. (By way of comparison, have charges as serious as those alleged in this article just cited been brought against the largest Pentecostal denomination, the Assemblies of God? I think not.) And regardless of whether there is another side to the storyline of this article attacking the Southern Baptist Convention (which I cite as one example of many), the report gets one thing right: "Without accountability, power corrupts. Religious organizations are no exception."

That, in reality, is the root of the problem, rather than charismaticism being the root of the problem, as claimed by the Strange Fire camp. And so, it is primarily the *superstardom* of these charismatic leaders that most likely (or, almost certainly) led to their demise, rather than the fact that they spoke in tongues or believed in divine healing.[61] Moreover, I can provide you with countless, easily verifiable testimonies of those who were set free from besetting sins and morally transformed after an encounter with the Spirit – and I mean countless. That's exactly what happened to me on December 17, 1971 when, after two years of heavy drug abuse (including shooting heroin and other drugs) I surrendered my life to the Lord, promising that I would never put a needle in my arm again, and I was free from that night on. Oh for more of the glorious power of the Spirit! (Bear in mind this was part of what the Spirit was doing worldwide at that time in the Jesus People Movement – although I had no idea of this when I came to faith – and yet Pastor MacArthur reviled that movement as well.)

The Strange Fire movement, then, not only committed the error of the genetic fallacy and followed the faulty reasoning of guilt by association, but it also fails to use equal weights and measures, a serious ethical issue according to the Scriptures.[62] Yet I believe it was Pastor MacArthur's zeal for the truth and for purity that motivated him, and I applaud him for his many years of leadership without the hint of a sexual scandal associated with him. I also understand how glaring and pronounced some charismatic failings have been, especially with the pervasive influence of the internet and Christian TV.

Still, to repeat, the Strange Fire movement would do best to abandon these faulty lines of argument, recognizing the wonderful things the Spirit is doing worldwide in the Charismatic Movement and standing side by side with those of us in leadership, helping us reduce the number of scandals by getting to the real roots of the problems, as well as helping us lay more solid foundations for biblical preaching and teaching. This is sorely needed in a God-birthed movement that is growing so rapidly, and contrary to the assertion of Phil Johnson that there is no baby in the bathwater,[63] there are tens of millions of healthy charismatic babies in the bathwater, not to mention millions of healthy charismatic adults giving them a bath. But we could sure use the help of our cessationist friends given the breadth and scope of this massive harvest.

Endnotes

[1] *Strange Fire*, xv.

[2] *Strange Fire*, xvii.

[3] Ibid., 20-31

[4] Ibid., 27. Craig S. Keener, in his review of *Strange Fire*, has also drawn attention to inaccuracies in Pastor MacArthur's presentation of the origins of certain charismatic beliefs. See http://pneumareview.com/john-macarthurs-strange-fire-reviewed-by-craig-s-keener/

[5] *To the Ends of the Earth*, 21

[6] Ibid.

[7] Ibid., 21-22.

[8] Ibid., 22

[9] According to *Strange Fire*, 286, n. 1, Jonathan Edwards taught that "a holy life is the only sure sign of personal revival," and I agree with this both scripturally and experientially. One would think, then, when Strange Fire leaders would be presented with evidence of thousands of people whose lives have been made holy through charismatic-based revivals, they would rejoice. Sadly, to date, that has not been the case, but I do hope that with further interaction that would change.

[10] For a selection of his quotes online, see https://kindle.amazon.com/work/frank-bartlemans-azusa-street-revival%25C2%2597-ebook/B001P86MLW/ B001P05N06/posts

[11] Ibid.

[12] Ibid.

[13] Cited in 1982 by David Wilkerson in his sermon "A Christless Pentecost," http://www.tscpulpitseries.org/english/1980s/ts820001.html. Wilkerson's own message remains important.

[14] Ibid.

[15] Ibid.

[16] http://christian-quotes.ochristian.com/William-J.-Seymour-Quotes/

[17] Ibid.

[18] Ibid.

[19] For a free e-book citing this and many more quotes, see http://www.evanwiggs.com/revival/history/azusa.html. The reader will be able to evaluate more about Azusa Street, positively or negatively, by reading this. For the larger picture of the holiness-Pentecostal connection, see Vinson Synan, *The Holiness-Pentecostal Tradition: Charismatic Movements in the Twentieth Century* (2nd ed.; Grand Rapids: Eerdmans, 1997); see also idem, *The Century of the Holy Spirit : 100 Years of Pentecostal and Charismatic Renewal, 1901-2001* (Nashville: Thomas Nelson, 2012).

[20] Anton Bosch, http://moriel.org/MorielArchive/index.php/ discernment/impressions-from-strange-fire. I cite this not to claim that Mr. Bosch and his ministry would agree with all of my positions, nor is it to agree with the tone of his article, but rather to indicate how ludicrous the charges brought at Strange Fire would seem to many Pentecostals, like Bosch, who could not begin to relate to many of the abuses attacked at the conference.

[21]This is a true story and not just a hypothetical illustration, and it is hardly the only one of its kind. The son of one of these women, for years a pastor in North Carolina, told me the account personally and in detail.

[22]E. W. Kenyon is mentioned several dozen times in *Strange Fire*; for a sympathetic study of Kenyon, see Joe McIntyre, *E. W. Kenyon: The True Story* (Lake Mary, FL: Charisma House, 1997)

[23]For an impartial study on Brownsville, written during the midst of the revival by an award winning journalist, see Steve Rabey, *Revival in Brownsville: Pensacola, Pentecostalism, and the Power of American Revivalism* (Nashville: Thomas Nelson, 1998).

[24]Anderson, *To the Ends of the Earth*, 11.

[25]http://www.informationclearinghouse.info/article4531.htm. In support of this, Sizer cites the respected Calvinist author Iain H. Murray, *The Puritan Hope: Revival and the Interpretation of Prophecy* (Edinburgh, Banner of Truth, 1971), 191. A major proponent of the Edward Irving-pre-trib rapture connection is Dave MacPherson, author of a number of related books; see http://post-trib.net/macpherson/tribpages.html For a pro-dispensational critique of MacPherson, see http://www.raptureready.com/who/Dave_MacPherson.html For my radio debate with Dr. Sizer on, "How Christian Is Christian Zionism?," go to http://www.youtube.com/watch?v=22jgGE4hELI&feature=c4-overview&list=UUbINn3x-intLp88Zrf8acpg

[26]http://www.founders.org/journal/fj09/article1.html

[27]See Brown, *It's Rock the Boat*

[28]John H. Gerstner, *Wrongly Dividing the Word of Truth: A Critique of Dispensationalism* (Brentwood, TN: Wolgemuth and Hyatt, Publishers, Inc., 1991), 68. For a direct response to this book by Richard Mayhue, then Vice-President and Dean, Professor of Pastoral Ministries at The Master's Seminary, see http://www.tms.edu/tmsj/tmsj3d.pdf

[29]*Wrongly Dividing the Word of Truth*, 69.

[30]Please listen for yourself to see if I am presenting this fairly: http://www.youtube.com/watch?v=R7aQjsDYbcQ&feature=c4-overview&list=UUbINn3x-intLp88Zrf8acpg

[31] See further Michael L. Brown, *Can You Be Gay and Christian?* (forthcoming; Lake Mary, FL: Frontline, 2014).

[32] I am friends with Messianic Jewish leaders who believe I should be more observant (meaning, in terms of Torah and even Jewish tradition), and I am friends with Christian leaders who think these Messianic Jews are in error. I consider Mike Bickle a friend, even though we have enjoyed roughly one meal together in the last decade and I have not spoken at any of his conferences since 1991 and he has not spoken at our school since 2002. To the best of my knowledge (and attested to by many who have worked with him closely), he is a godly man, focused on Jesus, living very simply, and devoted to the Word and prayer. I mention Mike because of some of the very strong accusations brought against him by the Strange Fire camp. I would suggest that those unfamiliar with his ministry read his book *Passion for Jesus: Cultivating Extravagant Love for God* (Lake Mary, FL: Charisma House, 2007). As for Dr. Peter Wagner, I encourage both friends and critics alike to evaluate him based on his overall ministry fruit and literary output. All of us, in fact, should be evaluated accordingly.

[33] http://www.christianpost.com/news/jewish-people-need-to-accept-jesus-urges-chosen-people-ministries-president-107676/

[34] John F. MacArthur, Jr., *Charismatic Chaos* (Grand Rapids: Zondervan, 1992).

[35] See, for example, http://www.canapologetics.net/luther_said.html.

[36] http://souldevice.wordpress.com/2011/10/19/from-farts-to-faith-interesting-surprizing-and-amazing-quotes-from-martin-luther/ for this and other quotes, with references.

[37] For the references for these quotes, see conveniently, http://www.canapologetics.net/luther_said.html

[38] See, conveniently, http://divdl.library.yale.edu/dl/FullText.aspx?qc=AdHoc&q=3153&qp=15; of course, Luther scholars will be quick to point out the larger context of this quote (seen in this link), which is one reason I post this: Sound bites can be misleading and we need to do due diligence to see what people really believe and teach.

[39] For the quotes on a Christian website critical of Luther, see http://www.jesus-is-savior.com/False%20Religions/Lutherans/truth_about_martin_luther.htm

[40] See, conveniently, William R. McGrath, *Anabaptists: Neither Catholic nor Protestant*, at http://www.pbministries.org/ History/William%20R.%20McGrath/the_anabaptists_part1.htm

[41] Ibid.

[42] Martin Luther, *Vom Schem Hamphoras (Concerning the Unutterable Name of the Lord)*

[43] See Michael L. Brown, *Our Hands Are Stained with Blood: The Tragic Story of the "Church" and the Jewish People* (Shippensburg, PA: Destiny Image, 1992), 52, and 192, n. 30.

[44] This is from Luther's infamous 1543 work, *Concerning the Jews and Their Lies*. In the pre-internet days, I could normally find this book in neo-Nazi catalogues. Today, it is widely available online, with minor variations; see, for example, http://prophets-priests-poets.info/2009/10/31/repost-separation-celebration/. For Luther's earlier, pro-Jewish stance, and for the Lutheran repudiation of this book, see Michael L. Brown, *Answering Jewish Objections to Jesus: Vol. 1, General and Historical Objections* (Grand Rapids: Baker, 2000), 127-135.

[45] Cited in the internet article by Jim Walker, "Martin Luther's Dirty Little Book: On the Jews and their lies," http://www.nobeliefs.com/luther.htm.

[46] Jim Walker, ibid.

[47] Some of this material was adapted from Michael L. Brown, *The Real Kosher Jesus* (Lake Mary, FL: Frontline, 2012), 1-4.

[48] See again http://www.canapologetics.net/luther_said.html, for references.

[49] See http://socrates58.blogspot.com/2007/03/did-martin-luther-deny-canonicity-of.html; it is commonly quoted that he also said, "The book of Esther I toss into the Elbe [River]. I am such an enemy to the book of Esther that I wish it did not exist, for it Judaizes too much and has in it a great deal of heathenish foolishness." The accuracy of this quote, however, is disputed. See ibid.

[50] Martin Luther, Letter to Chancellor Gregory Brück, 1524

[51] http://www.catholicapologetics.info/apologetics/protestantism
/calvin.htm

[52] http://moriel.org/MorielArchive/index.php/discernment/im-
pressions-from-strange-fire; I do understand why Pastor Lawson focused on
Calvin in his talk. The perception of Calvin's importance in the context of
Strange Fire, however, can hardly be downplayed.

[53] For my debates on Calvinism with two of my esteemed colleagues, Dr.
James White and Pastor Bruce Bennett, see
http://www.youtube.com/watch?v=dmeMOo4nINA and
http://www.youtube.com/watch?v=iR4SVqj04kg, respectively

[54] To cite just two of the very negative critiques of Calvinism, see George
Bryson, *The Dark Side of Calvinism: The Calvinist Caste System* (Costa Mesa,
CA: Calvary Chapel, 2004); Dave Hunt, *What Love Is This? Calvinism's Mis-
representation of God* (Bend, OR: The Berean Call, 2004). I'm quite aware
that my Calvinist friends have very strong responses (and reactions!) to these
books.

[55] For a response to this charge by a colleague of the Strange Fire leaders,
see
http://teampyro.blogspot.com/2013/10/what-lutherans-have-done-for-5-
centuries.html

[56] http://thecripplegate.com/strange-fire-a-call-to-respond-john-
macarthur/; for a response to this claim, see, e.g.,
http://www.internetmonk.com/archive/43911 ("This is John MacArthur's
vision of Church History. What a narrow and simplistic view it is!")

[57] Of course, this was not a matter of drug-induced young people telling
the church how to act; rather, it was a matter of pastors like Chuck Smith,
father of the Calvary Chapel movement, having the cultural sensitivity to
reach these young seekers where they were and introduce them to Jesus and
the Word.

[58] This was passed on to me by Messianic Jewish scholar Stuart Dauer-
mann, who heard it from Dennis Prager, who in turn learned it from his
mentor Yitz Greenburg; see
http://larrygellman.blogspot.com/2008/07/pluralism-our-last-and-best-
hope.html. A.W. Tozer made a relevant statement that is frequently cited,
namely that a religious hypocrite "is hard on others and easy on himself,
but a spiritual man is easy on others and hard on himself." Missions leader

David Shibley (see below, Appendix D), in his open letter to Southern Baptists (December, 2007), noted, "When G. Campbell Morgan was asked if he was a fundamentalist he replied, 'In doctrine, yes, but I abominate their spirit.'" Morgan also said, "There is a spirit that contends of the faith which is in conflict with the faith...All zeal for the Master that is not the outcome of love to Him is worthless." For these last two sentences, see G. Campbell Morgan, *The Letters of Our Lord* (London: Pickering & Inglis, n.d.), 27.

[59] http://stopbaptistpredators.org/index.htm

[60] http://www.abpnews.com/opinion/commentaries/item/3712-spending-gods-money#.UnHuW_kqj2k. The article makes for lurid reading.

[61] Is it possible that a charismatic leader gifted with a healing ministry could get drunk on the perceived power of that ministry? Certainly, and that is a very real danger, since, power can also easily corrupt. And to the extent that charismatics depart from the holiness roots of their faith and from grounding everything in the Scriptures, scandals can easily abound This is something those of us on the inside of the movement have addressed for years as well. Yet it is clear that the proverbial temptations (spoken from a male perspective) of "gold, glory, and girls" can bring down anyone, and there are more than enough leaders of large cessationist churches or ministries who have also become drunk with power or influence or money, to their own demise. To state this again: If the Strange Fire camp could recognize the vast amount of genuine good that is being accomplished through the Charismatic Movement and work together with the many solid charismatic leaders who are laboring on the front lines, we could do a much better job of combatting error together.

[62]For my article on this (address Jewish counter-missionaries), see
http://realmessiah.com/read/unequal-weights-and-measures

[63]http://www.youtube.com/watch?v=F2JAoNoCVDY

CHAPTER FIVE

TESTING THE SPIRITS: ANOTHER LOOK AT THE EVIDENCE

Pastor MacArthur devotes two chapters of *Strange Fire* to "Testing the Spirits,"[1] following the guidelines formulated by Jonathan Edwards in his 1741 work, The Distinguishing Marks of a Work of the *Spirit of God*, written during the Great Awakening. Based on these guidelines, Pastor MacArthur concludes that the Charismatic Movement has been weighed in the balance and found wanting.

Are the Edwards guidelines fair and reliable? I believe so. Are Dr. MacArthur's conclusions equally fair and reliable? I think not.

Let's first understand, however, what Jonathan Edwards was *not* saying in *The Distinguishing Marks*. To explain the background to this book, we need to remember that it is common during times of revival for there to be intense and unusual physical and emotional responses to the Spirit's work, such as weeping, crying out, shaking, falling into trances, and the like. These can be disruptive, alarming, and unsettling, and not all of this activity can be attributed to the Holy Spirit. Is it demonic? Is it simply emotionalism? Or is it a genuine response to the Spirit?

Edwards offered nine non-signs which *did not disqualify the work* in general from being of God. In other words, based on these things happening, you cannot say, "This proves that it is not sent from heaven." So, these nine signs are not "false positives" (as Pastor MacArthur states) as much as "false negatives."[2] And they are certainly not negative signs, meaning, "If you see these things happen, you know the work is not of God." Quite the contrary.[3]

The Nine "Non-Signs" of Edwards

Here, in excerpted form, are the nine non-signs, followed by a brief explanation of each:

> I. *Nothing can be certainly concluded from this, That a work is carried on in a way very unusual and extraordinary; provided the variety or difference be such, as may still be comprehended within the limits of Scripture rules.*

Generally speaking, if something is unfamiliar to us, we don't like it. We get used to one way of doing things, and right or wrong, that's what we tend to stay with. That which is ordinary becomes the equivalent of "that which is spiritual." But revival is anything but ordinary! The point Edwards is making is simple: Just because something is new and intense doesn't mean it's not from God, unless it clearly violates Scripture.

> II. *A work is not to be judged of by any effects on the bodies of men; such as tears, trembling, groans, loud outcries, agonies of body, or the failing of bodily strength.*

Physical manifestations like these neither prove nor disprove that the work is from God. On the one hand, when the Spirit is moving deeply on people's hearts and minds, it makes perfect sense that there would be some kind of outward effect or external release. On the other hand, someone could get worked up into an emotional frenzy and have the same kind of manifestations. So these things themselves prove nothing either way. Plus, the Bible does not give us the right to pass judgment based on certain physical responses or manifestations. I know that there are charismatics who think that someone falling or shaking like a leaf is proof that the Holy Spirit is moving powerfully, while to some evangelicals, falling or shaking is proof that the people are in the flesh. But the Word of God gives us no right to make sweeping judgments based on these things alone.

III. *It is no argument that an operation on the minds of people is not the work of the Spirit of God that it occasions a great deal of noise about religion.*

Yes, revival will draw a crowd, and it will get people talking. Even the secular world will be stirred, and the media will report both the good, the bad, and the ugly sides of the work. But that doesn't mean that God is not moving in the midst of it all, and that He is not the Author of the spiritual excitement. *It is impossible to have a quiet, unheralded revival.* As I have said many times, you can have controversy without revival, but you cannot have revival without controversy.

IV. *It is no argument that an operation on the minds of a people is not the work of the Spirit of God that many who are the subjects of it have great impressions made on their imaginations.*

Could you picture a sweeping, radical outpouring that impacted countless thousands of saints and sinners without having some kind of impact on the imaginations? And Edwards is quick to point out that God actually uses this faculty for His purposes. The Bible is full of images – about heaven, hell, and our intimate relationship with God – and these images can stir our imaginations, as can powerful preaching.

In any case, Edwards was certainly right when he said: "That persons have many impressions on their imaginations does not prove that they have nothing else." Just because their imaginations were touched doesn't mean that the whole work was a fantasy.

> V. *It is no sign that a work is not from the Spirit of God that example is a great means of it.*

It is easy to say that people are weeping, or collapsing, or shaking, or laughing just because they have seen other people do the same. But Edwards claims that learning by example is both reasonable and Scriptural, if, in fact, the work is from God. Again, you can't prove anything either way from this.

> VI. *It is no sign that a work is not from the Spirit of God that many who seem to be the subjects of it are guilty of great imprudences and irregularities in their conduct.*

People who have been touched will make mistakes and will at times act foolishly. We are human before revival, during revival, and after revival. Heavenly perfection is not here yet. And so Edwards was not exaggerating when he said that: "if we see great imprudences, and even sinful irregularities, in some who are great instruments to carry on the work, it will not prove it not to be the work of God."

Just think of the church of Corinth, empowered by the Spirit but guilty of foolishness and sin. Do the excesses, problems, and even moral failures in that church prove that the gifts of the Holy Spirit are not good? On a certain level, this principle invalidates one of the biggest criticisms of the Strange Fire camp, namely,

that prominent charismatic leaders have fallen into sin or foolishness. As grievous as this is, in no way does it disqualify the
larger movement.

*VII. Nor are many errors in judgment, and some delusions of
      Satan intermixed with the work, any argument that the
      work in general is not of the Spirit of God.*

These were very real issues that Edwards and other leaders
had to deal with in the Great Awakening, and again, recognizing the massive expansion of the Charismatic Movement in
the world in the last fifty years, representing the most rapid expansion of the gospel worldwide in history, it is not surprising
that there are "errors in judgment" and even "some delusions
of Satan intermixed with the work." This, Edwards states, is not
"any argument that the work in general is not of the Spirit of
God." Once again, this principle has been virtually lost on Pastor MacArthur, who judges the whole work by the errors and
delusions of some.

*VIII. If some, who were thought to be wrought upon, fall away
       into gross errors, or scandalous practices, it is no argument
       that the work in general is not the work of the Spirit of God.*

Remember Judas Iscariot? Does his fall from apostleship disprove the ministry of Jesus or throw into question the validity of the other eleven apostles? Or how about Church history?
Does the Church's unspeakably bloody persecution of the Jewish people negate the truth of the Gospel? Once more, if Pastor
MacArthur had only kept this principle before him and interacted more with the countless millions of fine Pentecostal and
charismatic believers, he would not have judged the (very good)
whole from the (very bad) part.

IX. *It is no argument that a work is not from the Spirit of God*
     that it seems to be promoted by ministers insisting very
     much on the terrors of God's holy law, and that with a great
     deal of pathos and earnestness.

My, how things have changed! In Edwards' day, the concern
was about too much hellfire preaching; nowadays, the concern
is about almost no hellfire preaching. Still, God can send His
Spirit in spite of an overemphasis on hell or an under emphasis
on hell.[4]

Reading *Strange Fire*, it is clear that Pastor MacArthur *does*
disqualify the Charismatic Movement because of some physical and emotional manifestations, some scandals and impro-
prieties, and some errors in judgment and delusions, the very
thing that Jonathan Edwards urged against, using the principle
that we are to judge by the whole, not the part. The Strange Fire
camp would argue, however, that Pastor MacArthur's methodology is right because the Charismatic Movement *as a whole* is
corrupt. We will see, however, that that is hardly the case.

What Does It Mean to Judge within the Limits of Scripture Rules?

Before looking at the five true signs of revival (or, of a move of
the Spirit) that Edwards gives, let's return to the principle that
Edwards mentioned in his first "non-sign," above, namely, "That
a work is carried on in a way very unusual and extraordinary;
provided the variety or difference be such, as may still be com-
prehended within the limits of Scripture rules." Many Christians
take this to mean that if something is not explicitly written in the

Bible, it is automatically forbidden. But that was not Edwards'
point, as can be seen from these extended citations:

> The influence persons are under is not to be judged of one
> way or other by such effects on the body; and the reason is
> because the Scripture nowhere gives us any such rule. We
> cannot conclude that persons are under the influence of
> the true Spirit because we see such effects upon their bod-
> ies, because this is not given as a mark of the true Spirit;
> nor on the other hand, have we any reason to conclude
> from any such outward appearances, that persons are not
> under the influence of the Spirit of God, because there is
> no rule of Scripture given us to judge of spirits by, that
> does either expressly or indirectly exclude such effects on
> the body, nor does reason exclude them...
>
> Some object against such extraordinary appearances
> that we have no instances of them recorded in the
> New Testament, under the extraordinary effusions of the
> Spirit. Were this allowed, I can see no force in the objec-
> tion, if neither reason nor any rule of Scripture exclude
> such things...[5]

He also wrote:

> I do not know that we have any express mention in the
> New Testament of any person's weeping, or groaning, or
> sighing through fear of hell, or a sense of God's anger; but
> is there any body so foolish as from hence to argue that
> in whomsoever these things appear, their convictions are
> not from the Spirit of God?...
>
> Why then should it be thought strange that persons
> should cry out for fear, when God appears to them, as

a terrible enemy, and they see themselves in great danger of being swallowed up in the bottomless gulf of eternal misery? The spouse, once and again, speaks of herself as overpowered with the love of Christ, so as to weaken her body, and make her faint. Cant. ii. 5, "Stay me with flagons, comfort me with apples; for I am sick of love."[6]

Well said! He continues:

From whence we may at least argue that such an effect may well be supposed to arise from such a cause in the saints, in some cases, and that such effect will sometimes be seen in the church of Christ. "It is a weak objection, that the impressions of enthusiasts [emotionalists] have a great effect on their bodies. That the Quakers used to tremble is no argument that Saul, afterwards Paul, and the jailer did not tremble from real convictions of conscience. Indeed all such objections from effects on the body, let them be greater or less, seem to be exceeding frivolous; they who argue thence, proceed in the dark, they know now what ground they go upon, nor by what rule they judge. The root and course of things is to be looked at, and the nature of the operations and affections are to be inquired into, and examined by the rule of God's word, and not the motions of the blood and animal spirits.[7]

So then, how do we evaluate an alleged work of the Spirit based on God's Word? As J. I. Packer and many others have observed, the main scriptural tests are moral (how are you living?) and creedal (what do you believe?).[8] Edwards broke these down into five simple principles, meaning, if an apparent work of the Spirit produces these things, then it must be a genuine work of

God. I personally believe them to be true because: 1) They are in harmony with scriptural tests; 2) Jesus taught plainly that Satan cannot cast out Satan, which means that even if the devil can produce counterfeit miracles, he cannot (and will not) produce good, lasting, Jesus-exalting fruit;[9] and 3) the flesh cannot give birth to spirit/Spirit, and so, human efforts and emotionalism will not result in true conversions and genuine disciples.[10]

Edwards' five positive signs of a genuine work of God can be put in the form of five questions: 1) Does the work cause the Jesus of the Scriptures to be exalted? If so, "it is a sure sign that it is from the Spirit of God." 2) Does the work turn people against Satan's kingdom by turning their hearts away from sin and worldliness? If so, "this is a sure sign that it is a true, and not a false spirit." 3) Does the work produce a greater love and esteem and honor for the Scriptures? If so, it is "certainly the Spirit of God." 4) Does the work lead people to the truth? If so, "we may safely determine that it is a right and true spirit." 5) Does the work result in love to God and man? If so, "it is a sure sign that it is the Spirit of God."

The First Test

I'm sure that many of you reading this list are checking it off in your own life and in your congregations or ministries and saying, "No doubt about it! It is the Spirit of God moving mightily in the midst of the Charismatic Movement." Pastor MacArthur, however, comes to the opposite conclusion, arguing with regard to the first test, the exaltation of the Jesus of the Scriptures, that: 1) Charismatics exalt the Holy Spirit more than Jesus; 2) some Word of Faith teachers deny aspects of the deity of Jesus; and 3)

Charismatics have a mixture of odd beliefs, including Catholic Charismatics.[11]

This is as remarkable as it is regrettable, and in response, it could be argued that: 1) Reformed Christians exalt doctrine and sometimes even Calvin more than Jesus; 2) the fact that some Charismatic teachers might be in doctrinal error about Jesus is absolutely not an indictment of the countless thousands of charismatic teachers who are not in doctrinal error about Him; 3) Protestants (even Reformed Protestants) have a mixture of odd beliefs, including Reconstructionism.

As author and teacher Frank Viola notes in his critique of *Charismatic Chaos* and *Strange Fire,*

> Throughout his books, MacArthur continually uses the phrase, "Charismatics believe" ... such and such. "Charismatics think ... such and such." And then "the charismatic movement is guilty of ..."
>
> This is simply false. It would be accurate to say, "*some* charismatics believe"... or even "many charismatics believe..." or "some in the charismatic movement believe ..."
>
> Using MacArthur's logic and approach, one could easily write a book about the toxicity of the Reformed movement by painting all Reformed Christians as elitist, sectarian, divisive, arrogant, exclusive, and in love with "doctrine" more than with Christ.
>
> And just as MacArthur holds up Benny Hinn, Todd Bentley, Pat Robertson, et al. to characterize the charismatic world, one can hold up R.J. Rushdoony, Herman Dooyeweerd, R. T. Kendall, or Patrick Edouard, et al. to characterize Reformed Christians. Or Peter Ruckman and

Jack Hyles, et al. to characterize Fundamentalist Baptists. Or William R Crews and L.R. Shelton Jr., et. al. to represent Reformed Baptists.

My point is that charismatic, Reformed, and Baptist people would strongly object to the idea that any of these gentleman could accurately represent their respective tribes as each of them have strong critics within their own movements.

Even so, the game of burning down straw man city with a torch is nothing new.[12]

Now, I'm sure some of my Reformed friends reading these lines find this very offensive, saying that their appreciation of "the doctrines of grace" and the teachings of Calvin only enhances their love for Jesus. I do accept that, even though I sometimes hear more glorying in doctrine in these circles than I hear glorying in the Lord.[13] In the same way, the moving of the Spirit in charismatic circles points us to Jesus – in our worship, in our witness, in our personal lives – and one of the most common results of a person being healed or delivered by the Spirit of God is that they immediately begin to confess Jesus as Lord.

Perhaps to those outside charismatic circles, it appears as if tongues and prophecy and healing are the main focus for us. (I'm sure in some places that is the case, just as it's the case that in some circles, other secondary things become the main focus.) But to those of us within these circles, the moving of the Spirit in these different ways is just part of our spiritual lives, and all of it has the goal of exalting Jesus in our midst.

As for the legitimacy of writing off a movement of half a billion people because it has some false teachers or confused leaders, following this methodology would effectively eliminate virtually every denomination or identifiable Christian group on the planet. Shall I begin to name some serious errors, even Christological errors, in the cessationist camp? Does that therefore disqualify all cessationists? And may I remind you of a principle of fair judgment passed on by Dennis Prager, which he learned from his mentor Yitz Greenburg? "Don't compare the best things about your religion [or, ideology] to the worst things about someone else's."[14]

Again, it is unfortunate that the Strange Fire movement does this consistently, failing even to evaluate the doctrinal statements of the major Pentecostal denominations and Bible colleges and ministry schools and seminaries. With rare exception, Pentecostals and charismatics hold to a thoroughly orthodox Christology, and it is simply wrong for Pastor MacArthur to point to a few statements by a few TV preachers to discredit the orthodoxy of a multifaceted, worldwide outpouring of the Spirit. It's also worth mentioning that through the Charismatic Movement, many Catholics have become genuinely born-again, even if they have not yet repudiated all the errors of Catholicism. But even if none of them were truly saved, that would still not account for roughly 80% of the world's charismatics who are not Catholic. (According to estimates used in *Strange Fire*, there are roughly 100 million charismatic Catholics.)

So then, in response to Edwards' first sign, we can say that the Charismatic Movement passes the test with flying colors, since through the outpouring of the Spirit in the last century, hundreds of millions of lost sinners have been drawn to Jesus, turning away from idols, false religions, cults, and all kinds of deception, based on which he must conclude that this is definitely a work of the Spirit of God.

To give one case in point, as noted in a Pew Research report, "The share of the population that is Christian in sub-Saharan Africa climbed from 9% in 1910 to 63% in 2010."[15] This is truly remarkable, representing one of the greatest pro-gospel belief shifts in any largely populated region in history, and a large part of this shift is directly attributable to the twentieth century Holy Spirit outpouring in Africa, to which we'll return shortly. Yet because this movement is young and raw, because it some of it is mixed with deception and error, critics fail to see the beautiful forest because of the bad trees. This, as we have seen, is one of the biggest failings of the Strange Fire movement.

The Second Test

Moving on to the second test, which Dr. MacArthur rephrases as, "Does It Oppose Worldliness?", his conclusion again is completely negative, based on the alleged worldwide charismatic emphasis on the prosperity gospel coupled with a number of scandals among prominent charismatic leaders. In response, I would argue that: 1) He has misread or misunderstood the data regarding the prosperity gospel; and 2) the scandals, although prominent, are the exception to the rule – does anyone actually believe that most Pentecostal and charismatic pastors and leaders are immoral and corrupt? – and based on one of the earlier principles of Edwards, these scandals cannot be used to discredit the movement as a whole, which actually has turned multitudes away from sin.

Pastor MacArthur quotes Paul Alexander's book *Signs and Wonders*, stating that, "Over 90 percent of Pentecostals and charismatics in Nigeria, South Africa, India, and the Philippines believe that 'God will grant material prosperity to all believers who have enough faith."[16] This theme was reiterated throughout the Strange Fire conference, and Phil Johnson pressed it again during his appearance on my radio show. But is it true? And is there a reason that Dr. MacArthur all but ignored the fact that Pentecostalism worldwide is often a religion of the poor, even though this was noted in the same immediate context in which Alexander was quoted?[17] Why this significant oversight?

Let me first reiterate my complete and utter repudiation of the carnal prosperity message – meaning, the idea that Jesus died on the cross to make us rich – and let me state my agreement that it is spreading like wildfire in many parts of the world. I do not question this nor do I defend it, and, as mentioned above, in Chapter Two, I have addressed this forcefully for the last twenty-five years. At the same time, the Strange Fire camp is misusing the relevant data (unintentionally, I assume), also failing to look at mountains of other data that flatly contradict their conclusions.

In the aftermath of the Strange Fire conference, Mike Riccardi posted an article entitled, "Myths about the Strange Fire Conference," citing John T. Allen, *The Future Church*, 382–383, who noted that "the Pew Forum data suggests that the prosperity gospel is actually a defining feature of all Pentecostalism; majorities of Pentecostals exceeding 90 percent in most countries hold to these beliefs."[18] How then can I say that this data is wrong? How can I argue that most charismatics and Pentecostals worldwide are *not* seeking to emulate the lifestyles of some of "The Preachers of L.A."? It's simple. All I have to do is read the data, compare that data with other, more recent and comprehensive surveys, and then ask myself what I have witnessed firsthand in more than four decades of ministry in charismatic circles. Be assured that you're in for some real surprises, even from the primary survey used by the Strange Fire leaders.

The study being cited by John Allen is the October, 2006 Pew Forum survey, "Spirit and Power: A Ten Country Survey of Pentecostals."[19] One of the survey statements was, "God will grant material prosperity to all believers who have enough faith," and Christians were asked to express their agreement or disagreement with it. Based on the responses from ten countries, we have been told that 90% of charismatics worldwide believe in the "prosperity gospel."

What the Strange Fire camp did not emphasize strongly enough (or, at times, at all) was that:

1) A majority of the population in some of the countries surveyed is extremely poor, which means that "material prosperity" for many of these believers simply meant, "Having enough food for my family so we won't starve," or, "Having a roof over my head that doesn't leak." Is it so heretical to believe that God will grant that to His children?[20] (Note that, according to some estimates, 70% of the world's population lives on less than $3 per day.)

In the tribal regions where my friends at Love-N-Care Ministries plant churches in India, pastors (with families) can be supported *full-time* for $30 per month. I can't imagine anyone would accuse them of preaching a prosperity gospel if they felt that God wanted to supply them with a bicycle so they could travel to other villages and preach. Judging, however, by the caricatures presented in the Strange Fire movement, you would think that these impoverished charismatic Christians in the Two-Thirds World had pictures of Rolls Royces on their refrigerator doors, confessing one new vehicle for each member of the family. (Frankly, most of them would love to have refrigerators, but that would mean having electricity, which is still a luxury in many parts of the world.)

2) Looking at some of the ten countries surveyed in more depth, we see that in Brazil, 80% of Pentecostals and 61% of charismatics affirmed the material prosperity, but 70% of all other Christians affirmed it as well. Amazing! So, in this survey, which distinguished between Pentecostals and charismatics, the latter were actually *less* inclined to affirm the material prosperity statement than were other Christians in general. (Doing the math, it's easy to see that in Brazil, Pentecostals and charismatics combined had roughly the same beliefs about material prosperity as did the other Christians surveyed.)

The data is similar in all ten countries surveyed. For example, in India, 93% of Pentecostals and 95% of charismatics affirmed the material prosperity statement, compared to 87% of other Christians, while in Nigeria, 95% of Pentecostals affirmed the statement (Charismatics were not listed separately) compared with 93% of other Christians. How striking! This means that either the vast majority of *all professing Christians* hold to this same, false message (which then undermines the whole Strange Fire indictment against charismatics), or else the charismatic affirmation of the statement about material prosperity is far more innocent than it appears.

To repeat, this means that either a dangerous, carnal prosperity message has spread worldwide, infecting Charismatics
and non-Charismatics at almost the same rate, in which case
all of us need to do our best to combat it; or we are confusing
some TBN celebrity preacher getting rich off his TV audience
(or some celebrity Nigerian preacher, buying private jets while
his people barely get by) with the masses of Christians who simply believe that God will meet their (quite modest) needs; or it
is a combination of both, in which case, again, the whole argument of the Strange Fire movement falls to the ground.

But there's more. In October, 2010, in Cape Town, South
Africa, Pew Research Center's Forum on Religion & Public Life
surveyed 2,196 evangelical leaders from 166 countries and ter-
ritories who were attending the Third Lausanne Congress of
World Evangelization.[21] They found that: 1) "Nine-in-ten of the
leaders (90%) reject the so-called prosperity gospel, the notion
that God will grant wealth and good health to those who have
enough faith." 2) "Roughly half or more of the global evangelical leaders surveyed report that they have experienced or witnessed a divine healing (76%), received a direct revelation from
God (61%) and spoken in tongues (47%). These experiences,
often associated with Pentecostalism, are particularly common
among leaders from the Global South."[22]

Stop and chew on those figures for a moment. These are some
of the top evangelical leaders from around the world, gathering
for a ten-day conference on evangelism, and more than three-
quarters of them claimed to "have experienced or witnessed a
divine healing," more than six in ten said they had "received a
direct revelation from God," and almost half of them stated that
they have spoken in tongues – which puts half or more of them

in the Pentecostal or charismatic camp. Yet 90% of them reject the prosperity gospel. What does this tell you? And why aren't these stats being paraded by the Strange Fire camp?

These stats are also more in keeping with my experience as a leader serving in Pentecostal and charismatic circles over the decades, which is one reason that so many American charismatics are turned off by the lavish lifestyles of some of our celebrity preachers. (Note that the prosperity message is a relatively recent part of the charismatic movement, especially in its most aberrant forms.) But what many charismatic leaders *do* believe is that God wanted to raise up a mentality of provision rather than poverty *for the purpose of funding the spread of the gospel worldwide,* as argued by missionary statesman David Shibley in his book *A Force in the Earth.*[23]

And yet there's more. How is it right for Christians gathering at a conference in a lavish mega-church in suburban California to decry the fact that many impoverished Christians worldwide believe that God wants to meet their needs? Isn't there something incongruous about that? And isn't there something incongruous about claiming that the Spirit cannot be at work in the Charismatic Movement worldwide because it allegedly does not oppose worldliness while the salaries of some of the speakers at the Strange Fire conference could underwrite thousands of native, charismatic church planters in other parts of the world?

If American believers want to spend millions of dollars on lavish church buildings, that's between them and God. (Some of the finest churches in America are mega-churches, and their leaders are people of integrity.) And if a ministry board feels that a salary of hundreds of thousands of dollars a year is justified for its senior leader and there is nothing illegal taking place, then that is between that ministry and its constituents and God.[24] But, to repeat, there is something very wrong with living like kings, compared to much of the rest of the world, while rebuking our poorer brothers and sisters for believing that their needs can be met by their heavenly Father.

And yet there is more still. The very survey cited to support the carnal prosperity charge indicates that, according to other standards put forth by Edwards (and seconded by MacArthur), charismatics and Pentecostals are doing much better than the other Christians surveyed in most aspects of spiritual life. For example, in every country surveyed (including the United States): 1) Pentecostals, followed by charismatics, with a substantially higher percentage than the other Christians surveyed, agreed that "believers have a duty to convert others." Consequently, they shared their faith on a regular basis far more than did non-charismatic Christians. 2) Pentecostals, followed by charismatics, had a much higher view of the authority of Scripture than did non-Charismatic Christians, with Pentecostals leading "other Christians" in America by more than two-to-one. 3) Pentecostals, followed by charismatics, prayed much more regularly than did non-Charismatic Christians. 4) On moral issues, the survey pointed out that, "Pentecostals often stand out for their traditional views on a range of issues related to sexuality," meaning that here too, they pass the Edwards criterion of opposing worldliness with a much higher score than do their non-charismatic colleagues.

In sum, *the survey used by the Strange Fire camp to bludgeon charismatic believers actually points to them being far more committed to the authority of Scripture, personal evangelism, prayer, and personal holiness than their non-Charismatic compatriots,*

*while their beliefs about material prosperity are only marginally
higher than those of non-Charismatic Christians.* And so, one of
the central pillars of the Strange Fire movement is completely
false and misleading. Had the data been used rightly, it would
have suggested that a conference should have been held by cessationists asking for charismatic leaders from around the world
to show the cessationists what they were missing!

To repeat once more: There *is* a dangerous, carnal prosperity message spreading across America and into the nations, and
it must be corrected and stopped. But this is hardly a charismatic problem alone, and we do best not to frame it as such.
At the same time, the great majority of Pentecostal and charismatic believers do not hold to this carnal message, evidencing
spiritual vitality and health, especially outside America.

The Third Test

Pastor MacArthur summarizes the third sign as, "Does it point
people to the Scriptures?" Not surprisingly, his answer is a
strong no, in particular since charismatics believe that in different ways (obviously not in any way on a par with Scripture),
the Spirit is still speaking to God's people today. (For a further
response to this criticism, see Appendix B, below.)

As already noted, however, the survey wrongly used at
Strange Fire to bash charismatics indicates that here too, charismatics (especially those who belong to Pentecostal churches),
are doing far better than non-charismatic Christians. In my
view, though, this is not because charismatic theology points
to the Word more than, say, Reformed theology. Rather, it is

because the work of the Spirit in the lives of charismatics produces greater spiritual vitality, which in turn produces a greater hunger for the Word. This, after all, was Edwards' point, namely, that a real work of the Spirit leads people to the Scriptures.

In addition, because charismatics are often seeing the promises of the Word of God worked out in their lives on a regular basis, this too produces a greater interest and faith in the Word. (I'm not saying non-charismatics do *not* experience the reality of these promises; I'm simply suggesting another possible reason that Pentecostals and charismatics scored higher on this test than did their non-charismatic counterparts: The God of the Bible, by His Spirit, is doing many of the same things today, that He did back in biblical times.)

Anecdotally, in December, 1997, a staunch critic of the Brownsville Revival visited our school of ministry, bringing a message on discipleship to our student body. (To his credit, while a critic of the revival, he agreed to dialogue with me and meet with our leaders, which proved very fruitful in the midst of our differences.) He was surprised to hear the students give hearty "Amens" to his talk as he emphasized the importance of being students of the Word and living holy lives.

While he was with us, I asked the students my own survey question: "How many of you were committed believers, reading the Bible on a daily basis before being touched by the Spirit in revival?" Many hands were raised. I then asked, "How many of you are now reading the Word at least twice as much on a daily basis as you were before?" (And I clarified that I was not speaking of class assignments.) Virtually every one of those hands went up again, while many more went up when I asked how many were reading the Scriptures three times as much as before. I reached *five times* as much and then ended up my informal survey.[25]

What did this indicate? Simply that those truly touched by the Spirit develop a greater love for God's Word along with a greater faith in God's Word and a greater desire to submit to the authority of God's Word. That appears to be verified by survey data in terms of the Charismatic Movement as a whole.

Of course, I don't expect many of those in the Strange Fire camp to be impressed with this anecdotal survey, but there is something more tangible everyone can consider. It is noteworthy that Reformed and Baptist theological seminaries over the decades have often strayed towards liberalism, which is why more than eighty years ago, Westminster Seminary was formed when Princeton Theological Seminary began to deny the authority of Scripture. (Princeton was once a Reformed theological bastion.) In fact, theological apostasy is all too common in non-charismatic denominations, such as Lutheran, Methodist, Presbyterian. In contrast, Pentecostal denominations and seminaries have tended to remain theologically conservative with a high view of the authority of Scripture. This too is highly significant, pointing to yet another reason that the Strange Fire camp, while rightly rejecting the extremes and errors in the Charismatic Movement, should have been asking charismatic and Pentecostal leaders to join the conference and share the secrets of their real spiritual success.

The Fourth Test

Pastor MacArthur summarizes the fourth positive sign in Edwards' list as, "Does It Elevate the Truth?", claiming that, "The sad fact is that biblical truth has never been the hallmark of the Charismatic Movement, where spiritual experience is continually elevated above sound doctrine."[11] Yet again, this exaggerated, broadbrushed, and inaccurate statement is characteristic of the Strange Fire movement as a whole and it is, quite frankly, not true.

First, while charismatic churches may not be famous for systematically catechizing believers in basic Bible doctrine, the reality is that all the major Pentecostal denominations hold to evangelical fundamentals of the faith, and there is a clear line drawn between heresy and truth. In other words, Pastor Joel Osteen's regrettably ambiguous public statements about key doctrinal issues do not reflect the vast majority of charismatic believers, which is why there was such concern among them when Pastor Osteen, while on national TV, seemed to question whether salvation came only through Jesus. (He immediately clarified his beliefs on his website, reaffirming evangelical orthodoxy on this point.)[27]

Second, it can be argued that *cessationism itself* is guilty of serious doctrinal error, since a solid case can be made for the ongoing nature of the charismatic, New Testament gifts. (See below, Chapter Six.)[28]

Third, pointing back again to the Pew Forum, ten-country survey of 2006, it is noteworthy that Pentecostals specifically scored much higher than did non-charismatics when it came to affirming the wrongness of homosexual practice, prostitution, extra-marital sex, abortion, divorce, euthanasia, and drinking alcohol. (This was especially true in America, where Pentecostals have much higher conservative moral values, on average, than do non-charismatics.) Of course, I'm aware that there is ambiguity in terms of how many of the non-charismatic "Christians" in this survey are actually Christian at all. (That being said, Pastor MacArthur claims that the vast majority of charismatics are not actually Christian at all!) But it is clear that on any count, the Pentecostals held to high moral principles, based on the truth of the Scriptures. Check this off with a big "yes" on the Edwards list as well.

The Fifth Test

The last positive sign on the Edwards list was, "Does It Produce Love for God and Others?" (as summarized in *Strange Fire*). Here, Pastor MacArthur does a real disservice to charismatics, claiming that their love for God is suspect because, in the words of a Pentecostal theology professor, "We go crazy when we think about all God has done for us and with us. Even crazier than we get for our basketball team."[26] For Dr. MacArthur, this somehow equates to "irrational and ecstatic phenomena," to the point that he claims that it won't take long for anyone viewing TBN or another charismatic network to see people "even barking like dogs."[30] Seriously? And these TV networks somehow represent most charismatics?

How in the world does Pastor MacArthur jump from a Pentecostal describing how excited he and his fellow worshipers get about the Lord – more excited than they get at a basketball game – to accusing them of irrational behavior? And is it right for a cessationist to scream and yell at a football game, maybe even hugging the stranger next to him when his team scores in the game's final seconds for a dramatic comeback, and then sit like one of the proverbial "frozen chosen" on Sunday morning while his Pentecostal neighbor jumps for joy in the Lord next door? The words of Baptist evangelist Vance Havner come to mind here: "The same church members who yell like Comanche Indians at a ball game on Saturday sit like wooden Indians in church on Sunday."

I made brief mention of the well-known charismatic contribution to worship above, in Chapter Three, and I'll return to it again, below, in Chapter Nine. For the moment, however, we can simply state that outside of the Strange Fire circles, it is widely acknowledged that charismatics stand out as passionate, heartfelt, devoted worshipers of God.

Finally, Pastor MacArthur's attack on charismatics for their alleged lack of love for others is even more offensive than some of his other attacks, as he claims that because we believe in the value of speaking in tongues, which builds us up as we pray, we are guilty of focusing on self-edification. He also claims that our alleged lack of love is reflected in our supposed focus on material wealth.[31]

In response, it should be noted first that Paul himself said that he spoke in tongues more than the Corinthians did (1 Corinthians 14:18),[32] which would make Paul guilty of lacking love based on the John MacArthur criterion. In reality, those of us who pray in tongues do so to enhance our prayer lives and our intimacy with God, also knowing that praying in tongues (which is one of the ways we pray in the Spirit; see Ephesians 6:18) makes us stronger believers. In other words, this is not some selfish exercise we engage in, similar to feasting at a rich steak house while our neighbors starve; rather, it is like a football player lifting weights in the exercise room so he can help his team win games. In my own life, often before ministering the Word, especially overseas, it has been my habit to pray extensively in tongues as I meditate on the message I am about to preach, sharpening my spiritual focus and increasing my awareness of the Lord as I prepare to engage in sacred service to the lost and to the saved.[33]

Second, we pointed to a representative sampling of the countless social services provided by charismatic believers above, in Chapter Three, while the 2006 Pew Forum survey we have discussed in this chapter indicated that "Pentecostals tend to be more likely than non-renewalist Christians to say they trust people at their place of worship," while they were "involved with voluntary organizations" in comparable numbers to non-charismatic Christians. (We already saw that he was highly misguided to claim that charismatics disproportionately hold to a material prosperity gospel when compared to other Christians.) This is hardly a demonstration of lack of love to others.

Third, many have faulted the Strange Fire camp for what appears to be a conspicuous lack of love in their circles towards those they criticize and reject, to the point that it is all too common to find related posts and blogs mocking and vilifying charismatics in the strongest of terms. Yet somehow, this is considered acceptable and even godly. "After all, those charismatics deserve to be scorned!"

Some sections of *Strange Fire* read like the *National Enquirer* more than they read like a book written by a seasoned Christian leader, especially when detailing the failings and fallings of other leaders.[34] In fact, on page 64, Pastor MacArthur actually cites the *National Enquirer*, making reference to a picture of the then divorced charismatic leaders Benny Hinn and Paula White holding hands as they left a hotel in Rome. (They claimed innocence in the matter – God knows the truth – but the fact is that Hinn subsequently remarried his wife Suzanne, as noted, but without appreciation, by Pastor MacArthur.)

Now, according to my limited knowledge of the situation, there were no grounds for divorce for Paula White and her husband, and I do not see how they can rightly continue in ministry now, especially without even taking a break. And, as stated often in this book, I am not minimizing the scope and the nature of the scandals that have sometimes plagued the Charismatic Movement, including lack of proper discipline and restoration processes for fallen, celebrity preachers.

I will simply repeat that: 1) this is a symptom of celebrity and power more than anything else, and it does not represent the far, far greater majority of charismatic ministers who have not been involved in scandals;[35] 2) we could make quite a long list of divorced and discredited non-charismatic leaders (see above, Chapter Four); 3) the Strange Fire approach is sadly lacking in love for others, which would actually call it into question based on the last of the Edwards' criteria.

A Question for the Strange Fire Leaders

And this leads to a question that only Pastor MacArthur and the other Strange Fire speakers can answer, specifically, since they strongly indicted so many charismatics by name at the conference. Did they reach out to them privately in the past or present to speak into their lives or to appeal to them to repent or to point out what they believed to be their errors or to offer to help them where they believed they were weak? (For those who may have skipped the Preface, for months now, privately and publicly, I have been appealing for a face to face meeting with Pastor MacArthur, not to argue, but to advance the truth. I do hope that meeting will happen soon.) And would those attending the Strange Fire conference or those reading *Strange Fire* come away with a deeper love for their charismatic brothers and sisters, in particular the leaders who were mentioned by name? (I did not say pity, and I certainly did not mean scorn, but rather genuine love.)

From what I can tell so far, the answer would be a resounding no, and I since I started differing with the Strange Fire camp, lovingly and respectfully challenging their approach and their conclusions, I have had to remove mockers from my Facebook and Twitter accounts, just as in the past I have had to remove mocking gay activists and atheists. Now, in no way do I think that this speaks of cessationists as a whole, but I do think it is representative of the kind of fruit that the Strange Fire movement is producing, making it suspect on its own terms.

Of course, we will be told that this is a matter of fighting for the truth rather than being politically correct, but there is a right way to do this, which includes reaching out to those with whom you differ and being charitable and fair in one's conclusions, evaluating others as you would want them to evaluate you.[36] As Tamara Rice wrote on her HopefullyKnown.org blog, "It is better to be kind than clever," noting that,

Many writers have already pointed out the specific problems with Strange Fire (see list below), so I'll focus instead on the familiar colors that show up every time the condemnation paint is opened up …

— Sweeping generalizations (i.e., using the word "most" when "a small number" would be more accurate)
— Inaccurate representations of opposing views (i.e., minimizing or even leaving out the Scriptural basis for differing theologies and methodologies)
— Inflammatory language (i.e., demonizing and dehumanizing theological "opponents")

And to be perfectly honest, I'm weary of it. If the slightest hint of unorthodoxy frees us from the responsibility to be fair, to be honest, to be kind … then who are we, truly? To what end is all our rightness and cleverness going to lead?[37]

Perhaps the Strange Fire camp should meditate on verses like Hosea 6:6, "I desire mercy, and not sacrifice" (quote by Jesus in Matthew 9:13 and 12:7), or Jacob [James] 2:13, "For judgment is without mercy to one who has shown no mercy. Mercy triumphs over judgment." And perhaps, rather than divide over the meaning of tongues and prophecy and spiritual gifts in 1 Corinthians 12 and 14, more emphasis could have been placed on Paul's glorious teaching on love in chapter 13. Perhaps love and truth can be better joined together in the Strange Fire camp? Perhaps Pastor MacArthur's famous "grace to you" slogan could be fleshed out more consistently by his followers?

The Truth about Africa

On August 5, 2013, I responded to an article posted on the Grace to You website by African pastor Conrad Mbewe in which he indicted today's African charismatics in the strongest of terms. (Pastor Mbewe was one of the speakers at Strange Fire.)[38] In that article, I cited J. Kwabena Asamoah-Gyadu, Ph.D., Professor of Contemporary African Christianity and Pentecostal/Charismatic Theology in Africa at the Trinity Theological Seminary, Accra, Ghana, who observed that,

> Pentecostalism is a response to …cerebral Christianity and wherever it has appeared the movement has defined itself in terms of the recovery of the experiential aspects of the faith by demonstrating the power of the Spirit to infuse life, and the ability of the living presence of Jesus Christ to save from sin and evil.… The ministries of healing and deliverance have thus become some of the most important expressions of Christianity in African Pentecostalism.[39]

As for the quality of what is being produced, Evangelist Daniel Kolenda, the leader of Christ for All Nations and one of our ministry school grads, noted that, "The western brand of stale, cold, theoretic and purely cerebral Christianity that Africans have been offered by many of the [Western] evangelical denominations is laughable to them. For Africans, their faith must have real world consequences or it is worthless."And, he explained,

Some of the finest, strongest and most sincere Christians I have ever met anywhere in the world are in Africa. I personally know families who have lost family members who gave their lives as martyrs because of their confession of Christ. Many of the Africans Christians that I know have a faith in Christ so strong that it would put most Western Christians to shame. Their faith, humility and love for the Lord is an indictment of the indifference and unbelief so prevalent in the Western Church.[40]

One of my American friends hosted a pastor from Ghana who was visiting for a few weeks, and after attending several church services – after which the people inevitably went out for a meal together – the pastor said, "Now I see why nothing is happening in your churches! You spend all your time feasting; we spend ours praying and fasting."

Some of the finest students we have ever trained in our ministry schools have been African charismatic believers, marked by their devotion to Jesus, their passion for the lost, their willingness to sacrifice for the gospel, their solid lives of prayer, and their hearts for holiness. Their very lives are often a rebuke to those of us here in the West.

Without a doubt, with the rapid spread of the gospel in Africa, there are all kinds of serious errors, abuses, and foreign mixtures, but they are hardly limited to charismatic circles (quite the contrary) and they hardly represent the larger picture of what God is doing there. Those attending the Strange Fire conference would never know this, nor would they know about the wonderful things the Holy Spirit is doing around the world today which, despite evident flaws and failings, is undeniably a glorious work of God. As a result of this, with millions of sinners repenting and being saved, there is continual joy in the presence of God in heaven (see Luke 15:7, 10). Shouldn't we rejoice as well?

A Wise Assessment from a Wise Leader

In the opening chapter of this book, I mentioned that one of the respected leaders taking issue with the Strange Fire approach was Dr. Timothy George, Dean of the Beeson Divinity School of Samford University. In his article "Strange Friendly Fire," he wrote:

> One of the wisest appraisals of the charismatic movement as a whole has come from the estimable J. I. Packer. Like John MacArthur, he is Reformed in theology and a cessationist in his understanding of spiritual gifts. Packer finds in the New Testament both a creedal and a moral test for judging whether movements are truly inspired of God or not, principles the apostles themselves applied in letters like Galatians, Colossians, 2 Peter, and 1 John. Packer writes:
>
> > When we apply these tests to the charismatic movement, it becomes plain at once that God is in it. For whatever threats and perhaps instances of occult and counterfeit spirituality we may think we detect around its periphery (and what movement of revival has ever lacked these things around its periphery?), its main effect everywhere is to promote robust Trinitarian faith, personal fellowship with the divine Savior and Lord whom we meet in the New Testament, repentance, obedience, and

> love to fellow Christians, expressed in ministry of
> all sorts towards them—plus a zeal for evangelistic
> outreach that puts the staider sort of churchmen to
> shame.[41]

Dr. Packer, to his credit, accurately and fairly applied the
moral and creedal tests to the Charismatic Movement and came
to the right conclusion, namely, "it becomes plain at once that
God is in it," the exact opposite of Pastor MacArthur's conclusions. Why such a glaring discrepancy in their assessments?

It appears that just like Charles Chauncy, the chief critic of
the Great Awakening, the Strange Fire camp has focused on the
chaff whereas J. I. Packer, like Jonathan Edwards before him, has
focused on the wheat. As I wrote in *The Revival Answer Book*,

> Professor Conrad Cherry observed that "Chauncy metic-
> ulously assayed and reported the abundant impropri-
> eties of the revival, and abundant improprieties there
> were: ministers abandoning their own folds for an itiner-
> ant ministry, screamings and writhings by the congrega-
> tions, persons' neglecting their daily vocations to attend
> to things religious – Chauncy's list was endless." (Note
> that Chauncy's list is strangely reminiscent of the writings
> of some "defenders of the faith" who zealously and care-
> fully note every revival "abuse" and "excess.") Yet this is
> precisely where Chauncy made his fatal mistake, since,
> as Cherry notes, "These things in his judgment consti-
> tuted the very nature of the revival itself; the Awakening
> was not a work of God's Spirit but a despicable instance
> of wanton emotionalism." Sadly, this very same error is

being repeated by some leaders today who seek to protect the Church from errors and extremes but are actually
turning the hungry and thirsty away from the Spirit's life-
giving streams.

Now, this is not to say that Jonathan Edwards was
uninterested in guarding against abuses and correcting
excesses, and Cherry is careful to point out that it was
Edwards "who argued that more discriminating discernment was called for." But the fundamental approach of
Chauncy and Edwards was very different, since Edwards
emphasized that "the Awakening should be judged not in
terms of its excesses and errors alone but also in terms of
the *nature* of a true work of God which may appear even
in the midst of excesses." And that is what Chauncy totally
missed. For him, there was no revival taking place at all;
it was a sham, a counterfeit, a fraud. Critics of the Great
Awakening were unanimous in their verdict: It was *not* a
true *awakening*, nor was it *great*.[42]

It looks like history is repeating itself yet again.

Endnotes

[1] *Strange Fire*, 37-82

[2] Ibid., 34.

[3] The Edwards criteria was wrongly utilized in Hank Hanegraaff, *Counterfeit Revival* (rev. ed.; Nashville: Word, 2001), which I subsequently pointed
out, drawing a further response from him (see ibid., 275-277). In point of
fact, for several years, I had been reading Edwards' writings on revival with
interest and respect and when controversy arose during the Brownsville Revival regarding my citation of Edwards (I had actually cited him prior to that

outpouring, but the controversy arose during the outpouring), I consulted three of the top scholars involved with his work: Prof. Harry S. Stout of Yale University, who is one of the editors of the ongoing, multi-volume, annotated edition of the works of Jonathan Edwards; Prof. John Woodbridge of Trinity Evangelical Divinity School (where I served as a visiting professor), recognized as the one of the foremost Church historians today; and Prof. Doug Sweeney, now also at Trinity, and also one of the leading Edwards' scholars. To me, Edwards' points were perfectly clear, and I couldn't imagine how there could be any dispute about what he wrote or intended, and these scholars confirmed to me that my understanding was correct. Students of Edwards can readily evaluate the relevant issues for themselves. As for Hank Hanegraaff, he is a friend and colleague, despite our past differences.

[4]This material has been adapted from Brown, *From Holy Laughter to Holy Fire*, 224-228. The full text of Edwards can be found online here: http://www.biblebb.com/files/edwards/je-marksofhs.htm

[5]This is a continuation of the text from Edwards' second non-sign, cited above. See conveniently http://www.biblebb.com/files/edwards/je-marksofhs.htm

[6]Ibid.

[7]Ibid.

[8]We'll return to Dr. Packer's thoughts below.

[9]See Michael L. Brown, *The Revival Answer Book* (Ventura, CA: Renew, 2001), 120-161.

[10]Ibid.

[11]*Strange Fire*, 37-53

[12]*Pouring Holy Water on Strange Fire* (Gainsville, FL: Present Testimony Ministry, 2013), 9

[13]Cf. ibid., 10: "MacArthur accuses charismatics of being 'obsessed with the supposed gifts and power of the Holy Spirit' (Strange Fire, Advanced Reader Copy, p. 53). By the same token, one could say that all Reformed people are obsessed with Calvin's doctrine. But neither comment is fair nor accurate."

[14]See above, Chapter Four, n. 58.

[15]http://www.pewforum.org/2011/12/19/global-christianity-exec/

[16] *Strange Fire* 58-59, citing Paul Alexander, *Signs and Wonders* (San Francisco: Jossey-Bass, 2009), 63– 64; this charge is repeated several times in the book

[17] See *Strange Fire*, 285, n. 2, followed by the very next note, 286, n. 3.

[18] http://thecripplegate.com/myths-about-the-strange-fire-conference/

[19] http://www.pewforum.org/files/2006/10/pentecostals-08.pdf;

[20] Again, I am *not* defending the carnal prosperity message; I'm simply suggesting a different context for belief in "material prosperity." For a typical perspective from a charismatic leader, see David Yonggi-Cho, "Poverty is a curse from Satan. God desires that all His people prosper and be healthy as their soul prospers (3 John 1: 2). Yet much of the world has not really seen poverty as I have seen it. Especially in the Third World, people live their lives in despair, struggling to survive for one more day. I am from the Third World. I know first-hand what it is not to have anything to eat" (from Dr. Yonggi-Cho's *Fourth Dimension* [Seoul: Seoul Logos, 1979], 137-138, cited in Anderson, *To the Ends of the Earth*, 229) For the record, in some of the countries surveyed in the Pew Forum study (n. 19, immediately above), Pentecostals were not worse off than their non-charismatic Christian neighbors, occasionally surpassing them in income.

[21] http://www.pewforum.org/2011/06/22/global-survey-of-evangelical-protestant-leaders/

[22] "Seven-in-ten (70%) of those from the Global South, for example, say they have witnessed the devil or evil spirits being driven out of a person, compared with four-in-ten (41%) of the leaders from the Global North. Moreover, fully one-third of the Global South leaders (33%) describe themselves as Pentecostals, compared with only about one-in-seven of the leaders from the Global North (14%)."

[23] *A Force in the Earth: The Move of the Holy Spirit in World Evangelization* (Lake Mary, FL: Creation House, 1997), specifically chapter eight, "Prosperity's Purpose."

[24] To be clear, I am not advocating people getting rich off gospel work; I'm simply putting my concerns here in a larger context.

[25] It could be true that some students did this out of legalism (which could have been the case before revival as well), but there's simply no doubt that for

the vast majority, having been touched afresh by God, their hunger for His Word increased greatly

[26] *Strange Fire*, 71

[27] For my response to a recent interview with Pastor Osteen, see http://christiannews.net/2013/10/04/joel-osteen-god-absolutely-accepts-homosexuals/

[28] See also my debate on cessationism with Prof. Sam Waldron, http://www.youtube.com/watch?v=c0biTwj635I&feature=c4-overview&list=UUbINn3x-intLp88Zrf8acpg

[29] *Strange Fire*, 75

[30] Ibid.

[31] Ibid., 78

[32] Obviously, he didn't mean that he knew more foreign languages than they did!

[33] Cessationists will commonly object that for speaking in tongues to have value, it must be an intelligible, earthly language. But even if that were the case, if the one speaking in tongues did not understand the language, how would that be any different to them than if they spoke in a "heavenly" tongue (meaning, divinely given but not an earthly language)? Couldn't someone still raise the charge that it was gibberish *to the speaker*? That being said, it is clear from 1 Corinthians 14 that Paul is not dealing with earthly languages since he states, of the person speaking in tongues, that "no one understands him" (14:2), also saying that if he himself came to them speaking in tongues it would not benefit them unless he brought "some revelation or knowledge or prophecy or teaching" (14:6), which would make little sense if it was an earthly language, in which case he should have said, "If you don't happen to understand the particular foreign language I'm speaking, then all my tongue speaking won't help you." That's also why he wrote in 14:13 that the person who speaks in a tongue should pray that he can interpret it, as opposed to, "Whoever prays in a tongue should study and learn to interpret the foreign language that he is speaking." Why *pray* to interpret rather than to study to learn the language? And if an unbeliever came into the meeting and everyone was speaking in foreign languages, perhaps that unbeliever would be from a country that spoke that language and would be amazed and come to faith. Paul, to the contrary, says that he will think you're "out of your minds" (14:23). Paul also places interpretation of tongues as a supernatural spiritual

gift (first at 1 Corinthians 12:10), which again would make no sense if he was simply speaking about someone adept at learning languages.

[34]Of course, the rebuttal would be, "Well, it's not my fault if part of my book sounds like the *National Enquirer*. That's because the charismatic church looks the part." Again, this would be an exaggerated, untrue, and unfair statement.

[35]According to MacArthur, these failings are directly traceable to false doctrine, and since the congregations don't rise above their leaders, "the assembly is full of the same kinds of sins" (*Strange Fire*, 65-66). Interestingly, an ultra-Orthodox rabbi I was talking with pointed to the failings of the professing Church through the centuries as proof that Christianity itself was idolatrous.

[36]When writing *Hyper-Grace*, because I was going to "name names," I reached out to most of the main authors and teachers I differed with, letting them know where I found their position erroneous and asking for interaction, even offering to let some of them see what I was writing before it went to press. I did have gracious and open interaction with several of the teachers, although without a change in either of our positions.

[37]http://hopefullyknown.com/2013/10/25/because-it-is-better-to-be-kind/

[38]http://www.charismanews.com/opinion/in-the-line-of-fire/40503-is-african-charismatic-christianity-a-counterfeit; his article http://www.gty.org/Blog/B130724

[39]http://www.lausanneworldpulse.com/worldreports/464?pg=all. See further J. Kwabena Asamoah-Gyadu *Contemporary Pentecostal Christianity: Interpretations From an African Context* (Regnum Studies in Global Christianity; Eugene, OR: Wipf & Stock, 2013); and note also the relevant comments of Prof. Craig Keener in Appendix A, below.

[40]http://www.charismanews.com/opinion/in-the-line-of-fire/40503-is-african-charismatic-christianity-a-counterfeit

[41]http://www.firstthings.com/onthesquare/2013/11/strange-friendly-fire/timothy-george; the quote is from J. I. Packer, *Keep in Step with the Spirit: Finding Fullness in Our Walk with God* (repr.; Grand Rapids: Baker, 2005), 150. In keeping with the negative, critical mentality found all too frequently in the Strange Fire camp, Pastor Dan Phillips chooses to heap scorn on several other, somewhat related quotes from Packer's important

book, thereby seeking to discredit Dr. Packer's positive assessment of charismatics. See http://teampyro.blogspot.com/2013/11/a-word-about-j-i-packer-on-charismatics_6.html

[42] *Revival Answer Book*, 17. See further http://pneumareview.com/john-macarthurs-strange-fire-as-parody-of-jonathan-edwards-theology-by-william-de-arteaga/17/

Chapter Six

SOLA SCRIPTURA AND THEREFORE CHARISMATIC

C oming to faith in a Pentecostal church at the age of sixteen in 1971 and reading the Scriptures voraciously, I had no doubt whatsoever that the gifts and power Spirit described in the New Testament were for today. And I *did* see some amazing things happen in those early years in the faith, things that were undeniably supernatural and definitely from the Lord. (See Chapter Nine, below.) At the same time, I expected to see much more take place based on what I read in the Word and based on the stories I heard from the believers who had been around a lot longer than me.

"In the old days," they said with awe, "back in the 1950's, we saw incredible healings and miracles take place. And if you're faithful, you'll see those things happen too."

I also heard about outstanding signs and wonders happening in other parts of the world, but I couldn't help but wonder, "Why in the past but not in the present? Why over there but not over there?" To make things worse, there were some flakey things that took place – we actually got duped once by a charlatan – and as I started to get more educated, graduating from college with a major in Hebrew in 1977 and going straight into grad school, I became somewhat embarrassed of my Pentecostal heritage, turning strongly to Calvinism and a more intellectual approach to the Scriptures.

My Journey towards Cessationism

In 1977, I left the Pentecostal church, together with my bride of
eighteen months, Nancy, and our baby daughter Jennifer, looking for a Reformed congregation with some openness to the gifts
of the Spirit. But once there, I became less and less charismatic,
actually thinking to myself that I would be quite happy to discover that the gifts were not for today. All the Calvinist theologians I was studying were cessationists – in fact, my favorite Reformed publishing house, Banner of Truth,[1] was decidedly anti-
charismatic – and I got to the point where I wanted to be cessationist as well. I bought classic books like B. B. Warfield's *Counterfeit Miracles* and modern studies like Robert Gromacki's *The
Modern Tongues Movement*, studying the Scriptures afresh in
light of their arguments.[2]

And with my academic studies in graduate school focused
on the Old Testament and Semitic languages, I couldn't help
but notice how there seemed to be a lot more divine smiting
than divine healing, with biblical books like Job reinforcing my
incipient anti-healing theology.[3] I even had a five-point explanation as to why being slain in the Spirit was not from the Lord
and, to give you a striking example of how hard my heart had
become towards my Pentecostal roots, when my sister-in-law
Robin was miraculously healed at a meeting in New York City,
I completely rejected it. Talk about being resolute!

Robin had sustained a serious elbow injury in a work-related
accident that doctors could not fully repair, and so she learned
to live with the pain and the lack of full use of her elbow. She was
attending a gospel meeting with several thousand others when
the speaker announced that someone with a shattered left elbow

was being healed, at which moment the power of God touched her elbow and she was healed. But when she asked if she could testify at our next church service, we told her we already had a full service and she would have to wait.

Some weeks later, she was attending a Bible study I was leading, and she again wanted to share her testimony. She explained how, after hearing the speaker go through the Scriptures on the subject of healing, it seemed so clear to her that healing was for today. So she asked God to confirm His Word if her understanding was correct, and moments later, her condition was identified by the speaker and she was healed. In reply I said, "Well, Joni [Eareckson] asked for a sign from God, and she broke her neck and was paralyzed." (Regardless of how accurate my understanding was of Joni's story, this is what I said, a symptom of the hardness of my heart towards healing and miracles today.)

Sola Scriptura, Cessationism, and Continuationism

But I had a serious problem. The more I read the Word, *wanting* to prove cessationism true, the more I became convinced that it was exegetically impossible. The Scriptures did not teach cessationism. Then, when I would spend quality time with God in prayer, I would find myself speaking in tongues, which enhanced my intimacy with Him. So I accepted the fact that the gifts appeared to be for today, even though I remained skeptical of what was happening in Pentecostal-charismatic circles.

Then, in the early 1980's, we had an outpouring of the Spirit in our congregation marked by deep repentance and radical transformation, often accompanied by speaking in tongues and the manifestation of other gifts, including healing. Some people we prayed for were overcome by the Spirit – yes, they were "slain in the Spirit" – to my shock and mild embarrassment. (Remember that we didn't believe in these things at that time and most of those being touched had no exposure to them before, so this was hardly a matter of people exhibiting some "learned behavior.")

My own life was set ablaze for the Lord with a passion and devotion I had not known since my first years as a believer, and there was no doubt that God was mightily touching others in our midst. But what was I to do with my theology? What *did* the Word say about healing? What about the rest of the spiritual gifts?

Determined to get a better grasp on these things, I switched the topic of my doctoral dissertation from "Abbreviated Verbal Idioms in the Hebrew Bible: A Comparative Semitic Approach," to, "'I Am the LORD Your Healer': A Philological Study of the Root *RAPA'* in the Hebrew Bible and the Ancient Near East." (My graduate studies were at New York University, and so my focus had to be linguistic and textual rather than theological, since I was not studying in a seminary. My thesis was completed in 1985.) And the more I studied the Word, the clearer things became, regardless of whether or not I saw a single miracle with my own eyes.

Then, from 1992-1994, I determined to read through the Word intensively once more with a focus on divine healing, publishing the results in the Zondervan monograph *Israel's Divine Healer* (1995).[4] Since then, my views have not changed, and *the primary reason I am not a cessationist is because of the definite and clear testimony of the Word.* And while I have witnessed the Spirit's power in many ways over these last three decades, the basis of my theology is the Word, not my experience.[5] (I have also prayed for many people who were *not* healed, including close friends who ultimately died of their diseases, but, to repeat, the basis of my theology is the Word, not my experience.)

Theology Based on Experience or Based on the Word?

Interestingly, I have interacted with many cessationists who say, "I used to be charismatic," proceeding to describe the disappointments they experienced or the spiritual folly they witnessed, which led them to change their beliefs. In other words, because they did not see (or because of what they did see), they do not believe, which means that their theology is experience-based (or, at least experience-influenced). Still, all of us would agree that, regardless of our experiences positive or negative, we must bow to the testimony of the Word. What do the Scriptures say?

There are a number of fine books on the continuation of the gifts of the Spirit for today, some popular and some scholarly, and this is not the place to make an exhaustive, heavily annotated case for continuationism. Instead, I want to lay out the main lines of argument that seem clear and evident to me regarding this subject. Interested readers can continue their study in the books cited here, and whether we end up in agreement or disagreement, at least my cessationist friends can better understand what we believe and what we do as charismatics.[6]

Interestingly, at the Strange Fire conference, only one presentation, that of Tom Pennington, attempted to provide an exegetical foundation for cessationism, while the *Strange Fire* book does not present any kind of systematic argument for cessation-ism. (For a refutation of Pastor Pennington's arguments, see be-low, Appendix C.)[7] In fact, a man named Matthew, a professor at a cessationist seminary and himself a cessationist at present, posted this on my AskDrBrown Facebook page after the confer-ence: "Did you have concerns over the apparent lack of exegesis? Because that seemed like it should have been the foundation for the rest of the conference. But instead I got weak association ar-guments..." He also said, "The Strange Fire conference actually had the opposite effect on me. Am I too closed off to the Spirit?" When I asked him what he meant, he responded:

> Well I have a bit of a contrarian nature. So when I see one side being so broadly assailed I try to at least intel-lectually take that position. In this case I just couldn't ac-cept that virtually all charismatics were apostates. That led me to do some self examination and to be certain I am being truly Biblical in my own views. My cessation-ism has always been based on inductive arguments. I'm thinking that just isn't going to cut it when taking a hard-lined stance. When I was first saved I was overcome with the Spirit and acted in a way that the world would have thought foolish. So why am I far from that now?[8]

I appreciate his candor and openness, and again, the ultimate question is: What do the Scriptures say?

One leader who attended the conference and had previously defended Pastor MacArthur had a change of heart afterwards, noting how, in his view, John Calvin was often more important to the speakers than the Word itself.

Watching and subsequently digesting all this, I realized
with horror that Calvinists are, by definition, NOT Sola
Scriptura. They do not base their doctrines on Scripture
but primarily on Calvin who in turn based his doctrine
on that of Augustine. They are therefore, at least, twice
removed from the Scriptures.

The Sola Scriptura slogan is just that – a slogan. If
they really were committed to the Scriptures they would
not come up with TULIP, amillennialism, paedobaptism,
replacement theology and cessationism, to name a few.
These doctrines cannot be arrived at through a simple
study of the Scriptures, they have to be taught by someone
external to the Scriptures.[9]

Is this true? Would anyone become a cessationist based on
reading the Scriptures alone, newly saved and locked alone in a
room with a Bible, with the ability to read the original languages
fluently? I don't believe so, although some of my cessationist
colleagues would beg to differ.

Commenting on Pastor Steve Lawson's Strange Fire presentation entitled, "What Calvin Would Say to the Charismatic
Calvinists," one viewer sent me an email sarcastically entitled,
"We preach Calvin, and him glorified." Surely, though, every
speaker at the conference, including Pastor Lawson, who has
made many rich contributions to the Body, would agree that the
issue is not what Calvin said or what our experiences have been
but rather (to repeat), What do the Scriptures say? According
to Pastor MacArthur, "If Scripture alone were truly their final
authority, charismatic Christians would never tolerate patently
unbiblical practices-like mumbling in nonsensical prayer languages, uttering fallible prophecies, worshipping in disorderly

ways, or being knocked senseless by the supposed power of the Holy Spirit."[10]

Putting aside his characterizations of charismatic meetings, I agree with my brother that the Scriptures alone must be our final authority, so let's take a journey through the New Testament together, and as we do, would you pray with me for openness to the Word, regardless of where it leads? I pray the same for myself.

What Do the Scriptures Say?

In his review of *Strange Fire*, Prof. Thomas Schreiner, a top New Testament scholar and a cessationist, wrote:

> . . . it should be acknowledged that the arguments for a cessationist reading aren't open and shut. Nowhere does the New Testament clearly teach that supernatural gifts have ceased. A good argument can be made for such a reading; indeed, I think the case for cessationism is convincing, and the warnings MacArthur raises are salutary. Still, we must admit there are some solid arguments on the other side as well. For example, a good case for the continuation of the gifts until Jesus' second coming can be made from 1 Corinthians 13:8-12.[11]

How interesting that Prof. Schreiner points to the very text (1 Corinthians 13:8-12) sometimes used by modern cessationists to argue that the gifts ceased with the completion of the New

Testament canon (an utterly untenable view increasingly abandoned by cessationists),[12] and he cites it to argue for the opposite, namely, that "a good case" can be made "for the continuation of the gifts until Jesus' second coming." And note carefully his words, which are all the more telling given the larger context of his review and his pro-cessationist position: "Nowhere does the New Testament clearly teach that supernatural gifts have ceased."[13]

Reformed Pastor John Carpenter, who holds a Ph.D. in Church History with a focus on the Puritans, notes candidly: "Even responsible cessationists will concede, the Bible doesn't teach cessationism. Scripture has no explicit cessationist statement."[14]

In short, it can be demonstrated that:

1. The New Testament clearly states that these supernatural gifts *will* continue until Jesus returns.

2. The New Testament encourages the use of these gifts.

3. The New Testament never states that the gifts will cease in this age.

4. In light of the consistent, multifaceted testimony of the Scriptures, the burden of proof is clearly on the side of the cessationists, since they must tell us where the Word of God states plainly that the normal, expected, and encouraged practice found in the New Testament is not to be the normal, expected, and encouraged practice today.

5. Therefore contemporary, documented reports of healings and miracles, performed in the name of Jesus for

the glory of God and for the good of the Church and the
world, should be embraced rather than scorned.

On a historical level, Morton Kelsey noted that "the practices
of healing described in the New Testament continued without
interruption for the next two centuries."[15] This testimony from
Justin Martyr is typical: "For numberless demoniacs throughout
the whole world, and in your city, many of our Christian men
exorcizing them in the Name of Jesus Christ ... have healed and
do heal, rendering helpless and driving the possessing devils out
of the men, though they could not be cured by all the other ex-
orcists, and those who used incantations and drugs."[16]

In the third-fourth centuries, there are accounts like this,
from the monastic leader Anthony of Egypt (251-356). He was
highly regarded by Athanasius (298-373), who spoke of the miracles God performed through this desert father. (On a side note,
it is obvious that Athanasius could not be called a cessationist,
even if these stories were all myths. In other words, these early
Church leaders believed that things like this were still taking
place.) In his account of Anthony, Athanasius wrote:

> Often he spoke days beforehand of those who were com-
> ing to him, and sometimes a month before, and of the
> cause for which they came. For some came simply to see
> him, some came through sickness, some suffering from
> devils. And all thought the toil of the journey no trouble
> or loss... one came to him, having a devil. This demon was
> so dreadful that the possessed man used to eat the filth of
> his own body. St. Antony, pitying the youth, prayed and
> watched the whole night with him. (By the power of the
> Holy Spirit) St. Antony rebuked the demon, the youth was

at once made whole and then in his right mind, recognizing where he was, he embraced the old man.[17]

Not long after this, however, we see that Augustine (354-430) was skeptical about healings and miracles, stating clearly in his earlier writings that Christians should not look for the continuance of the healing gift.[18] But then he had a dramatic change of heart while completing his *magnum opus, The City of God.* There he wrote of the importance of documenting the miracles he and his community were witnessing, "once I realized how many miracles were occurring in our own day and which were so like the miracles of old and also how wrong it would be to allow the memory of these marvels of divine power to perish from among our people. It is only two years ago that the keeping of records was begun here in Hippo, and already, at this writing, we have nearly seventy attested miracles."[19]

How extraordinary! So, if we can see from the Word that such miracles are to be expected and then, by God's grace, we witness such miracles in our day, we should respond with gratitude and awe as Augustine did, trading in our skepticism for appreciation.[20]

The Miracles of Jesus and the Kingdom of God

Without doubt, healing the sick and driving out demons played a major role in Jesus' ministry, to the point that Matthew offered this summary:

> And he went throughout all Galilee, teaching in their synagogues and proclaiming the gospel of the kingdom and

healing every disease and every affliction among the people. So his fame spread throughout all Syria, and they brought him all the sick, those afflicted with various diseases and pains, those oppressed by demons, epileptics, and paralytics, and he healed them.(Matt 4:23-24; see also Matt 9:35: "And Jesus went throughout all the cities and villages, teaching in their synagogues and proclaiming the gospel of the kingdom and healing every disease and every affliction.")

Jesus Himself summarized His ministry in similar terms when warned by some Pharisees about Herod's evil intentions towards Him: "Go and tell that fox, 'Behold, I cast out demons and perform cures today and tomorrow, and the third day I finish my course.'" (Luke 13:32) And when He sent out His disciples to proclaim the good news while He was still with them, Mark records that "they went out and proclaimed that people should repent. And they cast out many demons and anointed with oil many who were sick and healed them" (Mark 6:12-13).

This was in harmony with the fact that He "gave them power and authority over all demons and to cure diseases, and he sent them out to proclaim the kingdom of God and to heal" (Luke 9:1-2). Or, as recorded in Matthew 10:7-8, when Jesus sent the Twelve out, He said, "And proclaim as you go, saying, 'The kingdom of heaven is at hand.' Heal the sick, raise the dead, cleanse lepers, cast out demons. You received without paying; give without pay."

Do you see this important connection between the kingdom of God and healing? Wherever the kingdom (= rule) of God drew near, Satan's domain was broken, as light overcame darkness, captives were delivered, the sick were healed, and demons were driven out. Note again the words of Jesus just cited: The apostles were to announce the imminent arrival of the kingdom of God *and then* heal the sick and drive out demons. Or, in reverse order in Luke 10:8-9 with reference to the seventy He sent out: "Whenever you enter a town and they receive you, eat what is set before you. Heal the sick in it and say to them, 'The kingdom of God has come near to you.'"

So, according to Matthew 10 (and Luke 9) they were to proclaim the good news of the arrival of God's kingdom through Jesus the Messiah, after which they were to heal the sick and set the captives free to demonstrate the arrival of that kingdom. In Luke 10, they were to heal the sick and then say, "The kingdom of God has come near to you." In other words, "Look at what just happened. Look at the miracles you have witnessed. God's kingdom has come near!"

This was the same point Jesus made in Matthew 12 where it is recorded that "a demon-oppressed man who was blind and mute was brought to him, and he healed him, so that the man spoke and saw" (Matt 12:22; note that there is often a close connection between demons and disease in the Gospels).[21] When the religious leaders claimed He was driving out demons by the power of Satan, He responded, "if it is by the Spirit of God that I cast out demons, then the kingdom of God has come upon you" (Matt 12:28; in Luke 11:20 the text reads, "if it is by *the finger of God* that I cast out demons, then the kingdom of God has come upon you," which points the reader back to Exodus 8:19).

The point of all this is simple: These miracles were not just impersonal acts of power announcing the inbreaking of the Messianic kingdom, like trumpets announcing the approach of royalty. They were *signs* – meaning indicators – of the inbreaking of the Messianic kingdom. This is what happens when the rule of God arrives! And since the Messianic kingdom did not leave the earth when Jesus ascended to heaven (where does the Bible say it did?), there is every reason we should expect to see the continuance of these miracles as the kingdom of God spreads around the earth, culminating with its full manifestation when Jesus returns. As Prof. D. A. Carson explained with regard to the words of the Lord's prayer, "Your kingdom come, your will be done, on earth as it is heaven" (Matthew 6:10), whoever reads these words in Matthew's Gospel "perceives that the kingdom has already broken in and prays for its extension as well as for its unqualified manifestation."[22]

As I wrote in *Israel's Divine Healer* in the section on "Healing and the Kingdom of God,"[23]

According to the testimony of the evangelists, Jesus was called "King of the Jews" by the Magi at his birth (Matt 2:2) and by the Romans at his death (Matt 27:37; Mark 15:26; Luke 23:38; John 19:19). When he began his public ministry, he took up the message of John the Baptist: "'The time has come,' he said. 'The kingdom of God is near. Repent and believe the good news!'" (Mark 1:15; cf. Matt 4:17 with Matt 3:2). Wherever he went, this was his theme (cf. Matt 4:23, 9:35), and his healing acts were directly linked to the inbreaking of the kingdom (cf. Luke 4:40-44, 9:10-11). Thus, when he sent his disciples out to preach the coming of the kingdom of God, he commissioned them to heal and exorcise in conjunction with this proclamation: "As you go, preach this message: 'The kingdom of heaven is near.' Heal the sick, raise the dead, cleanse those who have leprosy, drive out demons" (Matt 10:7-8a; cf. also Luke 9:2, "and he sent them out to preach the kingdom of God and to heal the sick"). Luke 10:8-9, the commissioning of the seventy-two, is especially clear: "When you enter a town and are welcomed, eat what is set before you. Heal the sick who are there and tell them, 'The kingdom of God is near you.'" *Miracles of healing and deliverance announced the inbreaking of the reign of God* (cf. above, 4.2.2, on Isaiah 35).[24]

In particular, Jesus made reference to the conflict between the kingdom of God and the kingdom of Satan in his exorcisms:[25] "If Satan drives out Satan, he is divided against himself. How then can his kingdom stand? ... But if I drive out demons by the Spirit of God, then the kingdom of God has come upon you" (Matt 12:26, 28).[26] As noted by Mueller, and reflecting the consensus of New Testament scholarship, these acts of deliverance were "an element in the struggle for the establishment of eschatological salvation. ... His exorcism of demons, and with it the victorious struggle against Satan on earth, are visible signs of the advent of the eschatological time of salvation in which God alone will reign."[27] (See further, below, 5.2.2.) This concept is also found in the longer ending of Mark, where the first sign to accompany the believers is: "In my name they will drive out [*ekballō*] demons" (16:17b), the usage of *ekballō* being suggestive of the LXX's rendering of *gārāš*, "to drive out," used frequently with reference to the conquest of Canaan (see, e.g., Exod 23:28-30; Deut 33:27; less frequently, but in similar contexts, *ekballō* renders the Hiphil

of *yrš*, "to dispossess"; see, e.g., Exod 34:24; Deut 11:23).
Thus, just as the Israelites were commissioned by Yahweh
to drive out and dispossess the Canaanites, thereby taking the promised land, so also the disciples were commissioned by Jesus to drive out and dispossess demons,
thereby taking back what rightfully belonged to God and
making disciples for him, the new subjects of his kingdom (Matt 28:18-20; Col 1:13; Rev 1:5b-6). This gospel
of the kingdom was proclaimed by the early Church (cf.
Matt 24:14; Acts 8:12, 20:24-25, 28:23, 31), suggesting that
there would be a continuing pattern of miracles integrally
associated with the message, since the battle for the final
establishment of the kingdom of God raged (and rages)
on.[28]

Speaking then in the present tense, rather than *looking back*
to the kingdom of God in Jesus' days on earth or *looking ahead*
to the full manifestation of the kingdom when Jesus returns,
Paul wrote to the Corinthians, "For the kingdom of God does
not consist in talk but in power" (1 Cor 4:20; Paul actually challenged the Corinthians 4:19 to show him what power they had,
so this was clearly not simply an apostolic privilege). In light
of this direct statement, it is only fair to ask: When and where
did this change? When and where did the nature of this kingdom power become diminished? Where does the New Testament even hint at the idea that the kingdom of God that Jesus
inaugurated only paid a visit and then departed? And surely no
one would argue that the kingdom of God left the earth when
the New Testament canon was closed!

If the reign of God was only here temporarily during the
time of the Gospels, why did Paul speak of it in the present

in 1 Corinthians 4:20? (For the larger context of his words, which included miracles of healing, see 1 Corinthians 2:1-5, discussed below.) And what are we to make of the fact that Philip "preached good news about the kingdom of God and the name of Jesus Christ" to the Samaritans (Act 8:12)? And why does Paul connect the gospel of grace with the gospel of the kingdom (see Acts 20:24-25, where he speaks of testifying "to the gospel of the grace of God" as well as "proclaiming the kingdom")? And notice that he is still preaching this same message at the end of Acts while a prisoner in Rome: "he expounded to them, testifying to the kingdom of God and trying to convince them about Jesus both from the Law of Moses and from the Prophets. . . . He lived there two whole years at his own expense, and welcomed all who came to him, proclaiming the kingdom of God and teaching about the Lord Jesus Christ with all boldness and without hindrance" (Act 28:23, 30-31).

With the coming of King Messiah into the world, the Messianic kingdom has broken in – it is here already, but its full manifestation is still to come; it is "already but not-yet"[29] – and that's why Paul could write about our life in the kingdom of God in the here and now: "For the kingdom of God is not a matter of eating and drinking but of righteousness and peace and joy in the Holy Spirit" (Rom. 14:17). Once again, he was speaking in the present tense, describing our current spiritual experience in the kingdom of God while in this world. May I ask where we are instructed to deviate from the message that was preached in Acts? What biblical texts instruct us to?

Without a doubt, we will not "inherit the kingdom of God" until the future (see, for example, 1 Corinthians 15:50), and *in no way* do I subscribe to the "kingdom now" message that implies (or overtly states) that we will take over the world before Jesus returns. At the same time, there can be no doubt that the Messianic kingdom has broken into this world – has the Messiah come or not? – and the arrival of God's kingdom brings with it salvation, healing, and deliverance.[30] To repeat, the light drives the darkness out and the Spirit drives the demons out.[31] And just as many people turned to the Lord in the Gospels and Acts as the kingdom was preached and demonstrated in the power of the Spirit, the same thing is taking place worldwide today, as attested by missionaries, native church planters, and missiologists around the globe.[32]

The Divine Purposes of the Miracles of Jesus

For most cessationists, the miracles of Jesus are viewed primarily as *proofs* whose main function was to demonstrate to the world – and in particular to the Jewish people – that He indeed was the promised Messiah. Then, after His resurrection, the Holy Spirit confirmed the message of the apostles with similar "sign gifts" until the Church was "established." As expressed by Jonathan Edwards (in a quote we will return to later in this chapter),

> The extraordinary gifts of the Spirit, such as the gift of tongues, of miracles, of prophecy, &c., are called extraordinary, because they are such as are not given in the ordinary course of God's providence. They are not bestowed in the way of God's ordinary providential dealing with his children, but only on extraordinary occasions, as

they were bestowed on the prophets and apostles to enable them to reveal the mind and will of God before the canon of Scripture was complete, and so on the primitive Church, in order to the founding and establishing of it in the world. But since the canon of the Scripture has been completed, and the Christian Church fully founded and established, these extraordinary gifts have ceased. But the ordinary gifts of the Spirit are such as are continued to the Church of God throughout all ages; such gifts as are granted in conviction and conversion, and such as appertain to the building up of the saints in holiness and comfort.

The canon of Scripture being completed when the apostle John had written the book of Revelation, which he wrote not long before his death, these miraculous gifts were no longer continued in the church. For there was now completed an established written revelation of the mind and will of God wherein God had fully recorded a standing and all-sufficient rule for his church in all ages. And the Jewish church and nation being overthrown, and the Christian church and the last dispensation of the church of God being established, the miraculous gifts of the Spirit were no longer needed, and therefore they ceased; for though they had been continued in the church for so many ages, yet then they failed, and God caused them to fail because there was no further occasion for them. And so was fulfilled the saying of the text, 'Whether there be prophecies, they shall fail; whether there be tongues, they shall cease; whether there be knowledge, it shall vanish away." And now there seems to be an end

to all such fruits [i.e. extraordinary gifts] of the Spirit as
these, and we have no reason to expect them any more.[33]

Theologian Michael Horton, in harmony with this position,
has also stressed that the miracles of Jesus were *revelatory* in
that they disclosed aspects of the purpose and mission of the
Messiah. So, Dr. Horton explains, when Jesus fed the five thousand, He was showing the world that He was the Bread of Life,
and when He healed a crippled man on the Sabbath, He was
demonstrating that He, in fact, was the only one who could give
rest to the weary and was Himself Lord of the Sabbath, yes, the
Sabbath incarnate. In short, the healings of Jesus were a revelation of *who He was*.[34]

The problem with these positions is that they fail to appreciate that who Jesus *was* remains who He *is* (Hebrews 13:8) and
that most (or, without question, many) of His healings had no
revelatory, "sign" nature attached to them by the Gospel writers.
Rather, these healings: 1) often arose out of His compassion for
the sick and suffering and were acts of mercy and restoration,
in contrast with the spectacular signs requested by the religious
leaders (see further, below); 2) were an earthly expression of
His Father's heavenly will and a reflection of His character as
revealed consistently through His Word (see again, below); 3)
provided the evidence that the Messianic age – characterized
by salvation and deliverance! – had begun and that the kingdom of God had arrived in power (as opposed to merely paid
a visit); 4) were the precursors of the eschatological outpouring
of the Holy Spirit (see further, below); 5) were part and parcel of
the proclamation of liberty to the captives and "the beginning
of the end of Satan's reign"[35]; 6) were an integral part of the very
platform of Jesus (Luke 4:16-20), a foundational element of His

jubilee declaration; and 7) were intimately related to His work of forgiving sins (see, for example, Isaiah 33:24; Matt. 9:1-7; John 5:1-14; Jacob [James] 5:13-14).[36]

Now, there is no question at all that Jesus' healings and miracles also served to accredit Him as Messiah, and we all agree that in many ways, His miracles were unique in scope and nature (see especially Acts 2:21-22). There is absolutely no disagreement between continuationists and cessationists on this.[37] However, as Prof. Raymond Brown expressed it,

> Jesus' miracles were not only or primarily external confirmations of his message; rather the miracle was the vehicle of the message. Side by side, word and miraculous deed gave expression to the entrance of God's kingly power into time. This understanding of the miracles as an intrinsic part of revelation, rather than merely an extrinsic criterion, is intimately associated with a theory of revelation where the emphasis on the God who acts is equal to (or even more stressed than) the emphasis on the God who speaks.[38]

Thus, Jesus refused to give His critics an abstract demonstration of power, specifically, a sign from heaven (see, for example, Matthew 16:1-4). He did, however, freely point to *His miracles* as proof, since they attested to the very heart of who He was and what He came to do.[39] His healings were signs of His Messiahship much like the first droplets of rain are signs of a coming downpour.[40] That is to say, the healings of Jesus were a sign that He was the Great Physician, His exorcisms were a sign that He was the mighty Deliverer, and His miracles over nature were a sign that He was the Lord of all.

Prof. Craig Blomberg notes that,

> Other specific healing miracles also point by inference to
> the arrival of the kingdom or of the messianic age. When
> Jesus heals a deaf-mute, Mark describes the man as one
> who could hardly talk (*mogilalos* – Mark 7:32), a word
> found elsewhere in the Greek Bible only in Isa 35:6 (LXX),
> in which the prophet is describing the wonders of the age
> to come, including the fact that the "mute tongue" will
> "shout for joy."[41]

The age to come has broken into this age, and therefore healings and miracles remain part of the partial manifestation of
God's kingdom in this age, while we eagerly await the return of
Jesus and the full manifestation of His kingdom, at which time
all sin, sickness, and pain will be banished from our midst.

The Healings of Jesus and Believers Today

Before moving to Acts, let's look at the healings of Jesus in a little
more depth, asking the question: What does this mean for the
Church today?

First, as noted above, the healings of Jesus often arose out
of His compassion for the sick and suffering and were acts of
mercy and restoration, in contrast with the spectacular signs
requested by the religious leaders. As stated in Matthew 14:14,
"When he went ashore he saw a great crowd, and he had compassion on them and healed their sick." And it was out of compassion for the widow of Nain that He raised her son from the
dead in Luke 7:13-15. Can we appeal to His mercy and compassion to heal and work miracles today? And doesn't Paul attribute

the healing of his co-worker Epaphroditus to the mercy of God in Philippians 2:29? Of course, this does not mean that healing is guaranteed, only that it can be prayed for with expectation in light of the character of God as revealed in the person of the Messiah. What would Jesus do?

Second, His healings were an earthly expression of His Father's heavenly will and a reflection of His character as revealed consistently through His Word. This means that we can learn the nature of the Father by observing Jesus, His Son (doesn't John 1:18 literally say in the Greek that the Son exegeted the Father?)

As the Lord said to Phillip in John 14:

> "Have I been with you so long, and you still do not know me, Philip? Whoever has seen me has seen the Father. How can you say, 'Show us the Father'? Do you not believe that I am in the Father and the Father is in me? The words that I say to you I do not speak on my own authority, but the Father who dwells in me does his works. Believe me that I am in the Father and the Father is in me, or else believe on account of the works themselves." (John 14:9-11)

Jesus explicitly stated that He only did what He saw the Father doing (John 5:19; 8:28-29; 10:38-39), and when the sick came to Him, He healed them without fail (see, for example, Matthew 15:30-31). What does this tell us about the heart of God and the will of God?

In his last message at Strange Fire, Pastor MacArthur asked, "How did the Holy Spirit work in Christ? Did he knock him down? Did he make him look drunk? Did he cause him to fall, or

flop, or roll, or laugh hysterically, or bark, or babble, or talk gibberish?... People who make people do that are not Spirit-filled.
That's not what the Spirit does."[42]

The answer is simple: This is how the Holy Spirit worked
through the Messiah. The Spirit drove out demons through Him
and healed a multitude of sick folks through Him and spoke
through Him prophetically. Jesus is the same. The Spirit is the
same. The needs of the world are the same. Who decided to
change this? Where does the Bible say this changed?

Healing Is Still a Divine Blessing

Years ago, during my anti-healing days, I heard a Texas evangelist say on the radio, "You know, in Bible days, it was the
devil who made people sick and Jesus who made people well.
Today, some preachers tell us it's Jesus who makes people sick
and the devil who makes them well!" I was so frustrated with
what this simple preacher had to say, but I realized that, from
a biblical standpoint, he was making a valid point: throughout the Word, sickness, in and of itself, is never presented as
a good thing (although we can grow through it and some of
the godliest people in the world are sick or handicapped) and
healing, in and of itself, is never presented as a bad thing. Moreover, sickness is never connected to the blessing of God while
it is often connected to sin or Satan (note the frequent connection between driving out demons and healing the sick in the
New Testament);[43] in contrast, healing is often connected to the
blessing of God.

To repeat: This does *not* mean that every believer who is sick is demonstrating a lack of faith or must be in sin or under demonic power – how many believers have been brutalized by these notions? – but it does mean that a consistent biblical theology of healing would recognize healing and health as gifts from God, often signs of His blessing and grace, while sickness and disease would be viewed as negative conditions (in and of themselves) and it would be right and fitting for us to ask God for healing. And when Jesus came on the scene as the will of God in living color, He demonstrated the Father's heart towards the sick and the demonized. That's why Peter explained in Acts 10:38, "how God anointed Jesus of Nazareth with the Holy Spirit and with power. He went about doing good and healing all who were oppressed by the devil, for God was with him." That also explains the Lord's words in Luke 13 when He healed a Jewish woman who had been bent over for eighteen years. (Please read this account carefully.)

> Now he was teaching in one of the synagogues on the Sabbath. And behold, there was a woman who had had a disabling spirit for eighteen years. [The NET reads, "a woman was there who had been disabled by a spirit for eighteen years."] She was bent over and could not fully straighten herself. When Jesus saw her, he called her over and said to her, "Woman, you are freed from your disability." And he laid his hands on her, and immediately she was made straight, and she glorified God. But the ruler of the synagogue, indignant because Jesus had healed on the Sabbath, said to the people, "There are six days in which work ought to be done. Come on those days and

be healed, and not on the Sabbath day. Then the Lord answered him, "You hypocrites! Does not each of you on the Sabbath untie his ox or his donkey from the manger and lead it away to water it? *And ought not this woman, a daughter of Abraham whom Satan bound for eighteen years, be loosed from this bond on the Sabbath day?"* (Luke 13:10-16)

Yes, Satan, in keeping with his character and doing what he always does, had bound her, and Jesus, in keeping with His character and doing only what He saw the Father do, set her free. Is it possible that Satan is still binding people with sickness and disease? (Can you give me any clear scriptural statements that he has stopped?) And is it possible that Jesus is still setting the captives free? Is there evidence that either of their characters has changed? And is there scriptural evidence that what had been a *curse* under the Sinai covenant (severe sickness as divine judgment for disobedience) has become a *blessing* under the new and better covenant?[44] And, in light of the abundant promises for healing in the Old Testament, what do we make of 2 Corinthians 1:20, "For all the promises of God find their Yes in him"?

"Whoever Believes in Me" in John 14:12

Third, Jesus gave a universal promise in John 14:12 that implies that all believers can ask God to demonstrate His healing and miracle-working power through them, since the statement in John 14:12 is programmatic, as Jesus said: "Truly, truly, I say to you, whoever believes in me will also do the works that I do; and greater works than these will he do, because I am going to the Father." How is this not universal in scope, given that the identical Greek phrase *ho pisteuon eis eme*, whoever believes in Me, is always universal in application in John? (See John 6:35; 7:38; 11:25; 12:44, 46.) And while we can debate exactly what Jesus intended by the "greater works," it is difficult to escape from the conclusion that *whoever believes* in the Son will also perform miraculous signs, based on: 1) the immediate context (14:9-11, with the emphasis on miracles as the *works* done by Jesus); 2) the universality of the language used; and 3) the assurance which follows, guaranteeing the efficacy of prayer to the Father in Jesus' name.[45]

To expand on this last point, note the two verses that follow, namely John 14:13-14: "Whatever you ask in my name, this I will do, that the Father may be glorified in the Son. If you ask me anything in my name, I will do it." This underscores the fact that Jesus is not simply talking about His followers performing acts of kindness and mercy. Rather, He is saying that He will be leaving the earth but then sending the Spirit, who will empower us to do what He did, and more (which obviously includes mass conversions, as happened at Pentecost in Acts 2). He then reinforces this with the promise to ask the Father for "anything" in His name, and the answers would be to His glory. This promise cannot be limited to the apostles based on the language of "whoever believes in Me," nor can it limited to non-supernatural acts of service. The reverse is actually true.

As expressed by John commentators (and highly respected New Testament scholars) Merrill C. Tenney and F. F. Bruce, respectively:

> As the living Lord he continued in his church what he had himself had begun. He expected that the living church

would become the instrument by which he could manifest his salvation to all people.[46]

When, after the healing at the pool of Bethesda, Jesus affirmed that the works he did were those which the Father showed him, he added 'he will show him greater works than these, to give you cause for marvel' (John 5:20). Now he tells his disciples that they in turn would do what he did. That must have been surprising enough. But what were they to think when he went on to say that, because he was going to the Father, they would do even greater works than they had seen him do?[47]

Healings and the Dunamis of the Spirit

Fourth, the healings of Jesus were connected with the *dunamis* (power) of the Spirit, and that *dunamis* is still given by the Spirit to God's people through the ages. To explore this point, we'll start in the Gospels and then move into Acts and even the Epistles, tracing the word *dunamis*, power (in particular, miraculous power) in a number of key verses. And note that the plural, *dunameis*, is often translated as "miracles" in the New Testament (see, Matthew 7:22; 11:20, 21, 23; 13:54, 58; 14:2; Mark 6:2, 5, 14; 9:39; Luke 10:13; 19:37 Acts 2:22; 8:13; 19:11; 1 Corinthians 12:10, 28, 29; 2 Corinthians 12:12; Galatians 3:5; Hebrews 2:4).

In Luke 1:35, Gabriel informs Miriam (Mary) that she will conceive the Son of God in her womb when the Holy Spirit and God's *dunamis* come upon her, marking the first time in Luke that the Spirit and the power of God are joined together.

Thirty years later, after His time of testing in the wilderness, Jesus "returned to Galilee in the power [*dunamis*] of the Spirit" (Luke 4:14); in Luke 5:17, the *dunamis* of the Lord was present for Him to heal the sick; in Luke 6:19, *dunamis* was coming out of Him and healing all the sick; and in Luke 8:46, Jesus realizes that someone touched Him with faith for healing because He perceives *dunamis* going out of Him.

In Luke 9:1, He gives His disciples *dunamis* and authority "over all demons and to cure diseases" (see also 10:19) while in Luke 24:49, after His disciples have witnessed His resurrection and after He has opened their minds to understand the Scriptures (see Luke 24:44-48), He tells them, "And behold, I am sending the promise of my Father upon you. But stay in the city until you are clothed with power [*dunamis*] from on high." This is reiterated in Acts 1:8, where Jesus stated before His ascension, "But you will receive power [*dunamis*] when the Holy Spirit has come upon you, and you will be my witnesses in Jerusalem and in all Judea and Samaria, and to the end of the earth" (Act 1:8). This did not only mean boldness; rather, it referred in particular to the supernatural enduement of divine power to work miracles in Jesus' name, thereby testifying (= being witnesses) to His resurrection from the dead. This becomes particularly clear when it is remembered that the plural of *dunamis*, namely, *dunameis*, is used frequently to refer to miracles in the New Testament, as noted above.

We see then in Acts 4:33 that the apostles bore witness to the resurrection of Jesus with great *dunamis*, while in Acts 6:8, it is recorded that Stephen, "full of grace and power [*dunamis*], was doing great wonders and signs among the people," which indicates that this *dunamis* was not for the apostles only (confirmed again in 1 Corinthians 12:10, 28-29, where "working of miracles" – again, from the Greek *dunamis* – is given to believers in general, not only to the apostles). This is reiterated in Galatians 3:5 (speaking in the present tense to the believers there about the Spirit working miracles), "Does he who supplies the Spirit to you and works miracles [*dunameis*] among you do so by works of the law, or by hearing with faith" (Gal 3:5)?

Again, a simple question would be, If the Spirit that comes upon believers today carries the *dunamis* of God, why shouldn't we expect to see some of the same demonstrations of power that took place in the Gospels and Acts? When did the *dunamis* of the Spirit change? Where is it written or even hinted at that the Spirit no longer includes God's *dunamis*?

I fully understand that the gospel itself is the *dunamis* of God to save (Romans 1:16), but it also contains the *dunamis* to heal and deliver. *Based on New Testament evidence alone*, you can no more separate the gospel from being the power of God to save than you can separate the Spirit of God from being the power of God to heal and deliver. This is reiterated in Paul's words in 1 Corinthians:

> When I came to you, brothers, I did not come with eloquence or superior wisdom as I proclaimed to you the testimony about God. For I resolved to know nothing while I was with you except Jesus Christ and him crucified. I came to you in weakness and fear, and with much trembling. My message and my preaching were not with wise and persuasive words, but with a demonstration of the Spirit's power [*dunamis*], so that your faith might not rest on men's wisdom, but on God's power [*dunamis*]. . . .

For the kingdom of God is not a matter of talk [literally, words] but of power [*dunamis*] (1 Cor 2:1-5; 4:20, NIV).

Isn't the kingdom of God *still* a matter of divine power? In particular, when the gospel of Jesus is brought to virgin territory, to men and women who never heard the Savior's name before, they not be impressed when we tell them, "Look, we have a holy book, and 2,000 years ago, the stories in this book were confirmed with signs, wonders, and miracles, but no longer." To the contrary, when we preach the same Jesus that Paul preached in the power of the same Spirit, demonstrating the reality of the same kingdom, Satan's power will be vanquished, the sick will be healed, the demonized set free, and most of all, the lost will be saved, recognizing that, indeed, He is risen. Preaching Jesus Christ and Him crucified is totally harmonious with the demonstration of the Spirit's power. In fact, the two go hand in hand. (To be perfectly clear, I absolutely affirm the power of the gospel itself to save, without accompanying miracles; I am simply exposing the weakness of the argument "divine confirmation on a book 2,000 years ago, but no more.")

A Wicked and Adulterous Generation Seeks a Sign?

Today, we often hear people say, "I don't need to see a sign or wonder to believe, and only a wicked and adulterous generation seeks after such things. Signs and wonders actually distract from the preaching of the gospel and become a carnival side show."

A biblical response would be:

1. We are not seeking a sign. We are seeking the outpouring of God's Spirit on the sick and suffering for the glory of God.

2. We also believe whether we see or not, but our love for a hurting world moves us to pray for the sick and ask God to manifest His power.

3. We want the world to know that Jesus is risen from the dead, and one of the ways He demonstrates that is by pouring out His Spirit and working signs, wonders, and miracles through His people.

4. We're simply following the theology of the first century believers. When they were persecuted, they prayed these words: "And now, Lord, look upon their threats and grant to your servants to continue to speak your word with all boldness, while you stretch out your hand to heal, and signs and wonders are performed through the name of your holy servant Jesus" (Acts 4:29-30). Would you have told them their prayer was amiss? Would you have accused them of being wicked and adulterous people who sought for signs? Would you have told them their prayer was a distraction from the gospel? And where is there the slightest evidence in the New Testament that it is wrong for us to pray this way, especially in times of persecution?

The Outpouring of the Spirit Is for "the Last Days"

Having said all this, it's important to recognize *that the Book of Acts states explicitly that the miraculous working of the Spirit –*

especially the gift of prophecy – is to continue until the end of this age. Note carefully the words of Peter in Acts 2 as he stands with the eleven to explain the miraculous gift of languages (coupled with the sound of the rushing mighty wind) that has drawn the Jewish crowd:

> But Peter, standing with the eleven, lifted up his voice and addressed them: "Men of Judea and all who dwell in Jerusalem, let this be known to you, and give ear to my words. For these people are not drunk, as you suppose, since it is only the third hour of the day. But this is what was uttered through the prophet Joel: 'And *in the last days* it shall be, God declares, that I will pour out my Spirit on all flesh, and your sons and your daughters shall prophesy, and your young men shall see visions, and your old men shall dream dreams; even on my male servants and female servants in those days I will pour out my Spirit, and they shall prophesy. And I will show wonders in the heavens above and signs on the earth below, blood, and fire, and vapor of smoke; the sun shall be turned to darkness and the moon to blood, before the day of the Lord comes, the great and magnificent day. And it shall come to pass that everyone who calls upon the name of the Lord shall be saved.'" (Acts 2:14-21)

I highlighted the words "in the last days" because they are not in Joel's original Hebrew text, which simply says, "And afterwards," nor are they in the Septuagint, the Greek translation of the Hebrew Scriptures. Rather, Peter inserts those words to say, "This is now the period of the last days, the period of the outpouring of the Spirit on all flesh, the period when the gift of prophecy will be multiplied to many, along with dreams and visions."

Now, the rest of the New Testament makes clear that "the last days" began with the death and resurrection of Jesus. Listen to the testimony of the authors of the New Testament. Hebrews 1:1-2 states, "In the past God spoke to our forefathers through the prophets at many times and in various ways, but *in these last days* He has spoken to us by His Son, whom He appointed heir of all things, and through whom He made the universe" (NIV). Notice those key words: *in these last days*. The last days were inaugurated by Jesus Himself! This is underscored again in Hebrews 9:26 where it is written that He "has appeared once for all *at the end of the ages* to do away with sin by the sacrifice of Himself" (NIV).

Paul writes in 1 Corinthians 10:11: "These things happened to them [i.e., the Israelites] as examples and were written down as warnings for us, on whom *the fulfillment of the ages* has come" (NIV). The "fulfillment of the ages" had already come on the Corinthians, and they lived more than 1900 years ago! Peter could inform his readers that Jesus, who was "chosen before the creation of the world . . . was revealed in *these last times* for your sake" (1 Pet 1:20, NIV), and Jacob [James] strongly rebuked the worldly rich, saying, "Your gold and silver are corroded. Their corrosion will testify against you and eat your flesh like fire. You have hoarded wealth *in the last days*" (Jam 5:3, NIV; that is exactly how it reads in the Greek). Yes, these greedy people who died nineteen centuries ago, were guilty of hoarding wealth *in the last days*. And what about the testimony of John? "Dear children, this is *the last hour*; and as you have heard that the antichrist is coming, even now many antichrists have come. *This is how we know it is the last hour*" (1 John 2:18, NIV). Could anything be clearer? Were the apostles mistaken in what they wrote?[48]

There can be no possible question that the New Testament authors understood that they were living in the last days, and they lived with anticipation of the Lord's return. They did not live with some expectation that they were starting a unique work and once they left the earth things would change dramatically in terms of the activity of the Spirit, many centuries after which Jesus would return.

In sum, the last days are here right now and the last days have been here for many years. As John Calvin expressed it, ". . . the whole period of the new dispensation, from the time when Christ appeared to us with the preaching of his Gospel, until the day of judgment, is designated by the last hour, the last times, the last days . . . ."[49] And Peter declared that the outpouring of the Spirit with prophecy and dreams and visions was something that would take place "in the last days." Those are the days in which we live.

Will the last days be marked by deception and defection? Absolutely (see 2 Timothy 3:1; 1 Timothy 4:1; note also Matthew 24:4-13 for a potential end-time warning as well). Will they be marked by the outpouring of the Spirit in miraculous ways? Absolutely. Peter makes it totally clear in Acts 2:17, reinforcing this in Acts 2:38-39 where he tells his fellow Jews who have asked what they must do in response to his message, "Repent and be baptized every one of you in the name of Jesus Christ for the forgiveness of your sins, and you will receive the gift of the Holy Spirit. For the promise is for you and for your children and for all who are far off, everyone whom the Lord our God calls to himself."

Again, the text is quite straightforward. Peter has just explained that the miraculous phenomena which the crowds had witnessed was the result of the outpouring of the Spirit, a sign that the last days – the Messianic era! – had begun, and now he declared that the gift of this same Spirit was for all who would repent and be immersed, telling them that the promise was for them, their children, and "all who are far off, everyone whom the Lord our God calls to himself."

And note that it is likely that Peter in Acts 2:39 is referring back to the promise of the Spirit in Isaiah 59:21, "And as for me, this is my covenant with them," says the LORD: "My Spirit that is upon you, and my words that I have put in your mouth, shall not depart out of your mouth, or out of the mouth of your offspring, or out of the mouth of your children's offspring," says the LORD, "from this time forth and forevermore."[50] And so, Peter is saying that forgiveness of sins and the gift of the Spirit are promised to all believers in all generations. And, to repeat, he has already said that this last days outpouring of the Spirit included the profusion of the gift of prophecy along with visions and dreams. In addition, we have seen the explicit connection between the Spirit and God's *dunamis* – His miraculous healing power – and so *we have no exegetical grounds whatsoever* for saying that:

1. The Spirit that was poured out in Acts is different from the Spirit that is poured out today.

2. The last days outpouring of the Spirit has not continued throughout the last days.

3. We should not expect prophecy, dreams, visions, healings, and miracles as the Spirit continues to move in the earth today for the glorification of the name of Jesus and the good of His people.

The New Testament Clearly Teaches Continuationism

I respectfully challenge any cessationist to give me explicit scriptural testimony that nullifies what I have written here. Without question, *sola Scriptura* points to the ongoing miraculous acts of the Spirit until Jesus returns, and when Paul wrote to some of his congregations about the importance of the Spirit in their lives, speaking of the Spirit as a deposit for what was to come (see Ephesians 1:14), he was not simply speaking about the Spirit's witness in our hearts. He was also talking about the Spirit's active presence in our midst – convicting of sin, leading us into righteousness, and working miraculous gifts.

In keeping with this, he writes to the Corinthians (people whom Strange Fire critics would have had a field day criticizing) with these words of encouragement, which indicate that both he and they fully expected to see the ongoing manifestation of the gifts and power of the Spirit until Jesus returned:

I give thanks to my God always for you because of the grace of God that was given you in Christ Jesus, that in every way you were enriched in him in all speech and all knowledge–even as the testimony about Christ was confirmed among you–*so that you are not lacking in any gift, as you wait for the revealing of our Lord Jesus Christ*, who will sustain you to the end, guiltless in the day of our Lord Jesus Christ (1 Cor 1:4-8).

Later in the letter he writes,

To each is given the manifestation of the Spirit for the common good. For to one is given through the Spirit the utterance of wisdom, and to another the utterance of knowledge according to the same Spirit, to another faith by the same Spirit, to another gifts of healing by the one Spirit, to another the working of miracles, to another prophecy, to another the ability to distinguish between spirits, to another various kinds of tongues, to another the interpretation of tongues. All these are empowered by one and the same Spirit, who apportions to each one individually as he wills. For just as the body is one and has many members, and all the members of the body, though many, are one body, so it is with Christ (1 Cor 12:7-12).

Nowhere does Paul (or any other New Testament author) say that this impartation of the Spirit was given for a few decades, at most, and nowhere does he say that these gifts were given to confirm the apostles' message. Rather, they are the gracious workings of the Spirit through the body "for the common good."[51]

And as we continue reading in 1 Corinthians 13, as Thomas Schreiner noted, "a good case for the continuation of the gifts until Jesus' second coming can be made from 1 Corinthians 13:8-12," where Paul makes clear that tongues and prophecy will continue until the *eschaton*.[52] As Messianic Jewish scholar Arnold Fruchtenbaum points out (he is a dispensationalist and a non-charismatic), "We cannot actually prove exegetically that the gift of tongues has come to an end. While many use I Corinthians 13:10, they tend to interpret the word 'perfect' as referring to the canon of Scripture, but this does not fit the context... The gifts will come to an end when the body is complete, at the rapture."[53]

Note also how Paul classifies the way that God has arranged the Body in 1 Corinthians 12: "Now you are the body of Christ and individually members of it. And God has appointed in the church first apostles, second prophets, third teachers, then miracles, then gifts of healing, helping, administrating, and various kinds of tongues" (1 Cor 12:27-28). Even if you argue that apostles and prophets were just for the first century (see below for more on this), you certainly believe that teachers are for today. Yet "teachers" in this list are followed by "miracles, then gifts of healing," which are then followed by "helping, administrating, and various kinds of tongues." Where is the slightest hint in the text – *sola Scriptura*! – that we can somehow extract teachers, helpers, and administrators from this list, claiming that only these giftings and callings continue until today, while eliminating miracles, gifts of healing, and tongues? To be truthful, to do so is to do exegetical violence to the text.

The same goes for Paul's follow up questions: "Are all apostles? Are all prophets? Are all teachers? Do all work miracles? Do all possess gifts of healing? Do all speak with tongues? Do all interpret? But earnestly desire the higher gifts. And I will show you a still more excellent way" (1 Cor 12:29-30). Based on cessationist interpretation, the only thing that remains in the Body today from this list is teachers. What?[54]

And after laying out the more excellent way of love – which includes the way in which the gifts were to be manifested and used – Paul gives practical instructions on tongues and prophecy, speaking highly of both of them, in particular prophecy, if used rightly. And he closes this section with a final exhortation: "So, my brothers, *earnestly desire to prophesy, and do not forbid speaking in tongues.* But all things should be done decently and in order" (1 Cor 14:39-40). And remember that for Paul, "decently and in order" meant, "When you come together, each one has a hymn, a lesson, a revelation, a tongue, or an interpretation. Let all things be done for building up" (1 Cor 14:26).

Who Changed What the Word Says?

With all respect to my non-charismatic readers, I ask you plainly: On what scriptural basis do you *not* earnestly desire to prophesy? Paul tells us to earnestly desire to prophesy. On what scriptural basis *do you* forbid speaking in tongues? Paul tells us not to, and there's not a sentence in the Bible reversing either of these exhortations, nor is there a legitimate inference to that effect.[55] Peter told us this outpouring of the Spirit with signs and wonders was for this entire age. Why then aren't you seeking the gift of prophecy and allowing the proper use of tongues?

You might say, "Well, I just don't believe what you charismatics practice is real prophecy or real tongues." But that is actually beside the point, since, whatever true prophecy is and whatever real tongues are, they are to continue until Jesus comes and they are to be sought after for the good of the Church and the good of the world and the glory of the Lord.[56]

Paul exhorted the Thessalonians clearly, writing, "Do not quench the Spirit. Do not despise prophecies, but test everything; hold fast what is good" (1 Thes 5:19-21). Obviously, in this context, quenching the Spirit was connected to extinguishing prophecies, which somehow could be despised. As expressed by F. F. Bruce in his commentary to 1-2 Thessalonians,

> The verb "quench" is related to the figure of fire used in various places (e.g. Matt 3:11 par. Luke 3:16; Luke 12:49; Acts 2:3; Rom 12:11) to denote the Holy Spirit or his activity. As the context goes on to make plain, the activity chiefly in view here is prophecy. In this respect the Spirit may be quenched when the prophet refuses to utter the message he has been given, or when others try to prevent him from uttering it.[57]

Was it because, given the profusion of the gift of prophecy and with so many able to prophesy, there was sometimes immaturity in the use of the gift or possibly false words spoken? Otherwise, why would prophecies be despised?[58] What is clear is that prophecies were *not* to be despised, the Spirit was *not* to be quenched, and all things *were* to be tested, with the exhortation to hold on to the good. This is what we seek to do as charismatics, based on *sola Scriptura*. Can you give me any reason not to? Where does the Word explicitly tell us that this has changed? To the contrary, it doesn't.

To quote Dr. John Carpenter again:

> Further, the Bible doesn't call spiritual gifts "revelatory gifts" (or "sign gifts"). It calls them "charismata" (literally, results of grace; or alternately it calls them "spiritual

things"). "Revelatory gifts" is a term made up by cessationists to get us to the conclusion that they have ceased.
Calling them "ceased gifts" and then concluding from
that name that they have ceased, would be no more circular in reasoning. The term "revelatory gifts" is imposed
onto scripture and gives the illusion that cessationism is
a product of careful Bible study.

And so cessationism is a self-contradictory doctrine
that claims the Bible is sufficient so we don't need spiritual
gifts (that the Bible tells us we need) but we do need the
doctrine of cessationism (that the Bible doesn't teach.)[59]

So, I repeat my challenge, based on *sola Scriptura*: Since Paul
commanded us to seek prophecy and other spiritual gifts, what
biblical text negates this? Since he commanded us not to forbid speaking in tongues, what scripture says this only applied to
Paul's day and not to us today? Since he commanded us not to
quench the Spirit with specific contextual reference to prophecies, what portion of Scripture now nullifies this?

I'm giving the benefit of the doubt that you won't try to argue that by "prophecy" Paul actually meant preaching, since
that completely undermines the cessationist claim that the gift
of prophecy is not for today because it is revelatory. (For a
clear refutation of this line of argument, see Appendix C.) And
I'm giving the benefit of the doubt that you won't claim that
1 Corinthians 13:10 indicates that tongues and prophecy will
cease when the canon of Scripture is closed, one of the most
impossible interpretations put on a biblical text in the history of
interpretation – and a relatively recent one at that.[60] And if you
argue that signs and wonders were uniquely attached to New
Testament apostles and prophets and, since we no longer have

apostles and prophets, the gifts have ceased, I would point out that:

1. The gifts of the Spirit in 1 Corinthians 12 are not connected with apostles and prophets.

2. Miracles and wonders were performed by non-apostles and non-prophets in the New Testament (as with Stephen and Phillip in Acts 6 and 8).

3. The promise in Acts 2 was that the Spirit would be poured out on all flesh and that prophecy, dreams, and visions would become the norm for all believers in this age.

4. Universally worded promises like John 14:12 indicate that supernatural works were not limited to the apostles and prophets but to "whoever believes" in Jesus.[61]

The Prayer of Faith for the Sick

This is all reinforced in Jacob (James) 5, where it is written,

> Is anyone among you suffering? Let him pray. Is anyone cheerful? Let him sing praise. Is anyone among you sick? Let him call for the elders of the church, and let them pray over him, anointing him with oil in the name of the Lord. And the prayer of faith will save the one who is sick, and the Lord will raise him up. And if he has committed sins, he will be forgiven (Jam 5:13-15).

Let's look at this without presupposition, simply asking basic questions of application. Jacob (James) begins with, "Is anyone among you suffering? Let him pray." Has this changed at all? Was it only for the apostolic era? Certainly not.

Next he writes, "Is anyone cheerful? Let him sing praise. Has this changed at all? Was it only for the apostolic era? Certainly not.

Then he writes, "Is anyone among you sick? Let him call for the elders of the church, and let them pray over him, anointing him with oil in the name of the Lord. And the prayer of faith will save the one who is sick, and the Lord will raise him up. And if he has committed sins, he will be forgiven." Again I ask, Has this changed at all? Was it only for the apostolic era? Certainly not.

Once more, then, I ask my cessationist friends to supply me with one single verse that negates these verses or states that they only apply to the apostolic era. To the contrary, the complete reverse is true: All these exhortations should be a normal part of congregational life until the end of this age, as seen in the context that follows (Jacob [James] 5:16-20, which clearly remains applicable). The fact that we don't see more sick people healed doesn't negate this, unless we are basing our theology on experience, and again, it is impossible to argue that this only applied to the apostles, since here it is simply the congregational elders – not specifically apostles or prophets – who are charged with praying in faith for the sick. (I'm giving the benefit of the doubt here that you won't argue that it is the oil that heals the sick rather than the prayer offered in faith. Not only is this contrary to what the text states, but it would also mean that we need to find that miracle-cure oil in a hurry!)

As Prof. Peter H. Davids explains in his commentary on the Greek text of Jacob [James] 5: "In this circumstance the person is directed to "call the elders of the church." This at once indicates that the person is very ill (i.e. too ill to go to the elders so presumably he sends friends or relatives for the elders) and that the office of elder was already established in the church."[62] As for the oil: ". . . the function of the oil in James is not medicinal except insofar as it partakes of the eschatological oils (see Life Adam 36; Apoc. Mos. 9:3; Is. 61:3). Thus it is either the outward sign of the inward power of prayer or, more likely, a sacramental vehicle of divine power. . . as in Mk. 6:13."[63] As for the prayer:

> This is not a magical rite, nor an exorcism . . . but an open-ing to the power of God for him to intervene whether or not the demonic is involved. It is also interesting to note that this is not the special gift of an individual, unlike 1 Cor. 12:9, 28, 30, but the power of a certain office in the church (for which no NT passage suggests gifts of heal-ing were a qualification). This exercise of eschatological power as a duty of office is something not present in the synagogue elders. Yet it was a power regularly exercised in the church during the first centuries of its existence (cf. Kelsey, 104–199).[64]
>
> . . . It is a prayer of faith, i.e. the prayer which expresses trust in God and flows out of commitment to him, for only such prayers are effective (cf. Jas. 1:5–8; 4:3; Mk. 2:5; 5:34; 10:52; 6:6; Acts 14:9, where faith or lack of it is the condition for healing). The faith is that of the one who prays, i.e. of the elders who have ex officio healing power, not that of the sick person (who may or may not be in a condition to exercise much of anything). The promised result, which must have been normally the case . . . is that the power in the prayer will heal.[65]

To repeat my simple, *sola Scriptura* questions: On what basis do we hold that verse 13 of this chapter and, say, verses 19-20 of this chapter, are normative, while verses 14-15 are not? Based on what interpretive principle? Based on what other explicit scriptural texts? (Jacob [James] 5:14-15 are quite explicit.) And how can healing be the expected outcome of the prayer offered in faith if we are taught that healing is *not* to be expected today? Where does this text instruct the elders to pray, "Lord, if it be Your will to make this person sicker or to take him home, so be it. If it be Your will to heal him, so be it." I know that some godly elders pray that way, and they do so as not to be presumptuous before God, so I am not demeaning this or mocking the prayer. I'm simply asking if it comports with the words of the text here and if it comports with offering a healing prayer in faith. The principle of *sola Scriptura* drives me to pray, "Lord, why don't we see more healings taking place?"

Did the Gifts Begin to Wane in the Days of the Apostles?

Some cessationists claim that the healing gifts began to wane during the lifetime of the apostles, pointing to verses like 2 Timothy 4:20 in support, where Paul says that he left Trophimus ill in Miletus. Aside from the fact that the paucity of such texts actually argues *against* this cessationist claim – meaning, in comparison with the mountain of scriptural evidence on the other side – even this argument is easily refuted.

First, it is irrelevant to the instructions given to the elders here in Jacob (James) 5:13-14 as well as irrelevant to the continuing manifestation of the Spirit's gifts outlined in 1 Corinthians 12-14. Second, cessationists commonly claim that Paul himself suffered from an illness, based on texts like Galatians 4:13, which would mean that even in the height of his miracle ministry, he himself was sick at times (if this reading of the text is accurate).[66]

Third, we are not told why Trophimus was sick. (Was he recovering? Did he abuse his body through ministry overwork, in which case a miraculous cure might not be expected? Was he sick because of sin and Paul was politely covering him?) We simply do not know why he was sick, but to build any kind of theological framework on a verse like this is a counsel of despair. (For comments on Hebrews 2:3-4, see Appendix C.)

Fourth, the last chapter of Acts, certainly meant to leave the reader with a definite impression, describes a scene on the island of Malta where Paul ministered healing to the father of Publius, the chief man on the island, after which, "the rest of the people on the island who had diseases also came and were cured" (Act 28:9). Why put a verse like that towards the very end of your story if you want readers to understand that the healing gifts would be waning? Fifth, history tells us clearly the gifts of healing continued in the immediate generations after the apostles.[67]

In this light, it is worth noting that the longer ending of Mark, which was certainly not the original ending of the book, at the least contains a historical appendix that was quoted as authoritative by many of the Church Fathers. This means that whether it should be received as part of the canon or not, and whether it contains the actual words of Jesus or not, it was believed to contain accurate information. In that case, these verse would add further weight to the continuance of healing, tongues, and exorcisms *through the believers* (Mark 16:15-20).[68]

I repeat once more: The burden of proof is entirely on the cessationists here, since the testimony of the New Testament is decidedly against the cessationist viewpoint, the testimony of the early Church (meaning, the first two centuries, at least) is against it, and the testimony of the modern Church worldwide is against it. (See further Appendix A.)

The Need for Words and Power

We saw earlier that when Paul preached "Jesus Christ and Him crucified" to lost sinners in Corinth he stressed that his message did not come with words alone, "but with a demonstration of the Spirit's power," since, after all, "the kingdom of God is not a matter of words but of power" (1 Corinthians 2:1-5; 4:20). But weren't *his words* enough? Wasn't the scriptural message he was preaching sufficient? Why was additional testimony needed?

You might say, "But the canon was not yet completed and the whole Bible – which is our sufficiency – was not yet finished." I reply that first, the completed Bible does not add anything more to the fundamental message of Jesus Christ and Him crucified, and second, the completed New Testament canon explicitly speaks of the continuance of the gifts and never once speaks against it.

You might say, "But you don't understand. The Church was not yet established in the earth. Once it was established, it no longer needed divine confirmation." I reply that from the first century until now, it *still* has not been established throughout much of the world, and carrying a complete Bible to a heathen tribe in the jungles of Irian Jaya will not in itself prove to them that our God is the real God and that they should abandon the gods that they worshiped for millennia, nor will it help the sick and the demonized that will surely be brought for prayer. Again the question must be asked: Why were Paul's words concerning the need for miraculous confirmation of the message of Jesus Christ crucified valid for his day and age but not for today? What, *in principle*, has changed?

Also, when Paul wrote to Timothy about "the sufficiency of Scripture" in 2 Timothy 3:16-17, it had *nothing* to do with the completion of the canon, since the New Testament canon was nowhere near complete (or even conceptualized as such). Rather, he was speaking of the sufficiency of that Old Testament Scriptures (simply, the Scriptures at that time) that Timothy had known from his childhood. The point is that with an *already all-sufficient Word*, Paul still felt the need for confirming miracles when he preached, and that divine confirmation remains part of the preaching of the Word and the ministry of the Spirit to this day.

We saw earlier that the brilliant and gifted Jonathan Edwards had written:

> The canon of Scripture being completed when the apostle John had written the book of Revelation, which he wrote not long before his death, these miraculous gifts were no longer continued in the church. For there was now completed an established written revelation of the mind and will of God wherein God had fully recorded a standing and all-sufficient rule for his church in all ages.

The truth is that this "established written revelation of the mind and will of God wherein God had fully recorded a standing and all-sufficient rule for his in all ages" reveals God as the

Healer, the Messiah as the Healer, and the Church as a community of healing. As I wrote in *Israel's Divine Healer* in the section "Healing and the Holy Spirit,"

> The Book of Acts speaks of the Spirit and his work more than sixty times, and Paul's first letter to the Corinthians makes clear that the supernatural gifts they were enjoying – including healings and miracles – were manifestations of the Spirit, given freely for the common good (1 Cor 12:1-11; cf. also Gal 3:1-5). The prophesied time had come. No longer would the Spirit fall only on a select few prophets and servants, enabling them to perform mighty acts for God. Now, the Holy Spirit, who had come to indwell every believer (Rom 8:15-16; 1 Cor 6:19; Gal 4:6; 1 John 2:27; cf. also John 14:17b), would be poured out freely on them all (Acts 2:17-18; and cf. Num 11:29). The Church would be the community of the Spirit (1 Cor 3:16, speaking corporately; Eph 2:22).[69]

Edwards further noted, "And the Jewish church and nation being overthrown, and the Christian church and the last dispensation of the church of God being established, *the miraculous gifts of the Spirit were no longer needed* [my emphasis], and therefore they ceased."

With all respect to Edwards, and putting aside his unfortunate statement of replacement theology,[70] not only is there not a single statement in the Bible to support this, but it would make absolutely no sense to a demonized or sick person reading the Scriptures who could only ask, "Who changed things? When did the Bible no longer mean what it said? When did Jesus stop His healing and deliverance ministry by His Spirit?"

The truth is that nowhere in the Bible are we warned about *the supernatural* per se, or about prophecies or miracles or healings. Rather, we are warned about *counterfeit* prophecies and miracles and healings. And just as the warnings about false messiahs, false apostles, false prophets, and false teachers presuppose the true Messiah and true apostles and true prophets and true teachers, so also the warnings against counterfeit signs, wonders, and miracles presuppose true signs, wonders, and miracles.

And as much as discernment is a good thing, the general attitudes of skepticism and cynicism are not. As I wrote in *The Revival Answer Book.*

> The Bereans not only carefully examined the Word to verify the accuracy of Paul's preaching, but, as translated in the NRSV, "they welcomed the message very eagerly." In fact, the NRSV translates the beginning of Acts 17:11 with, "These Jews were *more receptive* than those in Thessalonica." This helps to explain the "therefore" in 17:12: "*Many of them therefore believed,* including not a few women and men of high standing." Are the modern contenders for the faith really Berean in spirit? Do they receive the contemporary reports of revival with openness and even excitement, hoping that this might possibly be the real thing, that, at last, their prayers for revival could be answered (if, in fact, they are praying for revival), that the Lord is truly visiting His people, or do they receive such reports with real suspicion and skepticism, if not deep-seated cynicism and even hostility?
>
> This is the difference between destructive critics (not all critics are destructive!) and hungry believers (not all

believers are spiritually hungry!), both of whom say, "I'm jealous for the real thing." The destructive critics sit on the sidelines, rejecting every effort that falls short of their seemingly-unattainable ideal. Some of them hardly shed a tear for the lost or give themselves to fasting because of the compromised state of the Church, yet they almost *hope* that the latest report of the "real thing" turns out to be just another passing fad, since much of their identity is based on finding fault. In contrast, the hungry believers are hopeful (although often doubtful) that the new move will really be "it," and they are profoundly disappointed when, yet again, a trickle is called a river. They hurt inside, since they have been praying and fasting and weeping and longing for revival. The hungry believers will not rest until revival comes; the critical believers will not rest when it does come! The sincere are grieved if the exciting reports of revival prove untrue; the cynical are grieved if the reports *are* true!

The Bereans were hungry for God, willing to receive a man of God with open arms, to give him and his message time, and then to study the issues carefully for themselves. Because of that humble and hopeful attitude, many of them believed. This reminds me of hundreds of leaders who came to the Brownsville Revival to "check things out," not wanting to believe things just because someone else gave them a glowing report, knowing all too well that much of what has been called revival in our day has been anything but revival. Yet they came, not to mock or attack, but rather to see for themselves, even if they were admittedly skeptical. And when the Lord Himself touched

them, when they saw sinners flocking to the altars to repent, when they observed the zeal and commitment of the
young people, when they heard for themselves the sim-
plicity and purity of the holiness message, and – best of all
– when the Spirit began to move in similar ways in their
own churches and ministries after they returned home,
they wrote back with the exciting news: "This is it!"

Truly, these men and women were Berean in spirit
(and not just because they ended up agreeing with our position!). Their attitude was cautious but open as opposed
to closed and obstinate. They were careful but not cynical.
There is quite a difference! And they took the time to find
things out for themselves.[71]

It is my hope and prayer that you too will be a noble Berean,
welcoming the testimony of the Word with an open and expec-
tant heart, and joining me in embracing the New Testament gifts
and manifestations of the Spirit because of *sola Scriptura*. I for
one am thrilled that "the gifts and the calling of God are irrevo-
cable" (Rom 11:29).[72]

Endnotes

[1] To this day, I prize many of the Banner of Truth titles and appreciate
greatly so much of their work.

[2] Benjamin Breckinridge Warfield, *Counterfeit Miracles* (New York: C.
Sribner's, 1918); Robert G. Gromacki, *The Modern Tongues Movement* (rev.
ed.; Nutley, NJ: Presbyterian & Reformed, 1972).

[3] Of course, I failed to realize the obvious, namely, that there was so much
smiting taking place in the Old Testament because of Israel's disobedience,

not because God was blessing His people with sickness. As for Job, the theology of that book is obviously much more complex; I treat it in brief in Michael L. Brown, *Israel's Divine Healer* (Studies in Old Testament Biblical Theology; Grand Rapids: Zondervan, 1995), 165-181. I'm presently working on a commentary on Job that will focus on issues of theodicy and theology, due out in about three years time.

[4] See immediately above, n. 3.

[5] For some edifying, God-glorifying accounts, see below, Chapter Nine.

[6] In alphabetical order, and including both popular and scholarly works, see Brown, *Israel's Divine Healer*; Mark J. Cartledge, *Charismatic Glossolalia: An Empirical-Theological Study* (Aldershot, Hants, England; Burlington, VT: Ashgate, 2002); Harvey Cox, *Fire from Heaven: The Rise of Pentecostal Spirituality and the Reshaping of Religion in the 21st Century* (Cambridge, MA: Da Capo Press, 1995); William L. De Arteaga, *Quenching the Spirit* (Lake Mary, FL: Creation House, 1992) Jack Deere, *Surprised by the Power of the Spirit: A Former Dallas Seminary Professor Discovers that God Speaks and Heals Today* (Grand Rapids: Zondervan, 1993); idem, *Surprised by the Voice of God: How God Speaks Today Through Prophecies, Dreams, and Visions* (Grand Rapids: Zondervan, 1996); Howard M. Ervin, *Conversion-Initiation and the Baptism in the Holy Spirit: A Critique of James D. G. Dunn, Baptism in the Holy Spirit* (Peabody: Hendrickson, 1984); Christopher Forbes, *Prophecy and Inspired Speech in Early Christianity and Its Hellenistic Environment* (Peabody: Hendrickson, 1997); R. Douglas Geivett and Gary R. Habermas, eds., *In Defense of Miracles: A Comprehensive Case for God's Actions in History* (Downers Grove: IVP, 1997); Gary Greig and Kevin Springer, eds., *The Kingdom and the Power* (Ventura: Regal, 1993); Wayne Grudem, *The Gift of Prophecy in the New Testament and Today* (Wheaton: Crossway, 2000); idem, *Systematic Theology: An Introduction to Biblical Doctrine* (Grand Rapids: Zondervan, 1994); idem and Stanley Gundry, eds., *Are Miraculous Gifts for Today? Four Views* (Grand Rapids: Zondervan, 1996); Eddie L. Hyatt, *2000 Years of Charismatic Christianity: A 21st Century Look at Church History from A Pentecostal/Charismatic Perspective* (Dallas: Hyatt International Ministries, 1998); Craig S. Keener, *Gift & Giver: The Holy Spirit for Today* (Grand Rapids: Baler, 2001); Craig Keener, *Miracles: The Credibility of the New Testament Accounts* (Grand Rapids: Baker, 2011); idem, *Three Crucial Questions about the Holy Spirit* (Grand Rapids: Baker, 1996); Henry I. Lederle, *Treasures Old and New: Interpretations of "Spirit Baptism" in the Charismatic Renewal Movement* (Peabody: Hendrickson, 1988); Peter Lord,

Hearing God (Grand Rapids: Baker, 1988), esp. the introduction; Kilian Mc-Donnell and George T. Montague, *Christian Initiation and Baptism in the Holy Spirit: Evidence from the First Eight Centuries* (Collegeville, MN: Liturgical Press, 1991); Frank Macchia, *Baptized in the Holy Spirit: A Global Pentecostal Theology* (Grand Rapids: Zondervan, 2006); Gary B. McGee, ed., *Initial Evidence: Historical and Biblical Perspectives on the Pentecostal Doctrine of Spirit Baptism* (Peabody: Hendrickson, 1991); George T. Montague, *The Spirit and His Gifts: The Biblical Background of Spirit-Baptism, Tongue-Speaking, and Prophecy* (New York: Paulist, 1974); Rich Nathan, *A Response to Charismatic Chaos* (Anaheim: Vineyard, 1993); Cecil Robeck, ed., *Charismatic Experiences in History* (Peabody: Hendrickson, 1985); Jon Ruthven, *On the Cessation of the Charismata: The Protestant Polemic on Postbiblical Miracles* (Sheffield: Sheffield Academic, 1993); Roger Stronstad, *The Charismatic Theology of St, Luke: Trajectories from the Old Testament to Luke-Acts* (Grand Rapids: Baker, 2012); Max Turner, *Power from on High: The Spirit in Israel's Restoration and Witness in Luke-Acts* (Sheffield: Sheffield, 1996); John Rodman Williams, *Renewal Theology: Systematic Theology from A Charismatic Perspective* (Grand Rapids: Zondervan, 1996).

My appreciation to my FIRE School of Ministry colleague Steve Alt for compiling this introductory reading list, which is not meant to be exhaustive.

[7] Justin Peters also addressed related issues at the conference, but Pastor Pennington's talk was the only one explicitly presenting an argument for cessationism.

[8] The comments were made on October 25, 2013, and can be found here: https://www.facebook.com/AskDrBrown/posts/774763252549279?comment_id=112461074&offset=0&total_comments=28&notif_t=feed_comment.

[9] Anton Bosch, http://moriel.org/MorielArchive/index.php/discernment/impressions-from-strange-fire.

[10] *Strange Fire*, 16.

[11] http://thegospelcoalition.org/book-reviews/review/strange_fire

[12] For a useful survey, see Rodney H. Decker's article, "A History of Interpretation of 'That Which Is Perfect' (1 Corinthians 13:10) with Special Attention to the Origin of the 'Canon View,'" now online at http://frankviola.org/theperfect.pdf.

[13] http://thegospelcoalition.org/book-reviews/review/strange_fire

[14]http://www.christianpost.com/news/recovering-from-strange-and-friendly-fire-107976/; he also notes (accurately so) that "the Bible doesn't call spiritual gifts 'revelatory gifts' (or 'sign gifts'). It calls them 'charismata' (literally, results of grace; or alternately it calls them 'spiritual things'). 'Revelatory gifts' is a term made up by cessationists to get us to the conclusion that they have ceased. Calling them 'ceased gifts' and then concluding from that name that they have ceased, would be no more circular in reasoning. The term 'revelatory gifts' is imposed onto scripture and gives the illusion that cessationism is a product of careful Bible study."

[15]Morton T. Kelsey, *Healing and Christianity* (New York: Harper & Row, 1973), 129, n. 1.

[16]*Second Apology to the Roman Senate*, cited in Kelsey, *Healing and Christianity*, 136. Out of many similar testimonies which could be cited, cf. Tertullian, *To Scapula* 4 (in Kelsey, ibid., 137): "And how many men of rank (to say nothing of common people) have been delivered from devils, and healed of diseases!" See further Hyatt, *2,000 Years of Charismatic Christianity*.

[17]*Athanasius. St. Antony of Egypt*, J. B. McLaughlin, translator (Rockford, Illinois: Tan Books, 1995), 72-73.

[18]See Kelsey, *Healing and Christianity*, 184-188.

[19]*City of God*, XXII.8, cited in Kelsey, *Healing and Christianity*, 185. See also the important statement in his *Retractions*, I.13.7 (also I.14.15), cited in ibid., wherein he specifically revises his earlier views. For some terrific, relevant quotes, see Eddie L. Hyatt, "The False Doctrine Behind the 'Strange Fire' of John MacArthur," posted November 12, 2013, http://www.charismanews.com/opinion/41728-the-false-doctrine-behind-the-strange-fire-of-john-macarthur.

[20]On November 11, 2013, when I asked for testimonies of miraculous healings to be posted on Facebook (meaning, testimonies the people were directly involved in), along with requesting listeners to my radio show to call in, I was overwhelmed with the volume of responses, many of them breathtaking. For some of them, go here:https://www.facebook.com/AskDrBrown/posts/786779731347631?comment_id=112530471

[21]See Brown, *Israel's Divine Healer*, 227-229, with extensive documentation.

[22] Here are the relevant comments in more expanded form, along with the comments of other top New Testament scholars. First, D. A. Carson, "That kingdom is breaking in under Christ's ministry, but it is not consummated till the end of the age (28:20). To pray 'your kingdom come' is therefore simultaneously to ask that God's saving, royal rule be extended now as people bow in submission to him and already taste the eschatological blessing of salvation and to cry for the consummation of the kingdom (cf. 1Cor 16:22; Rev 11:17; 22:20). Godly Jews were waiting for the kingdom (Mark 15:43), 'the consolation of Israel' (Luke 2:25)... But the Jew looked forward to the kingdom, whereas the reader of Matthew's Gospel, while looking forward to its consummation, perceives that the kingdom has already broken in and prays for its extension as well as for its unqualified manifestation" ("Matthew," in Frank E. Gaebelein, *Expositors Bible Commentary* [Grand Rapids: Zondervan, 1984], 8:170). According to Donald A. Hagner, "The gospel is itself, above all, the announcement that God's promised rule has now begun in and through the work of Jesus the Messiah (see [Matt] 3:2; 4:17, 23), so the disciples are thus encouraged to pray that what has begun in the ministry of Jesus, what they have now begun to participate in, may be experienced in all fullness..." (*Matthew 1-13* [Word Biblical Commentary; Dallas: Word, 1993], 148). According to Craig S. Keener, "If the kingdom were wholly future, one might despair of accomplishing any justice now; if one supposed that it were wholly present, the realities of this age would quickly terminate disciples' illusive utopianism. But because the Gospels affirm that in Jesus the kingdom is present in a hidden way, believers in him can begin to make a difference in their world now, contending for the reality to be consummated at Christ's return..." (*A Commentary on the Gospel of Matthew* [Grand Rapids: Eerdmans, 1999], 200, n. 172).

[23] For extensive bibliography through 1994, see Brown, *Israel's Divine Healer*, 215-217.

[24] Cf. W. Kelber, *The Kingdom in Mark* (Philadelphia: Fortress, 1974), 17: "Exorcisms and healings are the two principal approaches used to translate the kingdom program into action. In both cases Jesus intrudes upon enemy territory, challenges and subdues the forces of evil which are in the way of the fulfillment of the kingdom of God" (cited in Ruthven, *Cessation*, 117, end of n. 3).

[25] According to R. H. Fuller, *Interpreting the Miracles* (Philadelphia: Westminster, 1963), 40 (cited in Ruthven, *Cessation*), "Jesus interprets his exorcisms as the beginning of the end of Satan's reign."

^{26}The significant Lucan variant in 11:20 ("finger of God" for Matthew's "Spirit of God") points back to Exodus 8:19, as is widely recognized, reminding us that the ten plagues and the exodus are presented in the Old Testament as a conflict between kingdoms.

^{27}See Klaus Seybold and U. B. Mueller, *Sickness and Healing* (Eng. trans; D. W. Stott; Nashville: Abingdon, 1981), 117-118; for the uniqueness of this concept, cf. ibid., 118-19, and note Mueller's reference (117) to Satan's *future* downfall expected in *Assumption of Moses* 10:1 in contrast with his *present* downfall according to Luke 10:18-19; note, however, Rom. 16:20.

^{28}H. Alford, *The Greek Testament* (with rev. by E. F. Harrison; Chicago: Moody, 1968), who considered Mark 16:9-20 to be "*an authentic* [but non-Marcan] *fragment, placed as a completion of the Gospel in very early times*" (1:438), states regarding vv. 17-18: "This promise is *generally* made, without limitation to the first ages of the Church. *Should occasion arise for its fulfillment,* there can be no doubt that it will be made good in our own or any other time" (1:436-37, his emphasis throughout). He claims, however, that "we must remember that *semeia* are not needed where Christianity is *professed*," adding in woefully antiquated sentiments, "nor by missionaries who are backed by the influence of powerful Christian nations [*sic*]" (1:437, again, his emphasis). Nonetheless, he freely admits, "There are credible testimonies of miraculous powers having been exercised in the Church considerably after the Apostles' time" (ibid.). For a textual evaluation of the longer ending of Mark, cf. Bruce M. Metzger, *A Textual Commentary on the New Testament* (London/New York: United Bible Societies, 1975), 122-128.

^{29}This is the classic formulation articulated by George Eldon Ladd and others.

^{30}See, e.g., Grieg and Springer, *The Kingdom and the Power*.

^{31}In keeping with his overall theology, Pastor MacArthur believes that the power to drive out demons was only for the first century, apostolic era.

^{32}See further, below, Chapter 10.

^{33}From Chapter Fifteen of Jonathan Edwards' book *Charity and Its Fruits*, available online here: http://counterfeitmiracles.com/articles/johnathan-edwards-on-the-cessation-of-revelatory-gifts/.

^{34}This was Michael Horton's exact statement to me when he lunch in Pensacola, Florida, August 8, 1997; Cf. also Craig Blomberg, "Your Faith Has

Made You Whole," in Joel B. Green and Max Turner, eds., *Jesus of Nazareth: Lord and Christ: Essays on the Historical Jesus and New Testament Christology* (Grand Rapids: Eerdmans, 1994), 85, with reference to John 9:5 and 11:15.

[35] Quoting R. H. Fuller; see above, n. 25.

[36] For the question of healing and atonement, see Brown, *Israel's Divine Healer*, 197-198.

[37] That being said, I do not concur with Pastor MacArthur's statement that in the days of Jesus and the apostles, "Disease was, in effect, banished from Palestine." See *Charismatic Chaos*, 135 (the usage of "Palestine" here, of course, is anachronistic).

[38] In Raymond E. Brown, et al., eds., *The Jerome Biblical Commentary* (New York: Prentice Hall, 1968), 787. A further problem for the "mere confirmation" assessment of the miracles of Jesus is found in the proofs he gives to the disciples of John, for not only does he point to his healings of the sick and resurrections of the dead, but he adds: "the good news is preached to the poor. Blessed is the man who does not fall away on account of me" (Luke 7:18-23, here vv. 22b-23). Would anyone classify "preaching the good news to the poor" among "first-century confirming signs," and thus, as not applicable to today? Rather, both his miracles and preaching were part and parcel of his Messianic work of redemption and mercy. As I. H. Marshall notes (*Commentary on Luke* [New International Commentary on the Greek New Testament [Grand Rapids: Eerdmans, 1978], 178), "The era of salvation has arrived; it is the year of the Lord's favour, characterised by the preaching of the good news to the needy and the performance of mighty works."

[39] Cf. also Kelsey, *Healing and Christianity*, 99, "Far from using his healings as signs of power, he seemed embarrassed by them and told people not to speak of them. At times he even gave the impression that he would rather not have performed miracles, from a tactical point of view. But it was his nature to be hostile to illness and to heal the sick . . . . If Jesus saw himself as the Messiah, then he represented the essential nature of God himself and was his specific messenger, and his healings therefore sprang form the essential nature of God. . . . By dealing with them as the Messiah, the agent of God, Jesus laid the attitude of God toward sickness out on the counter where all could see it."

[40] Cf. also R. Latourelle, *The Miracles of Jesus and the Theology of Miracles* (Eng. trans., M. J. O'Connell; New York: Paulist, 1988), 293-294, who notes

that "in the Scriptures the miracles of Christ are regarded first of all as mani-festations of the power and love of God the Savior." Second, they signify "that the prophesied kingdom has come at last and that Jesus of Nazareth is the awaited Messiah; the miracles fulfill the Scriptures." Third, they signify "that is God's envoy"; fourth, "they accredit Christ as Son of God"; fifth, "they give an anticipatory glimpse of the glorious order introduced by the resurrection of the body and the transformation of the cosmos at the end of time."

[41] Blomberg, "Your Faith Has Made You Whole," 85.

[42] http://www.gty.org/resources/sermons/TM13-1/strange-fire-john-macarthur

[43] See again Brown, *Israel's Divine Healer*, 227-229.

[44] For the issue of the promise of healing in the Old and New Testa-ments, see Brown, *Israel's Divine Healer*; I fully realize that carnal prosperity preachers have misused these concepts in terms of finances. The difference, of course, is that Jesus did not go around making poor people wealthy; He did, however, heal the sick. In keeping with that, while He often rebuked cov-etousness and greed (see, e.g., Luke 12:15), He never said, "Woe to you who are physically healthy!"

[45] Cf. Grieg and Springer, *The Kingdom and the Power*, 393-397 ("Ap-pendix B: John 14:12 – The Commission to All Believers to Do the Works of Jesus"). Note also W. R. Bodine, "Power Ministry in the Epistles: A Reply to the Cessasionist Position," in ibid., 203-204, n. 8.

[46] Merrill C. Tenney, "John," *Expositor's Bible Commentary*, 9:146.

[47] F. F. Bruce, *The Gospel and Epistles of John* (Grand Rapids: Eerdmans, 1983), 300.

[48] This is not the place to address the larger question of preterism and its different understanding of the *eschaton* and some of these verses.

[49] From his *Institutes of the Christian Religion*, Chapter Eight, Section 7, http://www.ccel.org/ccel/calvin/institutes.vi.ix.html.

[50] My appreciation to Dr. Jon Ruthven for this observation; see his *On the Cessation of the Charismata*, 123, 195, 202.

[51] See further Appendix C.

[52] See again Decker, "A History of Interpretation."

[53]http://ariel.org/qna/qtongues.htm?; "To argue, as some cessationists do, that 'the perfect' [1 Cor. 13:10] has in view the completion of the New Testament canon or some other state of affairs prior to the Parousia is just not credible exegetically," citing cessationist scholar Dr. Richard B. Gaffin Jr.

[54]It can be argued fairly that many churches today reflect this lack: They are built almost exclusively on the ministry of teachers and therefore miss out on the rest of the dynamic spiritual life of which the New Testament speaks.

[55]This, of course, came up in my debate on cessationism with Dr. Sam Waldron; see http://www.youtube.com/watch?v=c0biTwj635I&feature=c4-overview&list=UUbINn3x-intLp88Zrf8acpg

[56]My colleague Steve Alt noted that, "McDonnell and Montague quote Eusebius, saying, 'Even anti-Montanist polemicists recognized that "the prophetic *charisms* must exist in the church until the final coming"' (*Christian Initiation*, 121, citing Ecc. His., 5:17), further confirming this point. They also quote Irenaeus, who refers to people who recognized the existence of false prophets and, on that basis, rejected all prophecy: 'They are truly unfortunate…who, realizing there are false prophets, take this as a pretext for expelling the grace of prophecy from the church' (*Christian Initiation*, 120, citing Ag. Her. 3, 11, 9)." Isn't this similar to what many cessationists do today?

[57]F. F. Bruce, *1 and 2 Thessalonians* (Word Biblical Commentary; Dallas: Word, 1998), 125.

[58]It does not appear from the context that Paul was suggesting that prophecies would be despised because they called for repentance, otherwise, why the exhortation to test everything and only hold on to the good?

[59]http://www.christianpost.com/news/recovering-from-strange-and-friendly-fire-107976/

[60]See again Decker, "A History of Interpretation."

[61]It is interesting to note that both "apostles" and "prophets" are mentioned as traveling ministers in the *Didache*, which dates to the second century – meaning, the idea that there were no more apostolic or prophetic leaders after the death of the Twelve Apostles is not historically accurate. Note also that a strong case can be made for the continuance of these giftings until the end of this age, as per Ephesians 4:11-16, despite the arguments raised in *Strange Fire*, 100-102.

[62] Peter H. Davids, *Commentary on James* (New International Commentary on the Greek New Testament; Grand Rapids: Eerdmans, 1982), 192.

[63] Ibid., 193.

[64] Ibid., 194.

[65] Ibid.

[66] Although Galatians 4:13 is commonly translated with "bodily ailment," or the like (which could certainly be possible in terms of Paul being sick), the identical Greek phrase in Romans 6:19 is rendered with phrases like "weakness of [your] flesh," or "human limitations," and a colleague whose doctoral work focused on Galatians insisted to me that this Greek phrase never meant "physical illness" in other Greek literature.

[67] See the discussion and references above, especially Kelsey, *Healing and Christianity*.

[68] See now Graham H. Twelftree, *In the Name of Jesus: Exorcism among Early Christians* (Grand Rapids: Baker Academic, 2007).

[69] *Israel's Divine Healer*, 220. An interesting insight into the eschatological dimension of the outpouring of the Spirit is found in the *magnum opus* of the ninth century Jewish philosopher Sa'adiah Gaon, entitled *Emunot weDeot* ("Beliefs and Opinions"), chapter 8, end. He explains there that one of the signs of the Messianic age will be that the spirit of prophecy will be on all the Israelites.

[70] Cf. Brown, *Our Hands Are Stained with Blood*; Michael J. Vlach, *Has the Church Replaced Israel: A Theological Evaluation* (Nashville: B & H Publishing, 2010).

[71] *Revival Answer Book*, 48-49.

[72] While this verse refers to God's dealings with Israel, the statement can easily be applied to other gifts and callings given by the Lord.

CHAPTER SEVEN

SHALL WE BURN ONE ANOTHER AT THE STAKE?

I f you have ever watched James Robison on TV, you have probably noticed his gracious and gentle demeanor. But he was not always like this. In fact, an unholy judgmentalism once fueled his fire. As he explained in his irenic November 1, 2013 article, "Let's Prayerfully Consider John MacArthur's Concerns,"

> Billy Graham advised me years ago when I criticized and challenged him because he worked with so many different Christian groups. In my bold stand for my view of truth, I was often harsh and considered by some "God's angry man." Billy's response in kindness was, *"I suggest you spend time with other believers you've been taught to avoid."* I did! The experience was transforming not only for me, but also transforming for those I reached out to (those outside my own camp, my basket that covered me).[1]

Now, Dr. Graham did not counsel him here to spend time with cult members or with liberal "Christians" who denied the Bible was God's Word and didn't believe Jesus rose from the dead. Instead, he advised him to "spend time with other believers you've been taught to avoid."

But what if your own view of who is truly saved is so narrow that you actually exclude from God's flock those whom He has included? What if you avoid other believers because you don't think they *are* believers?

As I wrote on October 28, 2013,

> It has been said that heaven, at one and the same time, will be a great eye-opener and a great mouth-closer. You will be surprised to see many people there, and many people will be surprised to see you there. How true this is!
>
> In the last week, I have been criticized for failing to condemn Joel Osteen and Creflo Dollar to hell while, on the other hand, I have been criticized for daring to take issue with their messages at all.
>
> Someone claimed that Bill Johnson was the "biggest wolf ever" [and "an enemy of the True Gospel"] while, on the other side of the spectrum, someone claimed that John MacArthur was guilty of blaspheming the Spirit.
>
> A Calvinist told me that Mike Bickle was a false teacher while someone else asked me how a Calvinist like James White could even be saved.
>
> I witnessed one pastor being attacked for saying that those who did not believe in divine healing were preaching a "different gospel" while this pastor, in turn, was condemned for preaching a "different gospel."
>
> And then were the lovely tweets like ... "Charismaticism is a cult of Satan"...

How can we possibly move forward in the midst of such division and name-calling?[2]

One of the most frequently quoted lines from the Strange Fire conference was Pastor MacArthur's statement, "We're not trying to divide the body of Christ with this conference. We're trying to identify the body of Christ." (This was actually tweeted out by #StrangeFire.) He further explained that, "There are others who criticized by saying, 'You're attacking brothers.' I wish I could affirm that. We've said this one way or another this week: this is a movement made up largely of non-Christians . . ."[3]

Attacking the Body of Christ or Identifying the Body of Christ?

As we saw in Chapter Five, above, this wholesale condemnation of several hundred millions Christians is totally unmerited. Unfortunately, it's not the first time in Church history that such divisions have come, and they have often been downright ugly. Just consider this comment from a pastor following the Strange Fire conference if you want to get an idea of how unpleasant the rhetoric can get once we start damning one another to hell: "Well, if John MacArthur wants to train his fire on them [meaning, the charismatics], I say good for him. CAIR [the Counsel on American-Islamic Relationships] may not actually *be* terrorists, but I'm all for exposing their giving of aid and comfort to terrorists."[4] What a horrific comment and what a pitiful analogy.

Is it any wonder, then, that Church splits in the past have been deadly – and I mean literally deadly, with the spilling of blood? Perhaps we can learn some lessons from the past that will help us learn how better to treat differences within the Body. And perhaps if we exercise some greater care in using the "h" word – namely, heresy – we will be able to interact constructively without damning one another in the process.[5] (I found it amusing that the very hour I was finishing this chapter, this comment appeared on YouTube: "Brown is sadly a heretic who needs to accept the one true faith of Christ." It was posted by a Catholic!)[6]

Learning Some Lessons from the Past

In his book *Jesus Wars: How Four Patriarchs, Three Queens, and Two Emperors Decided What Christians Would Believe for the Next 1,500 Years*, the respected Church historian J. Phillip Jenkins describes what happened in the fifth-sixth centuries A.D. in the aftermath of the Council of Chalcedon. There it was officially determined that Christian orthodoxy required the belief that Jesus had two natures, one divine and one human, rather than one divine nature only (incarnated for a season here on earth), which was the view of the Monophysites, who "were only defeated after decades of bloody struggle"[7] – and this despite the fact that they were both numerous and influential, claiming a direct tie to the apostles.

You might say, "I agree. Their views are heretical. We know that Jesus had two natures joined together in one."

I understand, and I agree with Chalcedon's theology here. But I cite this because of the way the controversy was handled. Jenkins continues: "Each side persecuted its rivals when it had the opportunity to do so, and *tens of thousands—at least—perished*. Christ's nature was a cause for which people were prepared to kill and to die, to persecute or to suffer martyrdom."[8]

What? Professing Christians literally *killing each other* over a doctrinal issue? Jenkins notes that the intra-Christian violence of the fifth-sixth centuries far overshadows the violence of the later Inquisition, and he cites Edward Gibbon's classic description of the "immediate aftermath of Chalcedon" in his *Decline and Fall of the Roman Empire*:

> Jerusalem was occupied by an army of [Monophysite] monks; in the name of the one incarnate Nature, they pillaged, they burnt, they murdered; the sepulchre of Christ was defiled with blood.... On the third day before the festival of Easter, the [Alexandrian] patriarch was besieged in the cathedral, and murdered in the baptistery. The remains of his mangled corpse were delivered to the flames, and his ashes to the wind; and the deed was inspired by the vision of a pretended angel.... This deadly superstition was inflamed, on either side, by the principle and the practice of retaliation: in the pursuit of a metaphysical quarrel, many thousands were slain.[9]

Are you shaking your head as you read this? Really, it's hard to imagine this happening, but it did. And there's more. Just look at how the "orthodox" and "true" Christians acted:

> Chalcedonians behaved at least as badly in their campaigns to enforce their particular orthodoxy. In the eastern city of Amida, a Chalcedonian bishop dragooned dissidents, to the point of burning them alive. His most diabolical scheme involving taking lepers, "hands festering and dripping with blood and pus," and billeting them on the Monophysite faithful until they saw reason...

This is absolutely demonic behavior, but it was justified in the name of the true faith. And there's more:

A sixth-century historian records how the forces of Constantinople's Chalcedonian patriarch struck at Monophysite religious houses in the capital. Furnished with supplies of consecrated bread, the patriarch's clergy were armed and dangerous. They "dragged and pulled [the nuns] by main force to make them receive the communion at their hands. And they all fled like birds before the hawk, and cowered down in corners, wailing and saying, 'We cannot communicate with the synod of Chalcedon, which divides Christ our God into two Natures after the union, and teaches a Quaternity instead of the Holy Trinity.'" But their protests were useless. "They were dragged up to communicate; and when they held their hands above their heads, in spite of their screams their hands were seized, and they were dragged along, uttering shrieks of lamentation, and sobs, and loud cries, and struggling to escape. And so the sacrament was thrust by force into the mouths of some, in spite of their screams, while others threw themselves on their faces upon the ground, and cursed every one who required them to communicate by force." They might take the Eucharist kicking and screaming—literally—but once they had eaten, they were officially in communion with Chalcedon and with the church that preached that doctrine.[10]

As sickening as this is to read, it's almost as sickening to realize what the consequences of these atrocities were:

In the long term, these schisms led directly to the collapse of Roman power in the eastern world, *to the rise of Islam, and to the destruction of Christianity through much of Asia and Africa.* Apart from Islam, the greatest winner in the conflict was European Christianity, or rather the fact that Christianity, for better or worse, found its firmest bastion in Europe. So much of the religious character of the world we know was shaped by this conflict over the nature of Christ. The mainstream church kept its belief that Jesus was fully human—but at the cost of losing half the world.[11]

Now, to be perfectly clear, I am *not* comparing the Strange Fire movement to these murderous, dastardly acts. But I *am* saying that we need to step back in the midst of our self-confident divisions over "orthodoxy" and start listening to each other and making efforts to understand each other before we pronounce each other hell-bound heretics. Surely there are lessons to learn from the past.

Drowning the Anabaptists

Many cessationists are Baptists, and, contrary to their Presbyterian colleagues, they hold strongly to believer baptism as opposed to infant baptism. The fathers of the Reformation, however, held to infant baptism, and they aggressively persecuted the Anabaptists (literally, the "re-baptizers") who held to believer baptism, along with other views that were considered fringe and even lunatic. Although Anabaptists as a whole have been labeled part of the "Radical Reformation," many Baptists and Mennonites (among others) proudly trace their lineage back to them.[12]

According to the Spurgeon.org website,

Many Anabaptist ideas made invaluable contributions to the Reformation. For example, these five tenets might be identified as Anabaptist distinctives:

- *Sola Scriptura* . . . .
- *Separation of Church and State* . . . .
- *Freedom of Conscience* . . . .
- *Believers' Baptism*—The anabaptists were the among the first to point out the lack of explicit biblical support for infant baptism. Most of them made no issue of the *mode* of baptism, and practiced affusion (sprinkling), however, so they were not true baptists in the modern sense of the word.
- *Holiness of Life* . . . .[13]

How did the Reformers deal with the Anabaptists? (Bear in mind that the Anabaptists, for the most part, also practiced non-violence, so they were hardly a physical threat to their theological opponents.) The WayofLife.org website cites examples taken from *A History of the Churches from a Baptist Perspective*:

... The Anabaptists and their leaders, including [Conrad] Grebel and [Felix] Manz, were thrown into prison. [Note that these were among the less radical of the leaders.]
... In December 1527, Felix Manz, Jacob Falk, and Henry Reiman were put to death by drowning. The council had decreed, *Qui mersus fuerit mergatur*, or "He who immerses shall be immersed." The Protestant leader Gastins wrote, "They like immersion, so let us immerse them" (*De Anabaptiami*, 8. Basite, 1544, cited by Christian). The Baptists were delivered to the executioner, who

bound their hands, placed them in a boat and threw them into the water. Some Protestants mockingly called this the "third baptism."[14]

Yes, Reformation leaders actually *drowned* the Anabaptists as the fit punishment for their Baptist beliefs.

The *History* next mentions Anabaptist theologian Balthasar Hubmaier, once a close friend of Huldrych Zwingli, leader of the Reformation in Switzerland, before Hubmaier determined that the Bible did not teach infant baptism:

> He wrote powerful books in defense of his faith and one was in defense of believer's baptism. He said, "The command is to baptize those who believe. To baptize those who do not believe, therefore, is forbidden." He was right.
>
> He also wrote one against persecution, titled "Concerning Heretics and Those That Burn Them." He taught that it is not the will of Jesus Christ to put men to death for their beliefs, that the churches are in the business of saving men, not burning them.
>
> He was thrown into prison by the Zurich Protestants in January 1526 and kept there for four months. His appeal to his old friend Zwingli was ignored. His wife also was in prison and his health was broken. He had just gotten over a sickness that was almost unto death.
>
> In this sad and discouraged condition, he was tortured on the rack by the Protestant authorities; and on April 6, 1526, the broken man agreed to recant his beliefs.
>
> The people of Zurich were summoned to the cathedral to hear the recantation of this well-known Baptist preacher. Zwingli first preached a sermon against the

heretics. Then every eye turned to Hubmaier, who went forward to read the recantation. As he began to do so in a trembling voice, he broke down weeping. As he swayed to and fro in agony, he was suddenly strengthened by the Lord. He shouted, "INFANT BAPTISM IS NOT OF GOD, AND MEN MUST BE BAPTIZED BY FAITH IN CHRIST!" Pandemonium broke out! Some screamed against him while others shouted applause. The Zurich authorities quickly took him back to the dungeon.[15]

Although he was ultimately released from prison and he returned to public ministry, "On March 10, 1528, in Vienna, he was burned to death at the stake, and he died in the faith that he preached. His faithful Christian wife was drowned eight days later."[16]

The *History* also notes that Luther was initially averse to putting alleged heretics to death, since "the Papists and Jews, under this pretence, have destroyed holy prophets and innocent men, so I am afraid the same would happen amongst ourselves, if, in one single instance, it should be allowed to be lawful to put seducers to death."[17] According to William McGrath, however, Luther turned against the Anabapists, calling for their extermination: "Sadder yet, Luther reacted with equal violence to the Anabaptists who tried to apply the principle of 'liberty' to themselves. Though he knew there were both nonresistant, harmless Anabaptists as well as a radical fringe of social revolutionaries, he condemned all together–favoring a policy of extermination."[18]

And then, the final twist:

In 1529, the imposing **DIET OF SPEIRS** (Speyer) pronounced the death sentence upon all Anabaptists. This
council was composed of both Roman Catholic and
Protestant princes and heads of state. They hated each
other and did not get along even in this Diet, but they
hated the Anabaptists even more!

... The proclamation of the Diet greatly accelerated the
program of extermination already in progress.

"Four hundred special police were hired to hunt down
Anabaptists and execute them on the spot. The group
proved too small and was increased to one thousand.
... thousands of Anabaptists fell victim to one of the
most widely spread persecutions in Christian history. ...
Burning faggots and smoldering stakes marked their trek
across Europe" (Halley).[19]

So, the Anabaptists were executed, burned at the stake,
drowned, and nearly exterminated. Today, respected Church
historians like William R. Estep recognize them as representing
an important stream in Christianity (see Estep's major volume,
The Anabaptist Story),[20] while contributors to an honorary volume for Southern Baptist leader Paige Patterson believe that is
was the Anabaptists, rather than the followers of Luther and
Calvin, who more fully returned to New Testament Christianity. The volume, edited by Malcolm B. Yarnell, III, professor
of Systematic Theology, director of the Oxford Study Program,
and director of the Center for Theological Research at Southwestern Theological Seminary in Fort Worth, Texas is actually
entitled, *The Anabaptists and Contemporary Baptists: Restoring
New Testament Christianity.*[21] So, the contributors to this book
claim that the Anabaptists were simply seeking to restore the

New Testament faith, yet they were butchered and almost exterminated *by their Protestant brothers and sisters* (and, at times, by Catholics as well).

Obviously, I'm not claiming that all people on all sides of this dispute were believers – only God ultimately those who are His (2 Timothy 2:19) – but it's clear that these were all Protestants, and even within their own house, there were murderous divisions. And these are just small snippets from Church history. What can we learn from all this?

Surely There Is a Better Way

For several months leading up to the Strange Fire conference, as well as in the weeks that followed, I made public and private appeals to Pastor MacArthur and his camp, urging them to tone down their rhetoric, to be more careful in whom they damned and whom they labeled "false teachers" or "false prophets," and to remember Paul's warning to the Galatians: "For the whole law is fulfilled in one word: 'You shall love your neighbor as yourself.' But if you bite and devour one another, watch out that you are not consumed by one another" (Gal. 5:14-15).

In an article posted October 24, 2013, [22] and based on these verses from Galatians, I laid out these five principles, which I submit here for your prayerful consideration with the hope that by following them, we can avoid unnecessary casualties.

1) **We really do need each other.** This is a fundamental principle of how the body operates: "As it is, there are many parts, yet one body. The eye cannot say to the hand, 'I have no need of you,' nor again the head to the feet, 'I have no need of you.'" (1 Cor 12:20-21)

I said it on the radio when speaking to Phil Johnson from Pastor John MacArthur's ministry,[23] and I'll say it again now. I honestly believe that I need John MacArthur and that he needs me. I say that without hyperbole and I mean it from the heart. (If your first reaction is scorn – in either direction – than I'd say this is something you need to work on.)

It would be arrogant for anyone to think that their group or denomination had it all – how much more arrogant would it be for an individual minister to think he or she had it all! – and the fact is we all have blind spots and we all have strengths and weaknesses.

Rather than despise others who appear to be weak where we are strong, we should instead ask, "How can I serve that brother or sister? And what do they have that I need? How can I learn from them?"

The attitude that Jesus condemned was this: "God, I thank you that I am not like other men, extortioners, unjust, adulterers, or even like this [fill in the blank]" (Luke 18:11).

2) **Surgeons cut carefully.** Sometimes we like to be bombastic and make sweeping statements. It sure rallies the troops and makes for good sound bites, and it sure feels good to be dogmatic. "You won't hear any compromise from this pulpit!"

But this is often more harmful than helpful, since we paint with such a broad bush that we condemn the innocent with the guilty.

If I start my sentence with, "Let me tell you something about those Baptists," whatever I say afterwards is virtually guaranteed to be inaccurate, since not all Baptists are the same [except on the most basic of doctrinal points]. It would be the same if I said, "The problem with those charismatics is that . . . ." Whatever comes next is not going to be accurate, even if it applies to many. And that means I will be guilty of speaking falsely against many others at the same time.

Why can't we be more nuanced in our words? Wouldn't that better honor the Lord?

3) Don't be hasty to call others false prophets or false teachers. Based on New Testament usage, a false prophet is a ravenous wolf in sheep's clothing and therefore a hell-bound sinner (see Matthew 7:15-20), while a false teacher is a nonbeliever (or backslider) who introduces damnable heresies to the church (see 2 Peter 2:1, where it states that they "secretly bring in destructive heresies, even denying the Master who bought them, bringing upon themselves swift destruction").

Because of that, I refuse to call a brother or sister in the Lord a false prophet or a false teacher, even if they prophesy falsely (in which case they need correction and are falsely called a prophet) and even if they teach something false (does anyone dare claim to have perfect doctrine on all points)?

It is therefore unbiblical to use the "false prophet" or "false teacher" moniker for believers who are in error, and we can deal with their error effectively and strongly without damning them to hell. (Are you 100% sure they are not saved? Without a doubt? Remember: I'm not talking about a cult member here but about someone who claims to be born again through faith in Jesus.)

And while there are absolutely times when it is right to address people by name – I have sought to do that in a godly way in these columns over the months; God will be the Judge – in many cases it is possible to deal with issues without naming names, which also avoids unnecessary division and strife within the Body.

4) Before we differ with each other we have to understand each other. In talking with a dear brother who attended the Strange Fire conference and is himself a cessationist, I realized how he thought of one thing when he said "charismatic" and I thought of another thing. It was easy to talk right past each other.

It's the same with "the prosperity gospel." Some people take it to mean that "God is able to make all grace abound to you, so that having all sufficiency in all things at all times, you may abound in every good work" (2 Cor 9:8), which is obviously biblical and true. Others take it to mean that Jesus died to make us rich and that the test of our spirituality is the abundance of our possessions. This is a dangerous and deadly deception (see Luke 12:15; 1 Timothy 6:6-11).

I know rich Christian businessmen who are absolutely committed to Jesus, living godly lives, and believing that God has given them wealth to help spread the gospel worldwide. And I don't see them as being attached to their money at all, although they pray for prosperity in accordance with many biblical texts. I know other people who are carnal and worldly-minded as they pursue prosperity with the help of some manipulating preachers. [24]

So, before pronouncing someone wrong, why not ask, "Can you define your terms for me?" You might actually be in agreement!

5) Major on the majors. I received an email today from a woman who is a financial supporter of my ministry and listens to my radio show by podcast every day. And she attends Pastor MacArthur's church, differing with him on a number of points.

And I regularly hear from other listeners who tell me, "I love your show and agree with you most of the time, but not all the time," which is exactly what I would expect. (As my guest Dr. Sam Storms said the other day, "I don't always agree with myself!")

We might have different burdens and callings – and we could make a good case for many of them – but that doesn't mean we're not part of the same Body, saved by the same Lord, working against the same devil, trying to reach the same world, and going to the same eternal destination.

If you keep the main things the main things and concentrate on driving down the center of the road, you're far less likely to fall into a ditch.

Let the exaltation of the Lord Jesus be our ultimate passion – to the glory of God and for the good of a dying world – and we will find far more in common with each other than we ever imagined. And rather than our biblical distinctives dividing us, they will enrich us.

To sum things up, there is error to be addressed and there is sin to be corrected, but we can do it a constructive way or a destructive way. What will it be?[25]

"My Lord, Stop Them!"

Do you remember what happened when Eldad and Medad, two of the seventy elders of Israel, didn't follow the proper protocol to receive an impartation of the Spirit through Moses?

> Now two men remained in the camp, one named Eldad, and the other named Medad, and the Spirit rested on them. They were among those registered, but they had

not gone out to the tent, and so they prophesied in the camp. And a young man ran and told Moses, "Eldad and Medad are prophesying in the camp." And Joshua the son of Nun, the assistant of Moses from his youth, said, "My lord Moses, stop them." But Moses said to him, "Are you jealous for my sake? Would that all the LORD's people were prophets, that the LORD would put his Spirit on them!" (Num 11:26-29)

Sometimes people just do things differently than what we're used to (the fact is that we are far more influenced by our environment and upbringing than we realize), yet we feel the need to shut them down out of our zeal for the Lord. Perhaps there is a broadness in God beyond our parameters? Perhaps there's a healthy balance between "anything goes," on the one hand, and "my way or the highway," on the other hand?

A similar instance occurred with the apostles in the New Testament: "John said to him, 'Teacher, we saw someone casting out demons in your name, and we tried to stop him, because he was not following us.' But Jesus said, 'Do not stop him, for no one who does a mighty work in my name will be able soon afterward to speak evil of me. For the one who is not against us is for us.'" (Mark 9:38-40)

How remarkable! First, Joshua wants to stop Eldad and Medad because they're prophesying in the camp instead of at the tent, where they were supposed to be, yet the Spirit still chose to touch them. In response, Moses asks Joshua if he's jealous for his sake ("Too much competition, Joshua?"), then he speaks God's heart: "I wish God would put His Spirit on everyone, not just these seventy!" Then, in Mark, John wants to stop a man who is driving out demons in Jesus' name because he is not part of their group. Jesus speaks God's heart again: "John, if someone is doing mighty works in My name, they can't revile Me in the next moment. People are either for Me or against Me, and he's obviously for Me." (For the question of counterfeit miracles see below, Chapter Ten.)

It was Pastor MacArthur himself who wrote, "In matters in which Scripture is not explicit there is room for difference of opinion."[26] The truth is that we often draw lines where Scripture does not, and we often pass judgment where Scripture does not give us the right to. As D. Martyn Lloyd-Jones noted, "We must be very careful to draw this distinction between essentials and non-essentials lest we become guilty of schism and begin to rend the body of Christ."[27] For these reasons (among others), I'm very hesitant to label anyone a wolf, a false prophet, a charlatan, a fraud, or a false teacher unless I know for a fact that they either deny one or more of the fundamentals of the faith (such as salvation through Jesus alone; His divine nature; His atoning death and resurrection; etc.) or that they are lying in the claims they are making or that they are living an immoral, godless life.

In my view, cessationism is a false and unbiblical teaching, but I would never think of labeling the countless thousands of godly cessationist leaders "false teachers." I feel the same way about dispensationalism and the pre-trib rapture, but I would never join Dr. John Gerstner in labeling it a "heresy."[28] And I am not a Calvinist and therefore disagree strongly with many of the tenets of Calvinism. Yet I would never for a moment damn my Calvinist colleagues to hell, something I was questioned for by a sincere man named Kevin on Facebook:

Dr Brown I've seen a lot of your debates and I love that you defend the faith and I know by your testimony that you're an ex-Calvinist, but you call James White your brother in Christ, but he believes that [Jesus] didn't die for the world and that God didn't commend His love towards everyone and so many other falsehoods. Isn't he in fact calling God a liar and not believing the record of the only begotten Son of God?[29]

Of course, I set the record straight, which is all the more reason I find it unfortunate, unnecessary, and unbiblical when an esteemed and influential leader like Pastor John MacArthur paints with such a broad bush that he inevitably lumps the good together with the bad, often exaggerating the number and nature of the errors he is addressing in the process. This truly does more harm than good, and once more, I urge my senior brother and his camp to reconsider their ways. In fact, it can easily put charismatics into a defensive more, which then makes it harder to receive the valid criticisms that he and others make.

John Calvin once remarked, "A dog barks when his master is attacked. I would be a coward if I saw that God's truth is attacked and yet would remain silent." I certainly concur with that sentiment. I simply urge carefulness, circumspection, and accuracy when we raise our voices, remembering that we will be judged with the same standards with which we judge others (Matthew 7:1-5).

Condemning the Good with the Bad

In an interview with Tim Challies posted in the aftermath of the Strange Fire conference,[30] Pastor MacArthur was asked to respond to the criticism of New Testament scholar and Baptist seminary professor Thomas Schreiner, who stated that *Strange Fire* painted with too broad of a brush, writing, "The clarion call of warning should be modified with clearer and more forthright admissions that many charismatics adhere to the gospel and are faithful to God's Word."[31]

In response, Dr. MacArthur referenced two sections in his book (pages 81 and 231) in which he affirmed some charismatics as true believers and, in a few cases, even respected colleagues. Unfortunately, in each of those sections (something not noted in the interview), he proceeded to make harsh, broad, and unfounded accusations, speaking of the alleged "systemic corruption and confusion" of the Charismatic movement, claiming that even the true believers "remain confused about the ministry of the Holy Spirit," and then writing: "As a result, they are playing with strange fire. By continually exposing themselves to the false teaching and counterfeit spirituality of the Charismatic Movement, they have placed themselves (and anyone under their spiritual care) in eternal jeopardy."[32] So much for the conciliatory comments!

At the close of the interview (specifically, the first part, posted November 4, 2013), Pastor MacArthur stated:

> I understand that some reviewers will find my tone too harsh and my brush too broad. But I think the problem is a whole lot bigger than anyone realizes. And it breaks my heart to think that hundreds of millions of souls are being caught up into a movement where they are being seduced by false forms of the gospel.

That is why I wanted to sound such a strong warning. And I'm willing to be accused of broad-brushing in order to get that message out.[33]

Unfortunately, this strategy is tantamount to blowing up an apartment building filled with law-abiding civilians because there are terrorists inside (actually, as noted above, a pastor actually used the "terrorist" word before). To repeat: This is unfortunate, unnecessary, and unbiblical.

In the previous chapter, we saw how the Charismatic Movement passed Jonathan Edwards' criteria with flying colors, meaning that it is not the tiniest minority of charismatics who are truly saved but rather the great majority. And so, I encourage you to heed Billy Graham's counsel to James Robison years ago: "I suggest you spend time with other believers you've been taught to avoid." It might just rock your world.

We are connected to each other because we are connected to the same Lord, as Bishop J. C. Ryle explained:

The true Christian regards all Christ's friends as his friends, members of the same body, children of the same family, soldiers in the same army, travelers to the same home. When he meets them, he feels as if he had long known them. He is more at home with them in a few minutes, than he is with many worldly people after an acquaintance of several years. And what is the secret of all this? It is simply affection to the same Savior and love to the same Lord.[34]

In the end, not only does Paul urge us to preserve the unity of the Spirit (see Ephesians 4:1-16), but Jesus made it clear that this is not just about us. The world is watching too: "By this all people will know that you are My disciples, if you have love for one another" (John 13:35).[35]

On June 18, 1739, John Wesley recorded this in his *Journal*:

> I left London early Monday morning. The next evening I reached Bristol and preached to a large congregation. Howel Harris called on me an hour or two later. He said he had been much dissuaded from either hearing me or seeing me by many who said all manner of evil of me. "But as soon as I heard you preach," he stated, "I quickly found of what spirit you were. Before you were done, I was so overpowered with joy and love that I had much trouble walking home."

I believe heaven rejoiced over this, and it in this spirit that Dr. George O. Wood, General Superintendent of the sixty-six million member Assemblies of God denomination, responded to the Strange Fire conference graciously, but with a clear, loving corrective:

> We trust the time will come when Dr. John MacArthur and those who share his perspective will acknowledge the great contribution that Pentecostals and charismatics are making in the evangelization of individuals without Christ. We pray God's blessings on their efforts to share his Gospel with the lost and dying world. Pentecostals and charismatics are their co-laborers in this effort so we ask that they would similarly pray for God's blessing on us as we seek to fulfill the Great Commission that God has given us all.[36]

> May it be so!

Endnotes

[1] http://www.charismanews.com/opinion/41617-james-robison-let-s-prayerfully-consider-john-macarthur-s-concerns, my emphasis.

[2] http://www.charismanews.com/opinion/in-the-line-of-fire/41529-be-careful-about-what-you-call-a-different-gospel To be clear, I am not grouping all these leaders together on a level plane nor am I saying that some of them do not need to be corrected strongly.

[3] http://thecripplegate.com/strange-fire-a-call-to-respond-john-macarthur/

[4] http://chantrynotes.wordpress.com/2013/10/29/two-quick-thoughts-about-strange-fire/

[5] While it is true that the Greek word from whence we get "heresy" simply means "division" (see 1 Corinthians 11:19 in the KJV and then in modern versions), and while the word can be used in a lesser sense to describe any kind of doctrinal deviation, in the strict sense of the word, it refers to a fundamental deviation from orthodoxy – ultimately, to the point that someone embracing the heretical view could not be called a true believer. That's why I'm very careful with what I call heretical, fully aware that we use that term all too freely against one another in the Body.

[6] This was posted on November 4, 2013, by a user identified as vatican-catholic.com, http://www.youtube.com/user/mhfm1

[7] J. Phillip Jenkins, *Jesus Wars: How Four Patriarchs, Three Queens, and Two Emperors Decided What Christians Would Believe for the Next 1,500 Years* (New York: Harper One, 2010), Kindle Location 122.

[8] Ibid., Kindle Locations 125-126, my emphasis.

[9] Cited in ibid., Kindle Locations 135-139.

[10] Ibid., Kindle Locations 146-155.

[11] Ibid., Kindle Locations 158-162, my emphasis.

[12] The Mennonites, of course, derive their name from the Anabaptist leader Menno Simons (1496-1561)

[13] http://www.spurgeon.org/~phil/anabapt.htm

[14] http://www.wayoflife.org/database/protestantpersecutions.html

[15] Ibid.

[16] Ibid.

[17] Cited at ibid.

[18] William McGrath, *Anabaptists: Neither Catholic nor Protestant*; see http://www.cbc4me.org/articles/Baptist/04-McGrath.pdf

[19] http://www.wayoflife.org/database/protestantpersecutions.html

[20] http://www.amazon.com/The-Anabaptist-Story-ebook/dp/ B004DI75MQ/ref=sr_1_1?ie=UTF8&qid=1383542269&sr=8- 1&keywords=anabaptist, my emphasis.

[21] Nashville: B & H Academic, 2013. I strongly encourage students of the Reformation to read the essays in this volume.

[22] http://www.charismanews.com/opinion/in-the-line-of-fire/41494- let-s-not-bite-and-devour-one-another

[23] http://www.lineoffireradio.com/2013/10/21/dividing-over-truth-or- just-plain-divisive-dr-brown-interviews-christian-leaders-regarding-the- strange-fire-conference/

[24] To read my chapter on the Prosperity Trap, go here: http:// askdrbrown.org/my-chapter-on-the-carnal-prosperity-message-from- 1990/

[25] http://www.charismanews.com/opinion/in-the-line-of-fire/ 41494-let-s-not-bite-and-devour-one-another

[26] John F. MacArthur, *First Corinthians* (MacArthur New Testament Commentary; Chicago: Moody, 1986), 27. Cf. also Charles Spurgeon, who said, "I believe that in public worship we should do well to be bound by no human rules, and constrained by no stereotyped order."

[27] *What is an Evangelical?* (Carlisle, PA: Banner of Truth, 1992), 90

[28] See above, Chapter Four.

[29] I corrected the typos in the post, which was on my public AskDrBrown Facebook page (https://www.facebook.com/AskDrBrown).

[30] http://blogs.christianpost.com/overflow/john-macarthur-answers- his-critics-18633/

[31] http://thegospelcoalition.org/book-reviews/review/strange_fire; note that Prof. Schreiner is a cessationist and was much more sympathetic to *Strange Fire* than I am

[32] *Strange Fire* 81; on 231 he wrote, "The Charismatic Movement is teeming with false teachers and spiritual charlatans of the worst kind, as can be aptly illustrated by turning the channel to TBN (or any of several smaller charismatic networks). Certainly I do not view my continuationist friends in the same light as these spiritual mountebanks and blatant frauds."

[33] http://blogs.christianpost.com/overflow/john-macarthur-answers-his-critics-18633/

[34] From his classic book *Holiness*; see conveniently http://www.truth-source.net/quotes/index?q_sort=authors_list&sort_author=J.C._Ryle

[35] See again http://hopefullyknown.com/2013/10/25/because-it-is-better-to-be-kind/

[36] http://www.charismanews.com/opinion/41509-george-o-wood-sets-john-macarthur-s-pentecostal-record-straight

Chapter Eight

SPIRIT AND TRUTH, RIGHT BRAIN AND LEFT BRAIN

The more I interact with my cessationist brothers and sisters, the more I see that in many ways, we are passing each other like ships in the night, and it has nothing to do with one side being committed to the Lord and the other not. Instead, it seems as if we sometimes have fundamentally different ways of looking at the same things – fundamentally different perspectives and, in a sense, fundamentally different "spiritual personalities." How can we better understand each other, learn from each other, and serve together to glorify Jesus and touch a dying world?

Now, my goal in writing this book is not to win a debate or to gang up on cessationists. Instead, it is to advance the cause of the gospel of Jesus in the power of the Spirit and on the foundation of the Word of God. Of course, from my perspective, that includes setting the record straight when necessary and correcting errors where I see them. But my intent is absolutely *not* to drive away those who differ with me but rather to draw them in.

Am I personally convinced that the Scriptures testify clearly to the ongoing nature of the gifts of the Spirit? Without a doubt. Do I believe that every child of God should experience these gifts on one level or another? Without question. (See Chapters Six and Nine.) At the same time it is clear to me that both charismatics and cessationists have unique contributions to make to the Church and to the world and that there are personality traits unique to each camp. With this in mind, I propose that we take a few minutes and make a real attempt to understand each other better, putting aside our theological differences and focusing instead on our "spiritual personalities." I truly believe it will be worth the effort involved.

Although a recent study has disputed some of the standard right brain vs. left brain paradigm,[1] there is no question that one person's strength is often another person's weakness, and vice versa. For example, it would be pure torture to force a creatively gifted, inspirationally motivated artist to work a nine-to-five job as a bookkeeper tasked with checking and rechecking financial ledgers, while it would be a total disaster to hire a meticulous, bean-counting, precision-oriented administrator to develop the creative arts program at a university.

Some people are totally analytical, others totally intuitive. Some people love to confront, others love to comfort. Some are didactic teachers, others motivational leaders. Some people are born to invent, others to research and record patents for inventions; some are born to lead armies, others to care for the elderly – and you had better believe these respective giftings are quite different.

Right Brain, Left Brain

One website lays out the common Right Brain-Left Brain contrasts as follows:

The Right Brain

According to the left-brain, right-brain dominance theory, the right side of the brain is best at expressive and creative tasks. Some of the abilities that are popularly associated with the right side of the brain include:

- Recognizing faces
- Expressing emotions
- Music
- Reading emotions
- Color
- Images
- Intuition
- Creativity

The Left Brain

The left-side of the brain is considered to be adept at tasks that involve logic, language and analytical thinking. The left-brain is often described as being better at:

- Language
- Logic
- Critical thinking
- Numbers
- Reasoning[2]

I don't want to oversimplify, but some of you are already find-ing charismatics and cessationists on this grid (again, in broad terms, since there are complete exceptions to these character-izations). Either way, the point is clear: We can see things dif-ferently, and we can have different perspectives and approaches and giftings, yet we can all function together as part of the same Body (or brain!).

The story is told about a pot-luck dinner a pastor called for one Sunday, feeling it was important for the church members to get to know one another better in order to deepen their fellow-ship in the Lord. But one of the elders, who was evangelistically gifted, protested, saying, "Pastor, we have no business sitting around for hours sharing a meal together when right outside our doors there are lost sinners we need to reach. How is this luncheon compatible with the Great Commission?" Another el-der with a strong prophetic gifting protested as well, saying, "But pastor, there is so much sin in the camp. There's no way God will bless our fellowship until we repent." Then another elder, who was gifted as a strong teacher chimed in saying, "Perhaps we need to understand what the word 'fellowship' actually means. Would it be possible for me to bring a message on the meaning of *koinōnia* after the meal is over?"

Yes, this is how the different giftings in the body operate. As Paul wrote in Romans 12, "For as in one body we have many members, and the members do not all have the same function, so we, though many, are one body in Christ, and individually members one of another. Having gifts that differ according to the grace given to us, let us use them" (Rom 12:4-6). (By the way, to illustrate these points, we could easily tell all kinds of stories about how people from *different cultures* respond to the same scenario, and having ministered overseas on well over 130 trips, I can attest firsthand that Germans respond differently than Indians and that Italians respond differently than Fins. You can have some fun testing this out multiculturally.)

Again, I'm not debating here whose theology is right, be it cessationism or continuationism or some variation in between. (You obviously know where I stand on that.) I'm simply suggesting that it is helpful to recognize the strengths and weaknesses of the *spiritual personality traits* commonly found on each side. Again, this will help us better understand each other and, more importantly, better complement each other in the Body.

So, even though, based on my beliefs, I would love to see every member of the Body operate in the fullness of the Spirit, which would mean becoming charismatic in the best sense of the world, I realize that, even if that were the case, certain distinctions would still exist among us based on gifts, callings, and personality traits. So the principles laid out here would apply even if our theological differences evaporated. And while I hope the simple reflections that follow will help my cessationist friends see what charismatics have to offer to the mix, I, for my part, am convinced that my cessationist friends have much to offer to us charismatics.

Spirit and Truth

Rich Nathan and Ken Wilson co-authored a fascinating, very practical book entitled *Empowered Evangelicals*.[3] In it, they write:

"You can't have your cake and eat it, too." It's an old, familiar adage. Mothers have quoted it for decades, especially to teenagers who notoriously want the freedom of adulthood without the responsibilities. Sometimes we just can't have it both ways.

But sometimes we can. We can, for example, experience worship that includes "spirit and truth," heartfelt intimacy, and thoughtful biblical exposition. We can pray for healing, believing God will heal, and still leave room for God to be God. And we can hear God's voice and feel God's leading, yet still respect God's Word as the ultimate source of revelation. Yes, we can have the best of both worlds. In fact, we believe God wants us to.[4]

They explain:

To us, the most exciting aspect is the marriage of the evangelicals' historic target-the salvation of the lost-with charismatic power to get the job done. Imagine a church that experiences joyful intimacy with God, that regularly sees sick people healed, that tunes in to God's voice and worships with body, emotions, and Spirit, but employs the power of the Spirit not for a "spiritual buzz" but for evangelism and world missions! Imagine churches that experience powerful spiritual life, but channel that life toward the world. We call such churches empowered evangelical churches.[5]

Pastor Nathan suggests "that Christianity would be much stronger and more biblical if the best emphases of evangelicalism could be combined with the best emphases of

Pentecostalism."[6] In a nutshell, that is what I am saying here, but from a little different angle.

Consider the words of Jesus in John 4:24, where He said that "God is spirit, and those who worship him must worship in spirit [or, Spirit] and truth." Obviously, there is total harmony between spirit (or, Spirit) and truth, and it is not a matter of either-or but of both-and. At the same time, Jesus is describing two elements here, spirit (or, Spirit) and truth, and on a certain level (and simply using this text to make a point rather than claiming that this was what Jesus meant), charismatics, who are people of the Spirit, can put more emphasis on spirit/Spirit, whereas cessationists, who are people of the truth, can put more emphasis on truth. Both are equally essential.

Consider also the Lord's rebuke of the Sadducees in Matthew 22:29, "You are in error because you do not know the Scriptures or the power of God." Knowing *both* God's Word and God's power are essential for spiritual soundness and fruitful ministry. Knowing one without the other leads to errors and extremes. Knowing neither is fatal. Jesus emphasized the importance of both.

But it is possible (and all too common) for believers to be so heavily into the Word (in terms of studying the Bible and learning the original languages and getting into proper exegesis and theology) that they lose the vibrancy of their fellowship with the Lord and lack greatly in the empowering of His Spirit (although this ought not to be the case, since both biblical study and spiritual passion should go hand in hand). On the flip side, it is possible (and all too common) for believers to be so heavily into the things of the Spirit (in terms of wanting to see God's power touch a dying world and cultivating worship and intimacy with

God) that they become sloppy in their study of Scripture and doctrinal foundations (although, again, this ought not to be the case).

To say it once more: Spirit and Truth are essential. Word and Power are essential. In Jesus, they find their perfect match.

In my own life, although I was intensely hungry for the Word as a new believer, reading the King James Bible cover to cover five times in the first two years and, for a stretch of six months, memorizing twenty verses a day, I also prayed for hours each day and enjoyed vibrant fellowship with God. But the church in which I came to faith was very narrow theologically, and academic study was almost frowned on. And so, when I got more heavily into academic study and theology (and this is no one's fault but my own), I actually ended up reading the Word itself less (and when I did read it, often trying to work on my Hebrew and Greek skills, I sometimes read it for comprehension more than for edification and direction) and, not surprisingly, I was praying far less. It's as if I went from one extreme to the other, finally bouncing back to the middle (that is, for me).

But "the middle" for me is quite extreme to others (I'm way too Pentecostal for some and not nearly charismatic enough for others; I'm way too scholarly for some and not nearly academic enough for others), and the fact remains that, *while Jesus was perfectly complete and perfectly balanced and perfectly combined Word and Spirit, knowledge and power, none of us do.* That's why we need each other so much to fulfill the Great Commission and bring maximum glory to the one we love so much.

I know that my Scripture-expositing, cessationist brethren sometimes listen aghast to the charismatic eisegetics of some TV preachers, while our Spirit-filled, charismatic brethren look aghast at the power-depleted ministries of some cessationist colleagues. Why not have *both* the accurate Word and the power of the Spirit? And can you really have an accurate understanding of the Word *without* acknowledging the Spirit's power for our day? And can you really walk in the fullness of the Spirit *without* being grounded in the Word?

A Practical Way to Help Each Other?

Writing in 1984 in the Foreword to the classic volume by D. Martyn Lloyd-Jones, *Joy Unspeakable*, Peter Lewis made these sage remarks:

> The past twenty years have seen the widespread growth of two radical and potentially mighty movements in Great Britain. These are the reformed movement with its stress on doctrine, expository preaching and total loyalty to Scripture; and the charismatic movement with its stress on the Holy Spirit's baptism and gifts, its strong sense of personal guidance and its bold inventiveness in worship.
>
> The weakness of the reformed churches have often been their traditionalism, their lack of evangelism and their contentment with sound doctrine sincerely approved. The weaknesses of the charismatics have tended to be their self-indulgent and sometimes uncritical enjoyment of 'experience', their lack of interest in doctrine and their naïvety in church polity.[7]

Perhaps this should have been required reading for everyone attending the Strange Fire conference? As Lloyd-Jones himself noted:

The trouble has generally been...that people have emphasized either experience or doctrine at the expense of the other...This is something that has been happening in the church from almost the very beginning...When the whole emphasis is placed upon one or the other, you either have a tendency to fanaticism and excess or a tendency toward a barren intellectualism and a mechanical and a dead kind of orthodoxy...[8]

Exactly! In that light, Lewis added this healthy warning:

Both of these groups have known considerable blessing in recent years, but *both may well expect an element of divine rebuke to enter their life if they do not now begin to learn from one another* [my emphasis]. Already the charismatic movement is finding the Spirit withdrawing his blessings and the devil sowing his confusion wherever doctrine is despised and neglected. Correspondingly, in many places the reformed movement is beginning to go stale; its congregations replete with sound doctrine but cramped in regard to experience and self-expression are looking wistfully at less instructed but often more effective congregations 'down the road'. In both camps, *a sense of something more* is beginning to rise up from the people.[9]

Thankfully, Lewis also noted that cross-pollination was beginning to occur as well – the very thing I am calling for here – with charismatics learning to appreciate expository and doctrinal preaching and reformed congregations learning to include more congregational participation in worship and praise.

Let me, then, give you some specific examples so you understand that this is not just some "Kumbaya," feel good, "let's all kiss and make up" chapter. I intend to be very practical.

Contrasting Our Strengths and Weaknesses

It is highly unlikely (to put it mildly) that your average cessationist would be taken in by some manipulative televangelist claiming that if you pick up the phone right now and make a pledge for $777 God will bless you with $7,777 next week. Yet there are all too many charismatics who *are* taken in by this kind of nonsense, causing cessationists to wonder at their extreme gullibility. (If you are a gullible charismatic reading this now, do *not* pick up the phone and call.)

On the other hand, it is highly unlikely (to put it mildly) that your average cessationist would obey an internal prompting of the Spirit to go up to a stranger and say, "I sense that you're suffering from a serious ailment and in need of prayer," proceeding to lay hands on that person for healing. Yet there are plenty of charismatics who would obey that same prompting and minister God's healing grace to the stranger, potentially resulting in that person's salvation as well. But when the charismatic shares this story with a cessationist friend, that friend is totally skeptical, saying, "Stuff like that doesn't happen today!"

What does this tell us? It tells us that cessationists tend to be more circumspect in their faith, making them virtually immune to these carnal fund-raising schemes. This is a real strength for them. But the flip side of this strength is that they are prone to skepticism, and so the very thing that keeps them from foolish-ness, when rightly used, is the same thing that causes them to fall into cynicism when wrongly used.

As for charismatics, they tend to be people of vibrant faith, ready to step out in obedience when they sense the Spirit at work. This is obviously a real strength for them. Yet the flip side of this strength is that they are prone to gullibility, and so the very thing that helps them believe, when rightly used, is the same thing that allows them to be so ridiculously gullible, when wrongly used.

Again, I'm aware that there are countless exceptions to these descriptions, but I'm also convinced that the broad categories I'm presenting are quite applicable as well. I trust that this is starting to make more sense.

Let's consider the subjects of love and truth, both of which are of paramount importance in the life of every believer. Many charismatics, stressing the importance of love, do not engage in public name calling, putting the emphasis instead on being open to receive from a wide variety of teachers. This, of course, can be very positive, avoiding unnecessary division and pro-ducing a broad spiritual spectrum. On the other hand, if not grounded in truth, this emphasis on love can lead to careless-ness and confusion, since it easily leads to an "anything goes" mentality. In contract, many cessationists emphasize the im-portance of being grounded in the truth, leading to doctrinal precision and open confrontation of error. On the other hand, if not grounded in love, this emphasis on truth can lead to heresy hunting, divisiveness and a prideful, censorious spirit. Could this be why most "discernment" ministries or "watch-dog" groups are non-charismatic? And could this be why many charismatics consider those groups to be mean-spirited and judgmental?[10]

The Baptist evangelist Vance Havner said it well:

> One may be as straight as a gun barrel theologically and as empty as a gun barrel spiritually. In fact, it may be that in their very opposition to evil men and false teachers these Ephesian saints had left their first love... so often it turns out that fundamental and orthodox Christians become so severe in condemning false doctrine, gnashing their teeth at every sniff of heresy, that they end up without love. One may do a right thing in a wrong way. The same Paul who wrote, "... though we, or an angel from heaven, preach any other gospel... let him be accursed," also wrote the love chapter to the Corinthians. *Unless we can get that combination we shall be theological Hawshawks and doctrinal detectives, religious bloodhounds looking for heretics but with hot heads and cold hearts.*
>
> Moreover, Ephesus [in Rev. 2:1-7] proves that religious activity without love calls for repentance. I have wondered what would be left nowadays if we eliminated from our church work all that is not the spontaneous expression of our heart's love for Christ.[11]

But I want to stress once more that this need not be either-or (as Havner himself said), and one of the most common arguments these days in favor of same-sex "marriage" is that "love is love" – as if you could redefine the truth of God's intent for marriage by the feeling of "love."[12]

As a new believer, I would sometimes hear a speaker "accidentally" have a slip of the tongue and refer to a "seminary" as a "cemetery." It was even an unspoken tradition in our Italian Pentecostal church that if you were truly anointed to preach, you didn't need notes. In keeping with this, when my best friend preached for the first time, two weeks before me, in August 1973 (both of us were eighteen years-old), he followed this counsel to a tee, resulting in a message that he and I subsequently nicknamed "Random Thoughts on Christianity."

At the same time, I have heard more than enough exegetically correct but utterly lifeless messages preached over the years, and having taught at eight leading seminaries, I have met more than enough students who used to be passionate in their walks with the Lord but got so heady and theological that they became a mere shadow of their former selves.[13] Doesn't this underscore our need for each other, helping the other side to avoid its weaknesses while learning from the other side's strengths?

"I Have No Need of You"

I know it's tempting for each camp to say, "We're doing just fine without you," but my understanding of the Body tells me that can't be the case. "The eye cannot say to the hand, 'I have no need of you,' nor again the head to the feet, 'I have no need of you.'" (1 Cor 12:21) So, one camp is strong in the Spirit but if not grounded in the truth can give way to foolishness; the other camp is strong in the Word but if not walking in the Spirit can give way to intellectualism. I personally love the Word and the Spirit, but I'm sure that I need others to complement me and help me stay the course. Otherwise, I will naturally gravitate one way or the other.

Charismatics emphasize freedom in God, being led by the Spirit and enjoying fellowship with Him. The weak side of this can be a tendency to fleshly license, which is deadly. Cessationists emphasize spiritual discipline, being more systematic in their approach to life and more "wisdom" based. The weak side of this can be a tendency to religious legalism, which is also deadly.[14] To repeat yet again, I know this is a caricature, and there are many exceptions to these descriptions, but wherever the shoe fits, wear it, since that will help you understand your brother or sister who, to carry out the idiom, is wearing the other shoe.

Charismatics emphasize spiritual power, but power, if not used properly, can easily lead to abuse, especially when mixed with fleshly pride. Cessationists emphasize biblical teaching, but teaching, if not done relationally (toward God), can lead to coldness, especially when mixed with intellectual pride.

So, one group emphasizes *heart*, which on the positive side leads to passion and on the negative side leads to emotionalism. The other group emphasizes *head*, which on the positive side leads to sobriety and on the negative side leads to rationalism. The cessationists look at the charismatics and say, "How can you be so crazy?" And the charismatics look at the cessationists and say, "How can you be so cold?" This reminds me of an account I read from Daniel Rowlands, the Welsh revivalist, replying to the criticism of John Thornton of England, in the early 1760's: "You English blame us, the Welsh, and speak against us and say 'Jumpers! Jumpers!' But we, the Welsh, have something also to allege against you, and we most justly say of you, 'Sleepers! Sleepers!'"[15]

Unfortunately, what we normally do is continue with our caricatures, either mocking charismatic excess or bashing cessationist deadness (which is the negative side of both) whereas what we should do is look for the best parts of each movement and join charismatic fervor with cessationist grounding. Just think of what happens when there is holy cross-pollination! To the extent that we have both Word and power, truth and Spirit operating in our lives life it will be life-giving for us and helpful for others

Now, to return to an earlier statement in this chapter, I *do* believe that the New Testament charismatic gifts are for to-day – and therefore, one way or another, for every believer – and therefore, just as I don't believe there were any theological cessationists in the New Testament congregations, I don't believe there should be theological cessationists today. But I understand that even if every believer embraced tongues and prophecy and healing today (whether or not they themselves practiced these things), all of us are wired differently and all of us are gifted uniquely by God. Plus, there are other manifestations of God's Spirit spoken of in the New Testament (see, for example, Romans 12:3-8), and so, the principles of which I speak still apply. I am simply applying the categories of "charismatics" and "cessationists" because of the nature of the Strange Fire vs. Authentic Fire debate.

The truth is, as much as there is some "charismatic chaos" there is also some "Baptist boredom," and while I as a charismatic leader have written sarcastic poems about the charismatic chaos, Vance Havner, as a Baptist leader, remarked about the Baptist boredom, famously quipping that "we start at 11 o'clock sharp and end at 12 o'clock dull." One group sometimes falls into fanaticism, the other group into formalism, and both are equally wrong and dangerous (although each group sees the other's weaknesses as being far more dangerous, tending to exaggerate them as well because they seem so foreign).

Wouldn't it be great if, through learning from each other and listening to each other, we could produce fire and faithfulness, power and precision, energetic worship and exegetical wisdom? After all, aren't we commanded to love God with all our heart and all our mind and all our soul and all our strength?[16] At the risk of sounding trite, the Word is the anchor for our souls, the Spirit is the wind for our sails. And the Spirit is "the Spirit of truth" (John 15:26).

In the words of Psalm 85:10-11, "Steadfast love and faithfulness meet; righteousness and peace kiss each other. Faithfulness springs up from the ground, and righteousness looks down from the sky."

May this describe our effective union in the Lord.

Endnotes

[1] http://www.livescience.com/39373-left-brain-right-brain-myth.html

[2] http://psychology.about.com/od/cognitivepsychology/a/left-brain-right-brain.htm. It was only after writing this chapter that I discovered some very analogous thinking in Daniel B. Wallace, et al, eds., *Who's Afraid of the Holy Spirit?*(Dallas: Biblical Studies Press, 2005), in particular in Wallace's important opening essay. He writes, "The Holy Spirit does not work just on the left brain. He also works on the right brain: he sparks our imagination, causes us to rejoice, laugh, sing, and create. Few Christians are engaged and fully committed to the arts today. Where are the hymn writers? Where are the novelists? Painters? Playwrights? A very high-powered editor of a Christian magazine told me a few years back that he knew of only one exceptional Christian fiction writer. What are our seminaries doing to

encourage these right brainers? What is the Church doing to encourage them?" (Kindle Locations 343-347)

[3] Boise, ID: Ampelon Publishing, 1995. My own story parallels Pastor Nathan's in many ways, although some of my conclusions differ in terms of Pentecostal vs. charismatic distinctives, but primarily on minor lines

[4] *Empowered Evangelicals*, Kindle Locations 78-82.

[5] Ibid., Kindle Locations 333-338.

[6] Ibid., Kindle Locations 28-29). The authors ask: "So what label should be given to Evangelical who regularly heal the sick in the power of the Holy Spirit, cast out demons, have a low-key perspective regarding tongues, and regularly receive prophecies? We have chosen to call such people 'Empowered Evangelicals.'"

[7] Martyn Lloyd-Jones, *Joy Unspeakable: Power and Renewal in the Holy Spirit* (Wheaton: Harold Shaw, 1984), 7.

[8] Martyn Lloyd-Jones, *Life in Christ: Studies in 1 John* (Wheaton: Crossway, 2002), 400.

[9] *Joy Unspeakable*, 7-8

[10] That being said, it's important to note that some of the top apologetics and cult-watch ministries, like Stand to Reason (Greg Koukl), CARM (Matt Slick), and the Christian Research Institute (Hank Hanegraaff) all believe in the continuation of the New Testament charismatic gifts.

[11] This is widely quoted and apparently first printed in Vance A. Havner, *Repent or Else! The Seven Churches of Revelation* (Old Tappan, NJ: Fleming H. Revell Company, 1957), my emphasis. (I do not have the original page location.)

[12] For more on this, see Brown, *Can You Be Gay and Christian?*

[13] Helmut Thielicke's *A Little Exercise for Young Theologians* (Grand Rapids: Eerdmans, 1961), still makes for good reading. More unsettling is Etta Linneman, *Historical Criticism of the Bible: Methodology or Ideology: Reflections of a Bultmannian Turned Evangelical* (Eng. trans., Robert W. Yarbrough; repr., Grand Rapids: Kregel, 2001).

[14] See Michael L. Brown, *Go and Sin No More: A Call to Holiness* (Ventura, CA: Regal Books, 1999), 147-162.

[15] Cited in Brown, *From Holy Laughter to Holy Fire*, 120.

[16] Mark 12:30 and Matthew 22:37.

CHAPTER NINE

A GOD TO BE EXPERIENCED

L ike many of you, I love the Scriptures and I love to study the Scriptures. And like many of you, I encounter God through His written Word, and it is through the written Word that you and I truly come to learn who He is. This was affirmed by the Pentecostal pioneer Smith Wigglesworth (1859-1947), who once said, "I can't understand God by feelings. I can't understand the Lord Jesus Christ by feelings. I can only understand God the Father and Jesus Christ by what the Word says about them. God is everything the Word says He is. We need to get acquainted with Him through the Word."[1] Absolutely!

At the same time, God has not called us into a relationship with a Book but into a relationship with Himself, and, as a former cessationist once remarked, the Trinity is not composed of the Father, Son, and Holy Bible but of the Father, Son, and Holy Spirit. It is through the Spirit that we have intimate relationship with God, as Paul expressed in his benediction to the Corinthians: "The grace of the Lord Jesus Christ and the love of God and the fellowship [*koinōnia*] of the Holy Spirit be with you all" (2Co 13:14). Are you enjoying real fellowship with God?

New Testament Greek scholar Daniel B. Wallace, who is not a charismatic, shares some of his own story candidly:

> Through the experience of my son's cancer, I came to grips with the inadequacy of the Bible alone to handle

life's crises. I needed [an] existential experience with God. I got in touch with my early years as a charismatic and began reflecting on how the Holy Spirit works today. I saw scripture in a new light and began wrestling with the question, If the Holy Spirit did not die in the first century, what in the world is he doing today?[2]

...While I still consider myself a cessationist, the last few years have shown me that my spiritual life had gotten off track—that somehow I, along with many others in my theological tradition, have learned to do without the third person of the Trinity.

But this did not hinder my academic work. Mine had become a cognitive faith—a Christianity from the neck up. As long as I could control the text, I was happy.[3]

Prof. Wallace then offers eleven tremendously insightful theses, including:

1) Although the sign gifts died in the first century, the Holy Spirit did not.

2) Although charismatics have sometimes given a higher priority to experience than to relationship, rationalistic evangelicals have just as frequently given a higher priority to knowledge than to relationship.

3) This emphasis on knowledge over relationship can produce in us a bibliolatry.

4) The net effect of such bibliolatry is a depersonalization of God...

7) Evangelical rationalism can lead to spiritual defection."

All of this leads me back to the question, Are you enjoying real fellowship with God?

The Meaning of Fellowship with God

The Greek word *koinōnia* includes the meanings of communion, close relationship, partnership, and fellowship, and elsewhere in the New Testament, it is used for devoted, godly, human relations (see Acts 2:42; Philippians 1:5). In contemporary, common Greek outside the New Testament, the Moulton-Milligan lexicon states that, "it is worth noting that the [noun] like the verb…is used specially of the closest of all human relationships…"[4] That means that the fellowship we enjoy with each other should, on some level, parallel the fellowship we enjoy with the Lord, as John expressed to his readers: "that which we have seen and heard we proclaim also to you, so that you too may have fellowship with us; and indeed our fellowship is with the Father and with his Son Jesus Christ" (1 John 1:3).

We get a glimpse of this from God's side in many passages in the Old Testament that express the depth of His love for His bride (or, His firstborn son, depending on the metaphor), the people of Israel.[5] In the New Testament, we see God's heart expressed through Jesus shortly before He was betrayed, as He said to His disciples, *"I have earnestly desired to eat this Passover with you before I suffer.* For I tell you I will not eat it until it is fulfilled in the kingdom of God" (Luke 22:15-16). These men were the Lord's closest friends (John 15:13-15), and He longed to enjoy intimate fellowship with them before He suffered. What a revelation of the heart of God!

Sadly, many believers seem unaware of the invitation to *fellowship* with God – to commune with Him intimately by His Spirit – to the point that their relationship with Him is primarily a matter of reasoned, intellectual response, hardly reflecting true *communion* with Him, hardly reflecting *a shared experience* with Him. It was that deep experience of God that radically changed my life in 1971, as I explained in my book *Hyper-Grace*:

On Dec. 17th, 1971, the revelation of God's love so flooded my heart that I told the Lord I would never put a needle in my arm again, and I was free from that moment on. No more heroin. No more speed. No more addiction to the needle. No more hallucinogenic drugs. Jesus truly delivered me!

For the previous six weeks there had been a tremendous battle in my soul, beginning Nov. 12th, 1971, when I first believed that Jesus died for my sins. This alone was a major breakthrough for a 16 year-old, rebellious, proud, Jewish rock drummer! Prior to that, I had mocked the message of the gospel and boasted about my sin, but as the believers in a little Italian Pentecostal Church in Queens, N.Y. prayed for me, the Holy Spirit began to convict me (although I had no idea they were praying for me), and I knew something was terribly wrong with my life.

Then, after the light went on in my heart in November, I wrestled with God, shooting heroin one day and going to church the next, until that memorable service on Dec. 17th. As the pastor's wife played the piano and we sang the old hymns—hymns which sounded like little ditties to me compared to the Led Zeppelin and Jimi Hendrix music I listened to day and night—I became overwhelmed by the joy of the Lord and received a dramatic revelation.

In my mind's eye, I saw myself filthy from head to toe, and then I saw myself washed cleaned with the blood of Jesus and clothed with beautiful white robes, only to go back and play in the mud. I was spurning God's love, a love that was poured out on me when I was a filthy, godless sinner. I was mocking the blood of Jesus, blood that was shed for me when I was stealing money from my own father and bragging about how deceitful I could be.

At that moment, God's goodness exposed my badness, and I surrendered my life to the Lord and said goodbye to the life I had been living. And it was not hard to make the radical break. What a Savior![6]

Well do I remember being flooded with the Father's love and joy as we sang hymns like, "I Come to the Garden Alone," hymns which could have hardly have been farther removed from my previous hard rock culture. Are the words to that old hymn familiar to you? This is the first verse, and then the chorus:

> *I come to the garden alone*
> *While the dew is still on the roses*
> *And the voice I hear falling on my ear*
> *The Son of God discloses.*
> ###
> *And He walks with me, and He talks with me,*
> *And He tells me I am His own;*
> *And the joy we share as we tarry there,*
> *None other has ever known.*

No one had to explain to me what this meant.

He's Alive!

Something else dramatic happened to me as a new believer, and it made God's nearness all the more real to me. Shortly before coming to faith, I had developed a bad case of hives which would spread up my lower back, then down my arms and eventually cover much of my body, causing a real, tormenting itch. We had no idea what triggered it, and even with special lotion and special baths, it took hours to get relief. Even when I got medicine from the doctor, it took about twenty-four hours for all the symptoms to disappear.

Then, as a brand new believer, the hives came back with a vengeance, and I remember getting up in the middle of the night and praying desperately by my bedside for healing, but I was so new in the Lord that I didn't know if He would hear me if I prayed alone. (One of my friends had told me about some promise in the Bible that mentioned two or more people agreeing together in prayer, and I was such a new believer, I didn't know if He would hear me unless someone else prayed with me!)

No healing came that night, but I did start taking the medicine every day, after which the symptoms disappeared for good and so, as per the doctor's instructions, I stopped taking the medicine. Then, on the bus to high school one morning, I noticed my arms were starting to itch, and when I rolled my sleeves up (it was winter) I was shocked to see that the hives had come back, and those ugly red blotches were now spreading up my arms. Worse still, because I thought the symptoms were gone, I had no medicine with me, and even if I had a pill with me, the medicine would take quite a few hours to have any effect.

We arrived at school and I was in a mild panic, as the hives had spread rapidly and looked and felt miserable (I'm talking about pronounced, ugly red blotches all over my arms and other parts of my body), and before anyone else came into our home room where I was the first to enter, another believer walked in, also brand new in the Lord. At last there was someone to agree with in prayer! We bowed our heads and prayed for healing and the next moment, other students started to fill the room, and I was temporarily distracted by their presence. The next moment (this was in less than two minutes), I realized that the itching had disappeared and when I rolled up my sleeves, the hives were entirely gone without a trace, and they never returned after that. Jesus really had risen from the dead and prayers really were answered in His name!

As we came together several a times a week to worship and pray and hear the Word in the little church where the Lord saved me, and as I met with the Father alone at home day and night, I began to experience that "joy that is inexpressible and filled with glory" (1 Pet 1:8, or in the King James that was so familiar to me back then, "joy unspeakable and full of glory"), that "peace of God, which surpasses all understanding" (Phil 4:7), and "the love of Christ that surpasses knowledge" (Eph 3:19). And how I related to the words of Fanny Crosby in the hymn, "Draw Me Nearer," where she wrote, "Oh, the pure delight of a single hour, That before Thy throne I spend, When I kneel in prayer, and with Thee, my God, I commune as friend with friend!"

That says it all. Communing with God, as friend with friend. That is what the fellowship of the Spirit means, and that is what

God invites us to experience. And on a certain level, it speaks of sharing our lives together with the Lord.

The Living God in Our Midst

During a recent Sunday morning worship service at my home congregation, my thoughts turned to my brothers and sisters in the Strange Fire camp. At one point, as we began to proclaim God's greatness in song, some of the congregants began to shout out the name of Jesus, and I said to myself, "What a shame that some cessationists would judge this to be a mindless, emotional display," not understanding the passion and the love and the realities of God that fuel our worship.

Then, during the time of corporate prayer, one of our leaders, who oversees our missions department, felt prompted to read from Psalm 27, which turned out to be the very text that was going to be used for the sermon (of course, he had no idea about that). And then, before the message, a visiting pastor who had been miraculously healed of inoperable bone cancer more than thirty years ago was asked to share his testimony, preaching in microcosm the very message that was about to come from the pulpit. How many times does something like this happen in our meetings? And should little "providences" like this really surprise us if the living God is in our midst?

I remember another service in my home congregation when I was going to preach from Psalm 112, and during the worship time, one of the leaders asked me if it would be appropriate for him to read a portion of Scripture to everyone. I told him to go ahead, thinking to myself, "He's going to read Psalm 112," which he then did, as he thought to himself, "I believe Mike is going to preach from this text tonight." The amount of times things like that have happened is beyond counting, and while it is hardly a proof of the reality of the Charismatic Movement, it's a reminder that the living God is in our midst and that we are part of His family. Isn't this part of our life in the Spirit and our walk with the Lord?

Last year, I was preparing to minister at a gathering for some of the most sold-out, Jesus-devoted men I know in America. Normally, at their annual gathering, I would preach along the lines of taking up the cross or stepping out in obedience, but this time, I felt led to focus on the error or hyper-grace, a theme that surprised me. The men had been praying together for some time before I arrived, and, to their surprise, they had felt prompted to pray for God to expose the error of hyper-grace, a term they were not particularly familiar with. What do you know! Obviously, they readily received the message I preached. The confirmation encouraged me as well.

One time, while ministering on a Saturday night to a small group of Pentecostals who met in a tiny building which could barely hold thirty people, the Spirit began to touch people dramatically, with some crying out and others weeping. But I noticed a young man in the front row looking around the room with a big smile on his face, mocking what was happening.

I said to myself, "Lord, it's not right that he is here in Your presence and You are touching people so dramatically, yet he is sitting there mocking."

Suddenly, as I opened my heart to God, I knew this man's sin, saying out loud (but without identifying him), "There's someone here who is mocking the meeting and completely skeptical about what is happening, but God wants you to know that He knows exactly who you are. You are a pickpocket, and before the service tonight you were actually boasting to someone here about how you had just picked someone's pocket and they had no idea."

Immediately, the smile went off his face, and he listened respectfully the rest of the night. The next day, the pastor called to ask about that particular word, and after I explained it, he confirmed it to me in detail, saying that the young man left the service a whole lot less skeptical than when he came in. Could this be related to what Paul spoke of in 1 Corinthians 14:25, where the outsider has the secrets of his heart revealed prophetically and he acknowledges that God is among us?

Please understand that this was an extraordinary event, and I struggle like everyone else to determine God's will in difficult situations, praying earnestly, asking the Lord to direct my paths and to shut the wrong doors and open the right doors, reminding Him that I'm just a sheep and that Jesus is the Good (and Great) Shepherd. Yet I also know that He speaks supernaturally at different times and that His sheep hear His voice. (See John 10:27, and note that there is nothing in the Bible that says that God will never speak to us outside of the Bible. If such a verse exists, please show it to me.)

Encountering the Father's Tender Love in India

Some years ago in India, I was talking with the son of the ministry leader, a young man named Suneel. (His father is Yesupadam, whose ministry I mentioned above, in Chapter Three). Suneel and his wife Kalpana had been married for three years but were unable to have children. So I prayed for them to have a baby by the time I arrived next year, and sure enough, it happened. Was it miraculous? I don't know, but we were all thrilled to hear the news.

When I arrived the following year and met the little baby, I asked Suneel, "What's his name?" He replied, "Uncle (which is a term of affection), you're going to name the baby!" (This is not uncommon in some countries.) After really praying about it, I named the boy Daniel, and to my relief, the parents were very happy as well.

A couple of years later, they had another boy, but this time they told me in advance that I was to name him during my next trip there. You definitely feel some pressure in situations like this! But the moment I prayed, I heard these words in my heart: "His name is Jonathan." And that assurance stayed with me until it was time to name him. Then, at the ceremony when I said, "His name is Jonathan," his mother began to cry, which really got my attention. Why was Kalpana crying?

She explained to me after the service that she wanted me to use the name of someone in the Bible who was a true friend and who would be a true friend to his older brother, and she immediately thought of David and Jonathan. But she said to herself, "But David fell, and I don't want to use that name." And then she prayed, "Lord, have Uncle name the baby Jonathan." That explains the tears!

A few years later, while back in India in December, 2012, in the first message at the pastors meeting, I was preparing to preach from 2 Timothy 4:7, but at the last moment, I decided to back up my text by a few verses, starting with verse 5 instead. After the meeting, Yesupadam came up to me and said, "Brother, 2 Timothy 4:5 was the theme verse for all our pastors for 2012, and now they have gathered together at the end of the year. It's as if the Lord is calling us to give account."

The next day, I received an email from my former personal assistant, Trent, who is now a missionary in the Philippines, saying that he was praying for God to speak through a dream to Andrea, a young lady who works in our ministry and who was on trip with me, along with her husband, Randy, who is also part of our ministry team, and their baby son Cyrus. I didn't realize that over the years, Andrea had had a number of undeniably prophetic dreams, including one with her having a son after doctors had told her for years that she could never conceive, let alone carry and deliver a healthy child. (She has actually had five miscarriages in less than three years, so little Cyrus really is a miracle child.)

That night, I preached a message on blessing out of barrenness, in the midst of which I quoted from the beginning verses of Isaiah 54, without having planned to do so before the message. After preaching, I laid hands on couples there that could have not children as well as praying for church planters who were struggling in their ministries. After the meeting, to my shock, Andrea told me that a few weeks before we left for India, she had a dream where she saw me preaching this exact message and then laying hands on the people afterwards. (Remember that Trent had emailed me before the meeting, saying that he was praying that God would bring confirmation through a dream given to Andrea.) Then, Yesupadam came up to me after the meeting and said with shock that the text I read from in Isaiah 54 was their theme for 2013!

Perhaps best of all, a couple in their thirties from our ministry school who had been interning in India came up for prayer, and that's when I first realized that they had been unable to have children for almost ten years. The wife had undergone a medical procedure in India, and they were hopeful that eventually, she would be able to conceive, and I don't know if the procedure helped or not. But this much we do know. Within a few days after we laid hands on her in that meeting she was pregnant, and she and her husband are now the very proud parents of a wonderful little boy.

And then for the icing on the cake. While being driven back to my hotel by Suneel, the young man whose sons I had named, I asked him if he and his wife considered having another child, and he said, "We would love to Uncle, but we can't." To my surprise, I felt a distinct impression that Kalpana would conceive and that she would have a girl and that I was to name the girl Nancy, but I said nothing to him other than that we would pray about them having another child. (Nancy is my wife's name, and the very thought of naming a little Indian girl "Nancy" was outlandish to me.)

The next day, on the way to the meeting, Suneel said to me, "Uncle, my wife was praying and she had the sense that we were going to have another baby, and it will be a girl, and you will give it the name Nancy." What a holy moment! Sure enough, she conceived again after not being able to for some years, and within the very week this book is scheduled to be released (early December, 2013), I should be in India, naming that little girl. (I personally believe that almost of all this is the result of the childlike and yet deeply mature faith of these precious Indian believers. I attribute none of it to my own spirituality.)

Why do I share these stories? I'm sure that plenty of you reading this book are far more spiritual than me, and that includes plenty of cessationists, many of whom lead godly lives that could put most of us to shame. And I am absolutely not "Mr. Prophet," walking around knowing the secrets of everyone's hearts. But sometimes, as part of our fellowship with the Lord, we enjoy life in the Spirit, and it includes special moments like these.

Are you really sure this is all demonic? Or do you think I'm lying? Or perhaps you believe it's all a series of uncanny coincidences? May I ask what verse in the Bible says that God will *not* speak and act like this today? And may I ask why some readers will say, "The Lord is wonderful! I can tell you similar stories of His grace in my own life," while others will say, "I knew that Michael Brown couldn't be trusted!"? Why the different responses?

Fellowship with God Is Both Rational and Relational

In *Strange Fire*, Pastor MacArthur writes that, "The Holy Spirit enables fellowship with God,"[7] noting how the Spirit produces in our hearts a profound love for God, how He draws us to the Father without fear, and how we "long to commune with Him – to meditate on His Word and to fellowship with Him in prayer."[8] At the same time, Dr. MacArthur seems to approach biblical faith in an almost exclusively intellectual way, writing elsewhere, "Biblical faith . . . is rational. It is reasonable. It is intelligent. It makes good sense. And Spiritual truth is meant to be rationally contemplated, examined logically, studied, analyzed, and employed as the only reliable basis for making wise judgments. That process is precisely what Scripture calls discernment."[9]

Of course, I understand his emphasis (in part) when writing about "the rationality of faith," which was the larger subject of the last quote, but consider his interaction with Todd Friel during a Q&A session at the Strange Fire conference:

> **Friel:** Let me play devil's advocate. "Your problem, Pastor MacArthur, is you like organs and cellos. This is our way of expressing ourselves in worship. What's the problem with our way of worshiping?"
>
> **JM:** It's mindless emotional hysteria. It's not about worship. Worship only goes high when understanding goes deep. The deeper your understanding of the truth of God, the higher your worship goes. Worship is directly correlated to understanding. The richer your theology, the more elevated your worship becomes. You don't have to turn the music on for me to worship. In fact, I sometimes wish the music would all go away, and that I didn't have to deal with sensations along with my thoughts. Low understanding of God, superficial, shallow understanding of God, leads to shallow, content-less, superficial hysteria. That's not worship. Why have you been singing hymns this week? Because there is rich theology in hymns. We don't have to go hysterical. We want your mind fully engaged.[10]

So those are the two alternatives? Either deep theological understanding or "mindless emotional hysteria"? What about just having an overflowing outburst of *love for Jesus*, which doesn't always come from a deeper "understanding of the truth of God"? What about spontaneous, overflowing joy in response to His goodness? Is the choice only between "shallow, content-less, superficial hysteria" and rich theology? Do we only enjoy fellowship with each other based on mental calculations and intellectual reflection? If not, why must that be the case with God?

Most revealing to me about Dr. MacArthur's approach to worship – frankly, I find it shocking – is his statement that, "I sometimes wish the music would all go away, and that I didn't have to deal with sensations along with my thoughts." What a cerebral approach to worship, as if music and sensations and thoughts cannot all work in harmony to enhance our worship of God, and as if we are to love Him only with the mind and not with our whole being.

Consider the exhortations of Psalm 150, and then reflect on Pastor MacArthur's words again:

> Praise the LORD! Praise God in his sanctuary; praise him in his mighty heavens! Praise him for his mighty deeds; praise him according to his excellent greatness! Praise him with trumpet sound; praise him with lute and harp! Praise him with tambourine and dance; praise him with strings and pipe! Praise him with sounding cymbals; praise him with loud clashing cymbals! Let everything that has breath praise the LORD! Praise the LORD! (Psa 150:1-6)
>
> Pastor MacArthur: "I sometimes wish the music would all go away, and that I didn't have to deal with sensations along with my thoughts."

How ironic, then, that he quotes men like A. W. Tozer and D. Martyn-Lloyd Jones in *Strange Fire* and often elsewhere, yet these great leaders were men of very different temperament when it came to the experience of God.

God Loves to Use Music

Now, I don't want to do to Pastor MacArthur and others in the Strange Fire camp what he has done to charismatics and say that his worship is wrong or lacking. So, while I accept the fact that it can be legitimate and rich *for him*, it seems strangely lacking *for me* and very hard to relate to. Can't he say that he is projecting his personal perspective on others who are not of like temperament? (Obviously, this ties in with some of the themes discussed in the last chapter.)

I was a rock drummer when I came to faith and I know the demonic, destructive power of music when it is used wrongly. All the more, then, do I value the right use of music, joined with words of praise and adoration and divine truth – even if they do not always contain the rich theology of a Charles Wesley or Augustus Toplady hymn. Many of the most wonderful times of worship I have experienced came when every part of my being was fully engaged, meaning, body, soul, and spirit given over to Him in adoration or celebration, sometimes while playing drums with the worship team, other times prostrate on my face while they played and sang, other times jumping and dancing and shouting (all these are solidly biblical forms of praise).

Of course, I recognize that there are times when the musicians or singers can hijack the worship, making it into a performance, but that can be the same in non-charismatic churches too, where the majesty of the choir or the power of the orchestra competes with the words being sung. And I agree that there are more than enough lightweight, mindless songs being written today. I am also all for periods of silent reflection and meditation. How life transforming and God glorifying those can be as well.

But it seems that Pastor MacArthur is imposing his approach to God on others, failing to recognize how the Scriptures themselves often connect the presence of God with music and worship or how believers can really get caught up with the Lord in meaningful, deep, life-changing encounters through extended times of song and prayer, and how our emotions and our minds (and even our bodies) can be given over in worship.

Is there no significance to a passage like this in 2 Kings 3:11-15, when the king of Israel called for Elisha to prophesy? "And Elisha said, 'As the LORD of hosts lives, before whom I stand, were it not that I have regard for Jehoshaphat the king of Judah, I would neither look at you nor see you. But now bring me a musician.' *And when the musician played, the hand of the LORD came upon him*" (2 Kin 3:14-15). There are other scriptural examples similar to this, yet for Pastor MacArthur, this seems totally foreign.[11]

Consider these further comments from the conference:

Friel: Why are young people drawn to that?
JM: I don't think it has to do with what the teachers are saying. I think it's the music. It's like getting drunk so you don't have to think about the issues of life. If you shut down the music, turn on the lights, and have someone get up there and try to sell that with just words, it's not going to work. You've got to have some way to manipulate their minds.

Actually, there's often a lot of teaching in charismatic meetings (and, on a related note, I find the same hunger for truth when I teach in charismatic seminaries as I do in cessationist seminaries), but Pastor MacArthur's larger point highlights what he is missing: The music can enhance our worship; it can help create an atmosphere where we can better focus on Him. Why disparage that just because it's not your cup of tea?

> **Justin Peters:** And all the healing crusades I've ever been to have always got the music going. Extended repetitive music that lulls people into the first stage of hypnosis. Disengage your mind and thought. You now become susceptible. And there are a lot of psychosomatic healings, all the time. But you don't see medically documented healings. People are very susceptible to emotionally-driven music that goes on for 17 minutes. It wouldn't work without the music.

Was David wrong, then, to have so much worship in the Tabernacle/Temple? Would it have been better if he had just written poems rather than writing psalms to be sung? And would Pastor MacArthur or Justin Peters have found much of this description to be a bunch of loud, distracting noise? Perhaps David, a man after God's own heart, knew something he didn't?

> The singers, Heman, Asaph, and Ethan, were to sound bronze cymbals; Zechariah, Aziel, Shemiramoth, Jehiel, Unni, Eliab, Maaseiah, and Benaiah were to play harps according to Alamoth; but Mattithiah, Eliphelehu, Mikneiah, Obed-edom, Jeiel, and Azaziah were to lead with lyres according to the Sheminith. Chenaniah, leader

of the Levites in music, should direct the music, for he
understood it. Berechiah and Elkanah were to be gate-
keepers for the ark...So all Israel brought up the ark of
the covenant of the LORD with shouting, to the sound of
the horn, trumpets, and cymbals, and made loud music
on harps and lyres."   (1 Chron 15:19-23, 28)

And was Paul missing something when he wrote to the Ephesians, "And do not get drunk with wine, for that is debauchery,
but be filled with the Spirit, addressing one another in psalms
and hymns and spiritual songs, singing and making melody to
the Lord with your heart" (Eph 5:18-19)? What's wrong with the
songs and melodies? Perhaps they actually help us to *engage* the
mind rather than *disengage* it? Perhaps they often *deepen* the
truths we are singing and *enhance* the worship we are offering?

> **JM:** You won't find that music in a Reformed church.
> Why? That's not who they are. They're going back to all
> the great Reformed teachers. Their world is sound theol-
> ogy, Bible exposition, obedience, discipline, order. This is
> a completely different stream. This is the world invading
> the so-called church and carrying it away with things that
> have nothing to do with the kingdom or the history of the
> church or sound doctrine.

Excuse me? Pastor MacArthur is actually claiming that a Reformed church is more biblical in worship because it uses older
music forms (many of which were simply the norm for the society in their age)?[12] He is claiming that following "all the great
Reformed teachers" whose "world is sound theology, Bible exposition, obedience, discipline, [and] order" takes the place of
the biblical mandates to raise our hands in prayer, or to kneel

before Him in prayer (or fall prostrate before Him in worship), or to clap or shout or dance in His presence, or to use soul-stirring instruments like cymbals or timbrels?[13] And would he have faulted the lame man who was healed in Acts 3 for entering the Temple "walking and leaping and praising God" (Act 3:8)? Was this proper decorum for the house of God? Had this joyful man engaged in enough serious theological reflection before engaging in such celebration?

Mind vs. Emotion?

For those who say I'm being unfair here, remember that many believers, especially those with a childlike gratitude to the Lord for His goodness, can respond like the healed man did – and the Lord is certainly pleased with it. Perhaps He is actually exuberant about it as well: "The LORD your God is in your midst, a mighty one who will save; he will rejoice over you with gladness; he will quiet you by his love; he will exult over you with loud singing" (Zeph 3:17).[14]

Pastor Tom Pennington and Pastor MacArthur also had this to say in response to a charismatic worship video that was played:

TP: The New Testament shows two groups of people. Those who aren't saved are driven by their feelings and emotions and their body's appetites. And those in Christ are driven by their minds, by their understanding of the truth. There's nothing about the mind in any of that [in the video].

JM: The attraction is the same thing as in a bar. It's a sensual experience that disconnects you from the realities of life.[15]

These comments are once again stunning to me. Pastor Pennington stated that "those in Christ are driven by their minds, by their understanding of the truth," which is somehow placed in total contrast with their emotions and feelings. Does not the truth affect our emotions and feelings? Do not *love* and *fellowship* include emotions and feelings?

Oh yes, we base our beliefs and our understanding of God on the truth of His Word, as stated at the outset, but to make the contrast between these two groups as starkly as Pastor Pennington does (while agreeing with him about the wrongness of being *driven* by emotions, bodily appetites, or feelings) is to grossly overstate the case and to make our relationship with God far too much a matter of the head and far too little a matter of the heart. And could it be that the Corinthians or the Thessalonians (or even Peter or John) were not necessarily a bunch of Calvinistic theologians, yet they personally knew and experienced the Lord? And just because the words "fill me" were repeated a number of times in the video (obviously, in the midst of a longer time of worship, which would have framed the context of the prayer) hardly means that, "There's nothing about the mind in any of that [in the video]."[16]

What would these sincere leaders make of the sentiments expressed by the great Puritan leader Samuel Rutherford (himself a Calvinist, and revered by Charles Spurgeon): "A long time out of Christ's glorious presence is two deaths and two hells for me. We must meet. I am not able to do without Him." Would they have mocked sentiments like these if they were on the lips of an Arminian charismatic?

And what of the words of the W.H. Griffith-Thomas, co-founder with Lewis Sperry Chafer of Dallas Theological Seminary?

> It is, of course, essential to remember that theology is not merely a matter of intellect, but also of experience. Theology is concerned with spiritual realities, and must include personal experience as well as ideas ... The feeling equally with reason must share in the consideration of theology, because theology is of the heart, and the deepest truths are inextricably bound up with personal needs and experiences.[17]

Would such a comment have been scorned at Strange Fire if attributed to a TV preacher? To quote Baptist evangelist Vance Havner again:

> There are Christians and churches that boast of being mature when really they are spiritually frostbitten. We have developed a prejudice against feeling and emotion until amens would be no scarcer if they cost a hundred dollars apiece – and the real truth is, we have lost our first love...
>
> This accounts for a lot of church troubles. When we love the Lord we love the brethren. When we break up the fallow ground of our hearts we uncover roots of bitterness... There is a reckless enthusiasm about first love. It is not cold and calculating.[18]

As Leonard Ravenhill once said, "You can have all of your doctrines right – yet still not have the presence of God."

Hearts Aflame for the Lord

And shall I quote Jonathan Edwards here?

> True religion consists so much in the affections that there
> can be no true religion without them. He who has no reli-
> gious affection is in a state of spiritual death, and is wholly
> destitute of the powerful, quickening, saving influences of
> the Spirit of God upon his heart. As there is no true reli-
> gion where there is nothing else but affection, so there is
> no true religion where there is no religious affection.[19]

A textbook on American history notes that,

> Edwards became the ablest apologist for revivals in
> Britain and America. When Boston's Charles Chauncy
> (very much a man of the Enlightenment) attacked the re-
> vivals as frauds because of their emotional excesses, Ed-
> wards replied that, although no emotional response, how-
> ever intense, could prove by itself the presence of God in a
> person's soul, he insisted that intense feelings must always
> accompany the reception of divine grace. *For Edwards an
> unemotional piety could never be the work of God.* In ef-
> fect, Edwards countered Chauncy's emotional defense of
> reason with his own rational defense of emotion.[20]

Jonathan Edwards? Really? And what should we make of
the fact that his wife, Sarah, sometimes fell into trances lasting
hours at a time?

And what of A. W. Tozer, who wrote,

In spite of the undeniable lukewarmness of most of us we still fear that unless we keep a careful check on ourselves we shall surely lose our dignity and become howling fanatics by this time next week. We set a watch on our emotions lest we become overspiritual and bring reproach upon the cause of Christ. Which all, if I may say so, is for most of us about as sensible as throwing a cordon of police around a cemetery to prevent a wild political demonstration by the inhabitants.[21]

Tozer's quote reminds me of the saying that, "It's easier to cool down a fanatic than to warm up a corpse."[22] And it is reinforced by this wise observation from Prof. D. A. Carson, one of the world's top New Testament scholars:

> Because some wings of the church have appealed to experience over against revelation, or have talked glibly about ill-defined "spirituality" that is fundamentally divorced from the gospel, some of us have overreacted and begin to view all mention of experience as suspicious at best, perverse at worst. This overreaction must cease. The Scriptures themselves demand that we allow more place for experience than that.[23]

Dr. Sam Storms admitted that in his own life, one of the biggest factors that kept him locked into cessationism was fear:

> There is one more reason why I remained for years committed to the doctrine of cessationism. This one is not based on any particular text or theological principle; yet it exercised no less an influence on my life and thinking than did the other five. In mentioning this fact, I am in no way suggesting that others are guilty of this error. This

is not an accusation; it is a confession. I am talking about fear: the fear of emotionalism, the fear of fanaticism, the fear of the unfamiliar, the fear of rejection by those whose respect I cherished and whose friendship I did not want to forfeit, the fear of what might occur were I fully to relinquish control of my life and mind and emotions to the Holy Spirit, the fear of losing what little status in the evangelical community that I had worked so hard to attain.

I am talking about the kind of fear that energized a personal agenda to distance myself from anything that had the potential to link me with people I believed were an embarrassment to the cause of Christ. I was faithful to the eleventh commandment of Bible-church evangelicalism: 'Thou shalt not do at all what others do poorly.' In my pride I had allowed certain extremists to exercise more of an influence on the shape of my ministry than I did the text of Scripture. Fear of being labeled or linked or in some way associated with the 'unlearned' and 'unattractive' elements in contemporary Christendom exercised an insidious power on my ability and willingness to be objective in the reading of Holy Scripture.[24]

Speaking of the born-again soul in his sermon, "A New Creation," Spurgeon remarked, "It is filled with a divine enthusiasm which it once rejected as fanatical." How true! In keeping with this, G. K. Chesterton observed that, "Nobody, I suppose, will accuse the author of "Grace Abounding" of being ashamed of his feelings."[25] Rather, it seems as if John Bunyan wore his emotions on his sleeves. But what could possibly be wrong with that, as long as it is in harmony with God's nature and truth? That is part of our experience in Him, part of the communion we enjoy, part of worshiping Him with our whole beings, heart and mind, emotions and intellect, body and spirit.[26]

John Wesley, who was anything but an intellectual slouch (to the contrary, he was a brilliant, well-read, and thoroughly logical thinker) also found many people resistant to the idea of an emotion-filled response to God, noting in *A Farther Appeal to Men of Reason and Religion*:

> With regard to the Author of faith and salvation, abundance of objections have been made; it being a current opinion, that Christians are not now to receive the Holy Ghost.
>
> Accordingly, whenever we speak of the Spirit of God, of his operations on the souls of men, of his revealing unto us the things of God, or inspiring us with good desires or tempers; whenever we mention the feeling his mighty power "working in us" according to his good pleasure; the general answer we have to expect is, "This is rank enthusiasm [i.e., emotionalism]. So it was with the Apostles and first Christians. But only enthusiasts pretend to this now."
>
> Thus all the Scriptures, abundance of which might be produced, are set aside at one stroke. And whoever cites them, as belonging to all Christians, is set down for an enthusiast [emotionalist].[27]

Again, I find it ironic that Pastor MacArthur can quote men like Tozer and Lloyd-Jones with such approval, while Tozer actually compiled a book called *The Christian Book of Mystical Verse*,[28] while so many of his writings are replete with emphasis on our experience in God. As for Lloyd-Jones, one of his most widely read books is *Joy Unspeakable: Power and Renewal in the Holy Spirit*,[29] hailed as "magisterial and challenging" by J. I. Packer. In this book, Lloyd-Jones asserts that someone "can be regenerate without being baptized with the Holy Spirit,"[30] pointing to the emotion-filled, experience-rich nature of life in the Spirit.

A Close Relationship with the Risen Lord

Reformed charismatic leader Adrian Warnock captures the spirit of this in the chapter entitled "A Relationship with the Risen Jesus?" in his book *Raised with Christ: How the Resurrection Changes Everything*.[31] (Note that his book is endorsed by leaders like Dr. Al Mohler, President of the Southern Baptist Theological Seminary and Joni Eareckson Tada.) He writes:

> Many avoid showing any kind of emotion in response to God and are satisfied with studying God in a purely intellectual manner through Bible reading. We console ourselves with the idea that this is the "mature" approach and look down on those who are full of passion for a Jesus they claim to know. But a man who claimed to love a girl he had never met, but had only read letters she had written, would earn our pity. We were not promised a relationship with a book but with a person. Paul was not immature, and he wasn't foolish. He was passionate for his books (see 2 Timothy 4:13), but more so for his relationship with Jesus. There has to be a way for us to pursue a personal knowledge of Jesus without throwing away our biblical anchor. We can love the author of the book he left us, which is intended to reveal the person of Jesus to us.

Unfortunately, over the last few decades the controversy about whether or not the gifts of the Spirit are
for today has largely obscured the more fundamental
question—*are Christians today able to experience a truly
personal relationship with Jesus?* In other words, what exactly did Jesus mean when he promised, "I will never leave
you nor forsake you" (Hebrews 13:5) and "I am with you
always, to the end of the age" (Matthew 28:20)? As we
consider this question, let's leave aside for the moment
our opinions on the gifts of the Holy Spirit and focus instead on whether an experience of God is available to believers today.[32]

He answers, of course, in the affirmative, citing many respected theologians and leaders of past generations in support,
including Lloyd-Jones, who wrote that, "New Testament Christianity is not just a formal, polite, correct, and orthodox kind
of faith and belief. No! What characterizes it is this element of
love and passion, this pneumatic element, this life, this vigor,
this abandon, this exuberance—and, as I say, it has ever characterized the life of the church in all periods of revival and of
reawakening."[33]

Dr. Warnock cites philosopher Francis Schaeffer, who wrote:

Christianity is not just a mental assent that certain doctrines are true—not even that the right doctrines are true.
This is only the beginning. This would be rather like a
starving man sitting in front of great heaps of food and
saying, "I believe the food exists; I believe it is real," and
yet never eating it. It is not enough merely to say, "I am a
Christian," and then in practice to live as if present contact

with the supernatural were something far off and strange.
Many Christians I know seem to act as though they come
in contact with the supernatural just twice—once when
they are justified and become a Christian, and once when
they die…

Some Christians seem to think that when they are
born again, they become a self-contained unit like a stor-
age battery. From that time on they have to go on their
own pep and their own power until they die. But this is
wrong. After we are justified, once for all through faith
in Christ, we are to live in supernatural communion with
the Lord every moment; we are to be like lights plugged
into an electric socket. The Bible makes it plain that our
joy and spiritual power depend on a continuing relation
to God. If we do not love and draw on the Lord as we
should, the plug gets pulled out and the spiritual power
and the spiritual joy stop.[34]

These words of Schaeffer, one of the leading Christian intel-
lectuals of the twentieth century, should be taken to heart.
According to J. I. Packer,

Communion with God was a great thing; to evangelicals
today it is a comparatively small thing. The Puritans were
concerned about communion with God in a way that we
are not. The measure of our unconcern is the little that
we say about it. When Christians meet, they talk to each
other about their Christian work and Christian interests,
their Christian acquaintances, the state of the churches,
and the problems of theology—but rarely of their daily
experience of God.[35]

In support of this, Dr. Warnock supplies several more quotes from men like Charles Spurgeon (who accused people of being spiritually dead if they "have never felt anything of God" – with a clear emphasis on feelings) and John Owen (the theologian of theologians among the Puritans, who wrote, "I pray God with all my heart that I may be weary of everything else but converse and communion with him.") But it is this quote from Jonathan Edwards, so esteemed by John MacArthur (see above, Chapter Five), that I must reprint it in full here:

> I have sometimes had a sense of the excellent fullness of Christ, and his meetness and suitableness as a savior; whereby he has appeared to me, far above all, the chief of ten thousands. And his blood and atonement has appeared sweet, and his righteousness sweet; which is always accompanied with an ardency of spirit, and inward strugglings and breathings and groanings, that cannot be uttered, to be emptied of myself, and swallowed up in Christ. [It appears that Edwards became quite emotional when this happened to him!]
>
> Once, as I rid out into the woods for my health...and having lit from my horse in a retired place, as my manner commonly has been, to walk for divine contemplation and prayer; I had a view, that for me was extraordinary, of the glory of the Son of God; as mediator between God and man; and his wonderful, great, full, pure and sweet grace and love, and meek and gentle condescension. This grace, that appeared to me so calm and sweet, appeared great above the heavens. The person of Christ appeared ineffably excellent, with an excellency great enough to swallow up all thought and conception. Which continued, as near

as I can judge, about an hour; which kept me, the bigger part of the time, in a flood of tears, and weeping aloud. I felt withal, an ardency of soul to be, what I know not otherwise how to express, than to be emptied and annihilated; to lie in the dust, and to be full of Christ alone; to love him with a holy and pure love; to trust in him; to live upon him; to serve and follow him, and to be totally wrapt up in the fullness of Christ; and to be perfectly sanctified and made pure, with a divine and heavenly purity. I have several other times, had views very much of the same nature, and that have had the same effects.

I have many times had a sense of the glory of the third person in the Trinity, in his office of Sanctifier; in his holy operations communicating divine light and life to the soul. God in the communications of his Holy Spirit, has appeared as an infinite fountain of divine glory and sweetness; being full and sufficient to fill and satisfy the soul: pouring forth itself in sweet communications, like the sun in its glory, sweetly and pleasantly diffusing light and life."[36]

What a picture of how mind and heart, truth and emotion fit together, producing a stunning experience with God. He longs for these times with us as well, as humbling and overwhelming as that sounds. But that is the heart of our Father, expressed to us through His and mediated by His Spirit.

God's Deep Desire to Fellowship with Us

As mentioned above, about the time this book is scheduled for release, I'm scheduled to leave for India, marking my twenty-first annual ministry trip there with Love-N-Care Ministries, led by Yesupadam. On our first trip there in 1993, after two full days of travel to arrive at our main destination, we then traveled by car another five hours up a dangerous mountain road to the tribal region of Paderu. I will never forget stopping on the side of the road while the old-model cars needed to add water to their radiators, looking at the monkeys in the trees. Yes, this was the most rural part of the world I had ever seen, and there were even warnings about a man-eating tiger that had attacked some of the villages where we were heading.

After one of the meetings, we were introduced to a little Indian pastor named Paul who was well known to my colleagues there. (The tribal people were smaller than the average Indians because of nutritional deficiencies, and I remember thinking that he was very small even among them.) His colleagues began to tell us about his devotion to the Lord and the work he was doing for the kingdom, including the time that God spoke to him and said, "I want you to care for orphans by faith the way George Mueller did," after which he went into the village to ask the other Christians, "Who is George Mueller?" (You can take this or leave this, but I have no reason to doubt it in light of the fruit of his life.)

During one particular season, he would get up very early in the morning to meet with God in the jungle, walking to his destination while it was still totally dark. And as he prayed, a light would shine on the area where he was, staying with him until he got up to leave. He did this day by day, enjoying this extraordinary communion with his Savior.

One day, he got up a little later than his habit had been, even though it was still dark out. But as he made his way into his special prayer place in the jungle, he was shocked to see the light already shining there. God was waiting to meet with Him! Absolutely overcome and humbled, he fell to his hands and knees and crawled into the light to spend time with the Lord. I hear the words of Jesus again as I write this, thinking of what He said to His disciples at the Last Supper: "I have earnestly desired to eat this Passover with you before I suffer."

Can you relate to a God like that? Can you relate to corporate services where hundreds or thousands of young people and old people are so hungry for Him that they are ready to burst, that from the depths of their souls they are crying out – not in the words of a song but out of the depths of their souls – asking Him to visit in power, asking Him to pour out His love afresh, asking for an encounter with Him? Is there anything unscriptural about this?

Dr. Lloyd-Jones asked,

Do we go to God's house expecting something to happen? Or do we go just to listen to a sermon, and to sing our hymns, and to meet with one another? How often does this vital idea enter into our minds that we are in the presence of the living God, that the Holy Spirit is in the church, that we may feel the touch of his power? How much do we think in terms of coming together to meet with God, and to worship him, and to stand before him, and to listen to him? Is there not this appalling danger that we are just content because we have correct beliefs? And we have lost the life, the vital thing, the power, the thing that really makes worship worship, which is in Spirit and truth.[37]

What a contrast to the sentiments expressed at Strange Fire!

Can you relate to times alone with Him in prayer when you are so burdened for the Lord's intervention in a dying world that "the Spirit helps us in our weakness," interceding "for us with groanings too deep for words" (Rom 8:26)? When you are so overcome with the glory and presence and purity of God that you fall on your face, as the elders did in Revelation 4, proclaiming over again that He is holy and worthy? Of these elders it is written that "day and night they never cease to say, "Holy, holy, holy, is the Lord God Almighty, who was and is and is to come!" (Rev 4:8) Perhaps some charismatic repetition in worship is not as mindless and worthless as some think? Perhaps it is an expression of awe and adoration, or of hunger and thirst, or of joy and gratitude?

Millions have benefited from John Piper's many calls to experience the pleasures of God,[38] echoed by Sam Storms and others,[39] since it is the Lord Himself who calls us to enjoy fellowship with Him. The mind boggling truth is that He enjoys the fellowship too.

What a Savior. What a God. What a Friend.

Endnotes

[1] This is widely quoted but I do not have the original source. (Wigglesworth never wrote a book, but his sermons have been transcribed and widely distributed.)

[2] Wallace, *Who's Afraid of the Holy Spirit*, Kindle Locations 162-165.

[3]Ibid., Kindle Locations 162-181.

[4]J. H. Moulton and G. Milligan, *Vocabulary of the Greek Testament* (repr., Grand Rapids, Baker Academic, 1995), 351

[5]See, for example, the imagery expressed in Jeremiah 2 or Ezekiel 16.

[6]*Hyper-Grace*, 1-2.

[7]*Strange Fire*, 189-190.

[8]Ibid., 190

[9]http://www.gty.org/resources/print/articles/A304

[10]http://thecripplegate.com/strange-fire-panel-qa-1-macarthur-lawson-pennington-peters/

[11]See, for example, the conspicuous role of music in 1 Sam 10:5; 2 Chronicles 5:11-14; 20:1-22.

[12]How small minded we can be! There is a big Body out there, and the God we serve is a big God, full of variety and surprise. There are cultural differences in His Church, as well as differences of doctrinal emphasis, differences of call and anointing, and differences of burden. One style of worship may be wonderful to one group and woeful to another. A turned on, black Pentecostal service may be glorious to some and gross to others, while a quiet Presbyterian service may be delightful to some and deathly to others. Yet both may be blessed by God! What is awesome to one group may seem awful to another. The first time my wife and I were in a worship service in India, we thought the music was demonic. The only time we had ever heard such sounds and tones before was in the context of Hinduism. Yet the songs were powerful Christian songs and the worship leader was a truly godly man, anointed by the Lord, and the music was simply Indian music, not Hindu music. We simply made a judgment based on previous cultural experience. It's so easy to do!

[13]It should be noted that the "tambourine" (Hebrew *tōph*), was a percussive instrument that was struck and not just shaken

[14]I'm obviously giving application to this verse as opposed to a strict, contextual exegesis

[15]http://thecripplegate.com/strange-fire-panel-qa-1-macarthur-lawson-pennington-peters/

[16] In my judgment, it would have been better for the panelists to give thanks to God that hundreds (or thousands?) of young people had chosen to gather together to worship God rather than get high or sleep together or play video games or watch TV, also recognizing that when the worship leader repeated "Fill me" a number of times, there was a context to the meeting up to that point, and so they were not praying to be filled with some abstract power (or worse) but rather with God's Spirit and love and power.

[17] See, conveniently, http://www.churchsociety.org/publications/principles/principles-introduction.asp

[18] Vance Havner, *The Seven Churches of Revelation*, available on-line at http://www.christsbondservants.org/Home_Files/wys- ch- Seven.Churches.pdf

[19] Available online here: http://www.ccel.org/ccel/edwards/works1.vii.ii.iii.html.

[20] John M. Murrin, et al., *Liberty, Equality, Power: A History of the American People* (United States: Wadsworth CENGAGE Learning, 2010), 128. See further Ann Taves, *Fits, Trances, and Visions: Experiencing Religion and Explaining Experience from Wesley to James* (Princeton, NJ: Princeton Univ. Press, 1999); for the descriptions of the religious ecstasies of Sarah Edwards and David Brainerd, see ibid., 66-67.

[21] From "The Missing Witness," http://lovestthoume.com/Preparation/MissingWitness.html

[22] For more on this, see the chapter "Now Don't Get Too Emotional!" in Brown, *The Revival Answer Book*, 199-219

[23] D. A. Carson, *A Call to Spiritual Reformation* (Grand Rapids: Baker, 1992), 191.

[24] In Grudem, *Are Miraculous Gifts for Today*, 204-205 (my appreciation to Facebook friend Steve Noel pointing this out to me); Daniel Wallace, in *Who's Afraid of the Holy Spirit*, is even more strong, claiming that, "as typical cessationists, we want to be in control at all times. Even when it means that we shut God out" (Kindle Locations 295-296).

[25] From his classic work *Heretics*; see http://www.ccel.org/ccel/chesterton/heretics.xv.html

[26] See also above, Chapter Eight.

[27] For a free online edition, see http://www.godrules.net/library/wesley/274wesley_h3.htm

[28] Reprint, Harrisburg, PA: Christian Publications, 1991.

[29] See above, Chapter Eight, n. 7.

[30] *Joy Unspeakable*, 32.

[31] Wheaton: Crossway, 2010; Adrian has graciously made this chapter available as a free download at http://wp.patheos.com.s3.amazonaws.com/blogs/adrianwarnock/files/2013/11/Raised- With- Christ- Ch.15- Excerpt.pdf It is used with permission here.

[32] *Raised with Christ*, 196-197.

[33] Cited in Warnock, *Raised with Christ*, 197.

[34] Francis Schaeffer, *Death in the City*, Chapter 9, in Francis A. Schaeffer, *The Complete Works of Francis A. Schaeffer: A Christian Worldview* (Wheaton: Crossway Books, 1996), cited in Warnock, *Raised with Christ*, 206.

[35] J. I. Packer, *A Quest for Godliness* (Wheaton, IL: Crossway Books, 1994), 215, cited in Warnock, *Raised with Christ*, 198.

[36] Warnock, *Raised with Christ*, 200-201.

[37] Martyn Lloyd-Jones, *Revival* (Wheaton: Crossway, 1987), 72, cited in Warnock, *Raised with Christ* 203.

[38] Most famously *Desiring God: Meditations of a Christian Hedonist* (rev. ed.; Portland: Multnomah Press, 2011).

[39] See especially Sam Storms, *Pleasures Evermore: The Life-Changing Power of Enjoying God* (Colorado Springs: NavPress, 2000). More recently, see Robert Morris, *The God I Never Knew: How Real Friendship with the Holy Spirit Can Change Your Life* (Colorado Springs, CO: Waterbrook Press, 2011); Francis Chan, with Danae Yankoski, *Forgotten God: Reversing Our Tragic Neglect of the Holy Spirit* (Colorado Springs, CO: David C. Cook, 2009).

CHAPTER TEN

MOVING FORWARD AFTER STRANGE FIRE

In my personal opinion, the Strange Fire conference and *Strange Fire* book (October, 2013 and November, 2013, respectively) will be significant for at least four reasons:

1. Strange Fire will serve as a negative landmark in the increasingly minority position of cessationism, as believers from all backgrounds continue to experience the gifts and power of the Spirit in ever-increasing numbers worldwide.

2. As a direct result of the conference and book, more believers will study the Scriptures afresh on the question of cessationism vs. continuationism, leading many to conclude that continuationism is true. As someone wrote, "Strange Fire will back fire!"

3. Pentecostals and charismatics who previously had no connection or even knowledge of each other will begin to discover one other, bringing more unity and cross-pollination, especially from some very different streams. Along with this, many non-hostile cessationists will begin to connect with many non-crazy charismatics, leading to mutual edification, building up the church, and even effective missions and evangelism work.

4. In keeping with one of the purposes of Strange Fire, charismatics will look more seriously at some of their most glaring and serious errors (both doctrinally and morally), speaking out more boldly and doing more consistent housecleaning. This, then, would be the only goal set forth in the conference that will be realized. Everything else will result in the opposite of what was intended.

Again, this is just my personal opinion, and time will tell if these insights prove true. What I can confirm is that, already, in these early weeks after the conference, numbers two and three, above, are beginning to happen.[1] So, where do we go from here? And what practical steps can we take?

This entire book was written as if there was a Strange Fire conference speaker (or attendee or blogger) sitting next to me and looking over my shoulder, challenging every point and coming back with a criticism or argument. (It's not uncommon for me to write like that, given my propensity to debate.) In light of that, I have made every effort to dot every "i" and cross every "t" – although, without doubt, the critics will claim that there are plenty of undotted i's and uncrossed t's. It will be up to other readers to sort the issues out and decide who and what is right.

But having a Strange Fire critic in my ear during these two intensive weeks of writing was not a bad experience at all. In fact, I came to appreciate my friends in this camp all the more (and be assured that quite a few wrote to me privately and through social media, so the "interaction" I had was far from an exercise in imagination). They are often sticklers for truth, prizing accuracy and precision, relating to the Lord and His Word in a particular way that makes it very difficult for them to see charismatics in a positive light. And so, these last pages are devoted in particular to those sympathetic to the Strange Fire message but with relevance for all of us in the Body.

1. *The Whole Bible is Wholly True. Believe It.*

We all know that we need to interpret and apply the Scriptures properly, and so when I say that "the whole Bible is wholly true," I certainly don't mean that we can indiscriminately point to any verse in the Word and say, "That applies directly to me today!" In fact, this reminds me of a humorous story from almost thirty years ago.

A woman who was attending night classes at the Bible school where I taught came to me with some questions, mentioning conflicts that her husband was having with her mother with whom she and her husband lived. When I suggested it wasn't the best living arrangement, she told me that her mother was very spiritual, getting "readings" from the Bible every day.

When I asked her what that meant, she explained that each day, her mother would open the Bible at random and point at a verse, and amazingly, the daughter claimed, it was just what her mother needed for the day. I explained to her that this was dangerous and that the Scriptures needed to be interpreted in context, and to prove to her that this didn't work, I opened my Bible randomly and pointed to a verse on the page, reading it out loud. The verse said, "Why bother the teacher anymore?" – at which point I said to myself, "Maybe this works after all!" In all seriousness, though, when I say that "the whole Bible is wholly true" and we should believe it, I mean that if the words or promises or exhortations or commands apply to us, we need to take God at His Word and believe and act on what He says.

The problem is that we sometimes ignore or avoid certain portions of Scripture because they are abused or overused by certain groups or because we once became obsessed with them (or were somehow burned by them). In my own life, about two years into my journey in the Lord, I decided that I needed to understand what the Word said about the rapture and Second Coming from a pre-trib standpoint, and so I got books by the main dispensational teachers like John Walvoord and J. Dwight Pentecost, buying into the system hook, line, and sinker, to the point that I tolerated no ambiguity on the point. If you believed the Bible truly and accurately, you had to be a dispensationalist.

A few years later, I reexamined the issue and ended up abandoning my pre-trib views (some of you are cheering and others are jeering), deciding that this was not what the Bible taught, and that has been my position ever since. At the same time, though, to avoid prophetic dogmatism, I ended up neglecting the careful study of some of the prophetic chapters of the Scriptures (including portions of Daniel and Revelation), leaving me with more uncertainty than God intended. Surely I should have *some* firm opinion on those chapters rather than just a host of interpretive options.

Some of you have gotten so turned off by the carnal prosperity message that you have become hostile to passages of Scripture that speak of giving and receiving and of sowing and reaping, thereby cutting off your nose to spite your face. In the process, you may have also hurt others that you have been called to bless, meaning, because you have become hostile to the thought of prosperity, you have forgotten that the Lord may want to prosper you *so you can give the money away to help the poor and to fund world missions.*

For a number of years, our ministry school was largely un-derwritten by one Christian businessman who believed that God called him to succeed in business so that he could bless the Body of Christ, and we watched with amazement as God pros-pered him and multiplied his funds. We have told him without exaggeration that, from a human perspective, our school would have closed years ago if not for his obedience, faith, and gen-erosity. Instead, we have had the privilege of training and send-ing into the field some of the finest missionaries and leaders you could ever meet. But if this brother had reacted against the car-nal prosperity message to the point that he developed a hope-less, small, poverty mentality himself, none of this would have happened. Do you see the point I'm making?

In short, *we should never develop our theology in a reactionary way*. If we do, we will almost always go from one erroneous ex-treme to another, over-correcting our course as we go.

In recent days, a good number of cessationists have con-tacted me, confessing that they hold to their theology because of bad experiences in the past or bad examples in the present. A man named Jason posted on my Facebook page, "I have seen so many abuses and heard so many false gospels from many men who put so much emphasis on performing the miraculous that I just fail to trust many of these men. It angers me when the Gospel is perverted and physical healing is sought more than spiritual healing." In response I wrote, "Don't be reactionary in your theology, be biblical. Otherwise, you are basing your the-ology on bad experiences." He agreed with this point.

Similarly, after I posted a request on Facebook for people to post testimonies of miraculous healings they or a family mem-ber had experienced – to be sure, cessationists believe in divine healing today, but as the exception rather than the rule – the page was quickly flooded with wonderful, Jesus-exalting testimonies. My initial post simply said this: "Have you personally experienced a miraculous healing in your life or in your immediate family? If so, please share it here (in brief). I plan to share some encouraging testimonies on the air today." But in the midst of all the testimonies, I found this comment from a man named Travis:

> How about, 'How many of you have not experienced miraculous healing even though you BEG God to be kind and merciful?' That is more prevalent an experience and more biblical than promising God's healing when it very well might not be God's plan to heal. Would you ask God to heal a man who lost a limb? 'Dear God, restore this man's lost limb.' Why not? B/c it's ridiculous to assume that God wants to heal everyone who asks.

Do you see how reactionary this is? Many times on the broadcast we have addressed the problem of suffering, and there was nothing in my post that stated that God would heal everyone all the time. I simply asked for Jesus-glorifying testimonies with which to encourage listeners, in keeping with the biblical pattern that recounts the many times people were healed rather than gives a record of all those who were not. What prompted such a reactionary response from Travis? I absolutely agree that if we're going to talk about healing we need to talk about those who are not healed as well. But there is a time and place for everything, and it is obvious that something was wrong in his response.

Is it possible that some hyped-up TV preacher shouting about "mountain moving faith" has caused you to react again biblical teaching on faith, moving you into such a safe, conservative spiritual lifestyle that the words of Jesus in Mark 11:22-24 have almost no meaning to you? Yet it was Jesus, not a Word of Faith teacher, who said, "Have faith in God. Truly, I say to you, whoever says to this mountain, 'Be taken up and thrown into the sea,' and does not doubt in his heart, but believes that what he says will come to pass, it will be done for him. Therefore I tell you, whatever you ask in prayer, believe that you have received it, and it will be yours."

How do verses like these apply to us today? And how do passages like Joshua 3, where the priests had to step into the river before the waters parted, or Luke 5, where Peter had to launch out into the deep before catching a miraculous amount of fish, speak to us today? To be sure, presumption is terribly dangerous, and emotional, pressure-driven decisions are certainly not from the Lord. But there are times when He calls us to step out in faith (have you read any missions' biographies in your life?), and it is often passages like these that He uses to prompt us.

Just because some charlatan abused the Bible doesn't mean that I can't use it rightly, and just because some teacher misinterpreted a verse doesn't mean that you should cut it out of your Bible. And just because some leader or denomination declared that certain parts of the Bible no longer apply to us today doesn't mean you have to accept that verdict when the Word seems plainly to say otherwise.

To repeat: The whole Bible is wholly true. Believe it.

2. *The Holy Spirit Is Moving around the World. Receive It!*

Yes, the Holy Spirit truly is moving around the world, and all of us should gladly receive what He is doing.

According to Prof. Alan Heaton Anderson,

> Pentecostalism has experienced amazing growth from its humble beginnings with a handful of people at the beginning of the twentieth century to some half billion adherents at the end of the century. There are many reasons, but perhaps the most important is that it is fundamentally an "ends of the earth," missionary, polycentric, transnational religion. The experience of the Spirit and belief in world evangelization are hallmarks of Pentecostalism, and pentecostals believe that they are called to be witnesses for Jesus Christ to the farthest reaches of the globe in obedience to Christ's commission. And they have been remarkably successful. They have contributed enormously to the southward shift of Christianity's center of gravity and provided a powerful argument against the inevitability of secularization.[2]

Amazingly, as he points out, most of this growth "has occurred in the very period when secularization was at its height in Europe." Indeed, "Pentecostalism is above all else a missionary movement" and "the fundamental conviction of pentecostals is that the power they receive through the Spirit is to evangelize all nations and so glorify Jesus Christ. It is estimated that Pentecostalism had reached fifty different nations within the first decade of its existence."[3] This reflects the missionary heart of God.

Anderson quotes Church historian and demographer Phillip Jenkins, who

> speculates that pentecostal and independent churches will soon "represent a far larger segment of global Christianity, and just conceivably a majority," resulting in Pentecostalism being "perhaps the most successful social movement of the past century." Considering that this movement had a tiny number of adherents at the beginning of the twentieth century, this is a remarkable achievement. The many varieties of Pentecostalism have contributed to the reshaping of the nature of global religion itself, with enormous implications. For example, its adherents are often on the cutting edge of the encounter with people of other faiths, sometimes confrontationally so.[4]

Some of you have been aware of this incredible growth, thinking to yourself, "This is the great end-time apostasy Jesus warned about! These are the counterfeit signs, wonders, and miracles!"

The problem with that line of thinking, as we have seen, is that Satan cannot cast out Satan, and if his kingdom is divided, it cannot stand (Matthew 12:25-26). And so, when multitudes of people really are turning from idols to the living and true God, putting their faith in Jesus, the Son of God, to save them from their sins and living a new life in Him, this is a cause for rejoicing. And when this Holy Spirit outpouring is marked by a passion for missions and evangelism coupled with a holy boldness to preach the gospel, and when the message of the cross is backed by divine power, helping to produce a wonderful harvest, we should all step back and give glory to God, doing whatever we can to help nurture and grow and strengthen and support this genuine movement of the Spirit.

Didn't Peter say almost 2,000 years ago that, "in the last days" God would pour out His Spirit "on all flesh," culminating with an amazing harvest of souls? (Note Acts 2:21, "And it shall come to pass that everyone who calls upon the name of the Lord shall be saved.") And didn't Jesus commission us to make disciples of the nations (Matthew 28:19), which at the least points to a harvest of souls from every nation, as described by John in Revelation 7? There he spoke of "a great multitude that no one could number, from every nation, from all tribes and peoples and languages, standing before the throne and before the Lamb, clothed in white robes, with palm branches in their hands, and crying out with a loud voice, 'Salvation belongs to our God who sits on the throne, and to the Lamb!'" (Rev 7:9-10)

As I read these scriptures and I see what God is doing around the world in terms of saving the lost (and for me, seeing Israel back in the land is significant as well), I am thrilled to be alive at such a time as this. To repeat, then: "The Holy Spirit is moving around the world. Receive it!"

You might say, "But a lot of things aren't being done right by these charismatic missionaries and evangelists. It's just too sloppy."

This objection, however, is reminiscent of the famous anecdote with D. L. Moody, according to which a lady once criticized him for his methods of evangelism in attempting to win people to the Lord. Moody's reply was "I agree with you. I don't like the way I do it either. Tell me, how do you do it?" The lady replied,

"I don't do it." Moody retorted, "Then I like my way of doing it better than your way of not doing it." Perhaps it would be better to help those doing the work around the world than to stand back and criticize them?

May I encourage you to make a fresh study of the Word, in particular the New Testament, examining what it says about the Holy Spirit, asking God to give you everything He has for you so that you can be more like Jesus and so that you can more effectively touch a lost and dying world? Jesus Himself assures us that if we ask for bread, our Father will not give us a stone. (See Matthew 7:7-11, and, with specific reference to the Spirit, Luke 11:9-13.)

May I also encourage you to read through the Book of Acts *minus* the miraculous works of the Spirit and the accounts that relate to those works (which eliminates almost the entire book!), asking yourself if that is what God intended for us or if, perhaps, the Acts of the Holy Spirit are continuing in similar ways to this day. Perhaps there is more to be had in the Lord and through the Lord and for the Lord than you realized before?

And may I encourage you to ask yourself the question, "Is it possible that in my zeal to reject the counterfeit, I have also rejected the true?" As you study the Word afresh, notice that for most of biblical history, God's people were guilty of rejecting the true at least as much as they were guilty of embracing the false. In fact, as you read through the Gospels and Acts, you will see that the greatest failing of many of the Jewish and Gentile hearers was that they rejected the true Messiah and the true Spirit. For them, this was a more relevant and serious sin than following counterfeits. One could even say that they followed the counterfeits *because* they rejected the true.

So, whatever healthy walls you have put up in your life to keep out the false spirits, be sure that they also don't keep out the Holy Spirit!

3. The Body of Christ is Multifaceted and Beautiful. *Embrace It.*

Recently, some well-meaning believers have urged me not to bother with John MacArthur, some claiming that he is hardly a believer at all. For example, a man named Gary posted this on the AskDrBrown Facebook page:

> I don't understand why or how you would give John MacArthur the slightest credibility. Like you, I became a Believer 42 years ago, and I've never heard MacArthur do ONE thing that showed he knows God any more than the Pharisees who had Jesus killed...
>
> He's hostile to God, a liar and a deceiver. Why pretend he's anything else?

Others have written to me in similar fashion, and I reject their approach in the strongest possible terms. (I imagine others have written to Pastor MacArthur and those in his camp in similar terms about me.) We are brothers in Jesus, and by God's grace we will spend eternity together. And even though my life and ministry seem full and blessed and filled to the max, I'm sure that I would be enriched if I could really get to know John MacArthur and Phil Johnson and Tom Pennington and other Strange Fire leaders. And I'm equally convinced that their lives would be enriched if they could really get to know me and other charismatic leaders.

It's interesting that Pastor MacArthur and others in his camp will point to fine leaders like John Piper (whom I don't know personally) and Wayne Grudem (whom I do know personally), recognizing them as brothers in the Lord despite their alleged theological errors regarding continuationism. After all, they are scholars, they are Calvinists, and they do not run around the building jumping and shouting like old-time Pentecostals. In some ways, they function as nice, token charismatics that the cessationists can readily accept. (I use these men as examples not to be derogatory but rather because they are so exemplary.) In the same way, perhaps I can readily embrace cessationists like the scholars who authored the book *Who's Afraid of the Holy Spirit?*, since they are not hostile towards charismatics and fully recognize the varied activities of the Spirit in the earth today. Perhaps they can be the nice, token cessationists in my world.

The fact is that God wants the Strange Fire camp to recognize as dear brothers and sisters the Pentecostals who jump and shout and run around the building because they are so excited about the Lord, and God wants the jumping Pentecostals to embrace the Strange Fire camp that hitherto rejected their spirituality. If God has accepted each of us through the gospel, who are we to reject one another?

In response to a question posted on Facebook as to whether God still raises the dead today, I posted a video with an amazing testimony from Africa, not knowing all the details myself but hearing about it from credible sources. My purpose was to stir healthy discussion and, if the account was true, to glorify the Lord.

Someone then posted a link from a watchdog group – a so-called discernment ministry – questioning the veracity of the

account and providing detailed charts (and I do mean detailed)
that claimed to prove that the story was not reliable, pointing
out alleged discrepancies in the various narratives. To be candid, it reminded me of New Testament critics ripping apart the
Gospels and trying to prove that they are not true because of
their alleged discrepancies. In fact, this discernment ministry
would have a field day with the resurrection accounts if it was
looking to disprove the Scriptures.[5]

At the same time, I realize that ministries like this do have
a purpose, since there certainly are fraudulent claims that are
made and dangerous teachings that are put forth. So, we need
the people of vibrant faith who are not afraid to visit the cancer ward of the hospital and confidently lay hands on the sick-
est person there, and we need the people who will cautiously
evaluate the claims of healing which are sometimes made pre-
maturely and even falsely. But in order to help each other we
will need to communicate with each other – openly, honestly,
publicly, and privately.

About thirteen years ago, I was involved in a very difficult
church-related split, one which brought pain and confusion to
many people, as much as we tried to avoid it. Yet God sustained
both of the entities involved, to our mutual surprise. "Lord, how
can You bless those people when they treated us so poorly?"
we thought to ourselves. "God, surely You won't sustain them
when they are so wrong in this matter!" those on the other side
thought to themselves. Yet, to repeat, the Lord blessed and sustained us both while we struggled to find common ground in
order to reconcile.

About two years later, the breakthrough came and reconciliation quickly followed, and for me, the key thing was to recognize that *God was for both entities involved in the split*, since He cared for both equally, loved the sheep involved in both groups equally, and wanted to bless all of us equally. (It was also important to realize that none of us were perfectly righteous either.) Once I grasped God's heart in all of this, it was no longer a matter of proving that our side was right or trying to win a debate about the issues but rather a matter of getting as low as possible to remove all offense, which mirrored the hearts of those on the other side of the split.

Well do I remember the night of reconciliation and the hugs and tears and laughs and renewed fellowship, and well do I remember how we smiled at one another and said, "I bet you were surprised to see how the Lord came through for us and sustained us!" Both of us, of course, nodded in agreement, and that night, to use the image of Psalm 133, the oil ran down Aaron's beard. Isn't it amazing how small-minded we sometimes can be when our Father's heart is so large and expansive?[6]

And so, in closing this book, it seems appropriate to cite all of Psalm 133, the opening words of which are well-known in Hebrew song (*Hinneh mah-tov u-mah-naeem shevet achim gam yachad*):

> Behold, how good and pleasant it is when brothers dwell in unity! It is like the precious oil on the head, running down on the beard, on the beard of Aaron, running down on the collar of his robes! It is like the dew of Hermon, which falls on the mountains of Zion! For there the LORD has commanded the blessing, life forevermore. (Psa 133:1-3)

Yes, *there*, in the place of unity and honor and respect and comradery, the Lord has commanded the blessing, and *there it is* that life will flow from us to touch a dying and lost world. Jesus deserves nothing less than that.

Endnotes

[1] Typical was this Twitter post from Nathan on November 13, 2013, "This whole discussion re: #StrangeFire inspired me to finally openly claim the charismatic label." Or this email from Tracey on November 11, 2013, "Before I became Reformed I conceded to the continuationist position and had many people lay hands on me to receive the Holy Spirit but I couldn't discern any effects like the people in Acts; so I became a cessationist after that experience. After recently listening to you over the Strange Fire Conference I have become a continuationist again and am seeking this thing all anew even though I am Reformed/Calvinistic."

[2] *To the Ends of the Earth*, 1.

[3] Ibid., 2.

[4] Ibid.

[5] Of course, I agree that there are answers to the apparent contradictions in the Gospels, and in no way am I comparing the Scriptures with contemporary claims of the miraculous. I'm simply talking about the attitude with which we approach things: Are we looking for truth with open and humble hearts, or are we looking to disprove and discredit? If the latter, we run the risk of missing the truth because of a wrong attitude.

[6] To be perfectly clear, I am not talking about some kind of broad ranging "Christian" ecumenism that in the end is anything but Christian. But surely there is a unity *among believers* that is precious in God's sight, is there not?

The Ongoing Evidence of Miracles, with Thoughts on African Charismatic Christianity

Craig S. Keener

B ecause this essay is being written before John MacArthur's book has been published, I respond here only to his prior public statements. Further response might or might not be warranted after the book actually releases.[1]

INTRODUCING THE DISCUSSION

Although I will strongly disagree below with some themes from Dr. MacArthur's conference, I do have some sympathy on at least some level. I cannot understand how anyone can see hard cessationism in the Bible, but the excesses of the most extreme charismatics sometimes make cessationism appear a more pleasant alternative. There have been times in my life as a Christian when I could have been tempted by my experience to affirm cessationism in some form—times of disappointment and even disgust at abuses in the name of the Spirit. People have, however, also abused the Bible, family relationships and other spiritual treasures that God has given us; we do not for this reason ordinarily reject these treasures.

Experiential Cessationism versus the Biblical Worldview

The main reason that I could never embrace cessationism, however, is that I am convinced that the biblical evidence is uniformly against it. That is, it is experience that has sometimes tempted me toward cessationism, and biblical authority that has prevented me from accepting it. Yet if I move beyond my personal experiences of some times in my life to a larger consideration of God's work in the world (and even in my life), even experience rules against cessationism. It is that issue I have been asked to address in this essay, but it does bear repeating that Scripture is the primary issue.

Indeed, hard cessationism's hermeneutic undercuts Scripture's authority in practice, because it keeps us from living in the spiritual reality of God's activity as depicted in many different periods in the Bible. This is especially true of the era since Jesus's first coming: he poured out his Spirit "in the last days" already at Pentecost (Acts 2:17-18). The Bible does not lead us to expect that he has since poured the Spirit back temporarily. Nor does the Bible suggest that we are any less in the last days than that first generation was. The radically Spirit-led character of the church in Acts, a striking contrast with its surrounding culture and an escalation of spiritual activity beyond the Old Testament, is an invitation to us.

I am producing a four-volume commentary on Acts, primarily focusing on historical questions. As a Christian, however, I do not read Acts or any biblical narratives exclusively for historical information; nor were these narratives meant to be read only that way. Ancient historians in general wrote history to provide models; certainly biblical history is meant to teach us no less (1 Corinthians 10:11; 2 Timothy 3:16-17). That is not to say that all of us replicate all the gifts and experiences reported in Acts, but that we can expect God to lead us in surprising ways as He led the church in Acts.

Because I am a biblical scholar, I would ordinarily approach this subject first (or even entirely) from a biblical perspective, but what has been requested of me here is instead a survey of some examples of miracles occurring around the world. I touch on the biblical evidence briefly in what follows, but those who would like to read my biblical argument can find it especially in my book *Gift & Giver: The Holy Spirit for Today* (Grand Rapids: Baker, 2001). Others have addressed the biblical arguments elsewhere. It is my impression that few scholars today would try to defend cessationism primarily from Scripture in any case.

Defining Language

Before beginning the survey, however, I should make some observations about the way I am using these terms. "Charismatic" is a broad label that includes a range of perspectives. I am an evangelical charismatic and use "charismatic" to mean a practicing continuationist—someone who not only believes in principle that biblical spiritual gifts are meant for the body of Christ after the first century (i.e., a noncessationist), but who also seeks to depend on the Spirit by using the gifts I have been given. In my case, this includes tongues in private prayer, sometimes prophecy, and most conspicuously and often, the gift of teaching.

Because "charismatic" in some circles has been hijacked to include any number of extrabiblical practices or teachings (such as prosperity teaching), I want to be clear at the outset that I am using the term in its broader, earlier sense. I have no attachment to the label and would welcome "practicing continuationist" as well. Since the Bible teaches that all God's people have *charismata*, or spiritual gifts, in the most biblical sense *all* Christians are charismatic. But in today's setting such a definition would muddy the waters, so I use the term as defined above.

The term "cessationist" is also used in very different ways. The hardest form of cessationism, much more common in earlier eras than today, rejects anything supernatural, not only postbiblical miracles but even demon possession. (Of course, no true Christian completely rejects everything supernatural, such as the new birth. In fact, the entire Christian life should be lived in the power of the Spirit, walking by the Spirit and bearing the Spirit's fruit.) More often cessationists believe that God may continue to perform miracles but that distinctively supernatural gifts have ceased. The distinction between "natural" and "supernatural" gifts is, however, a postbiblical distinction—it certainly does not appear in Paul's own lists of gifts.

The softest form of cessationism simply says that God does not *always* act in the miraculous ways we see in the Gospels and Acts. It allows, however, that he sometimes does so, especially where the gospel is breaking new ground. Such cessationism repudiates claims such as someone being able, for example, to always heal on command—a claim very few charismatics themselves would offer. Personally, I would not choose to call such an approach cessationism. Indeed, a large proportion of practicing charismatics and Pentecostals hold this position, including myself! Defining terms thus becomes important.

Today, when various movements vie for a wider hearing, some define labels broadly enough to invite people into a "big tent," only to narrow the label's meaning once newcomers have entered. It is important to be clear about what we mean—or at least about the wide range of senses in which the terms have been employed. I believe that most evangelicals (certainly most evangelical biblical scholars that I know) in the U.S. are theologically continuationists, in the sense that in principle they believe that gifts continue, even though most do not highlight most gifts or practice them in public worship.

Those who try to be continuationists in practice (welcoming *all* the gifts congregationally) are a smaller proportion, and this is what I mean by the general label "charismatic." (I say this even though I am ordained Baptist; that I personally welcome all the gifts does not mean all of them were able to function fully in all the congregations where I have ministered.) Yet even most cessationist evangelicals recognize many charismatic and Pentecostal Christians as allies in the gospel, and most Pentecostal and charismatic Christians in the U.S. either consider themselves evangelical (probably the majority) or regard evangelicals, including cessationist evangelicals, as allies in the gospel.

Most of my work is among evangelical scholars more generally; we each have different gifts to bring to the table, and we work together for the gospel in a setting of mutual respect. Most of these colleagues affirm the continuation of all the gifts but would not label themselves charismatic; some are even cessationist. Yet contrary to the denials of some critics, there are many of us charismatic biblical scholars and theologians, from a range of church backgrounds. We do make contributions to the larger evangelical world—for just a few examples out of many, Gordon Fee, J. P. Moreland, Wayne Grudem, my colleague Ben Witherington, and (hopefully!) myself.

SIGNS OF GOD'S COMPASSION

Certainly miracles continue today, as virtually all Christians except the hardest cessationists acknowledge. In the next section, I will survey some miracles that have supported the spreading of the gospel. In this section, I begin with some that for the most part simply met people's needs as an expression of God's compassion. Both sorts of miracles (and they do often overlap) were characteristic of Jesus's ministry. Because of the source of criticisms to which the book responds, I focus on accounts especially, though not exclusively, from two main kinds of circles. First, I include some reports from fairly conservative evangelical circles (some of the reports may even involve soft cessationists) and second, some from charismatic circles. I also include some others that I know well as credible, especially those I witnessed myself.

Documentation for these accounts and vast numbers of others appear in my book *Miracles: The Credibility of the New Testament Accounts* (Grand Rapids: Baker Academic, 2011). Despite some press the book receives, its purpose is to challenge not cessationism but antisupernaturalism—not the belief that dramatic miracles ceased but the belief that they cannot have ever occurred. The accumulation of cases, however, should challenge any idea that direct and obvious works of God barely ever happen today.

Earlier Miracles Expressing God's Love

Augustine discovered some of these expressions of God's love. At one time Augustine believed that miracles had ceased. He later explained that he never believed that God stopped doing miracles, only that they were very rare. But even on this point he changed his mind. True, he granted, healings do not always happen, but God is certainly still performing them. One example he narrates is that of his friend Innocent, who was suffering from an anal fistula and terrified about his surgery the next day. Augustine was among those praying with Innocent, and all were amazed at God's grace when, the next day, the surgeon discovered that the fistula had completely disappeared overnight. Augustine was himself healed, and noted that once his diocese began collecting reports, they documented seventy cases of miraculous healings in just two years. He notes that he knew of others not yet recorded.

If some of the critics in question might consider Augustine's generation too far from biblical truth, they might nevertheless appreciate French Huguenots or English Puritans. French Huguenots reported a number of healings; one of these was of Mary Maillard. She had been disabled all her life, but during a reading from the Gospels in 1693 she discovered that she was healed. Considering such Huguenot accounts, Puritan Cotton Mather wondered whether God was beginning a new "age of miracles." Miracles were also reported among the Moravians during the first Protestant missions movement.

In Britain's American Colonies, Mercy Wheeler's instant healing in 1743 sparked much discussion. She had been bedridden since 1726, but suddenly felt God's power, spoke what sounded to others like gibberish, and began to walk. Presbyterian minister John Moorhead also recounted healings that occurred during the First Great Awakening. A number of other healings were known in this period. Concerned not to compromise with "Catholics" by affirming "miracles," some chose instead to call these healings "special providences." Whatever the label, these healings were widely recognized as God's work.

John Wesley reports various experiences. In December 1742 a man named Mr. Meyrick apparently died; after Wesley and others prayed for the man, he opened his eyes and began to recover. During this period of revival, George Whitefield and the Wesley brothers tried to discern which experiences were God's work and which were merely human responses. The three did not always agree among themselves on particular cases, which were sometimes less than clear; nevertheless, a range of experiences, including healings, are reported. These also proliferated during the Second Great Awakening in the United States, a period in which massive numbers of unchurched people were evangelized and often recruited for the antislavery movement as well.

Presbyterian thinker Francis Schaeffer did not claim any special gift of healing, but he anointed people with oil based on James 5:13-18. Sometimes people were healed even of diseases that were supposed to be incurable. Some other conservative Presbyterian scholars have shared with me similar experiences.

More Recent Examples

Thousands of accounts could be offered today. In one study, 86.4 percent of Brazilian Pentecostals claimed to have experienced divine healing. In a different survey of Pentecostals and charismatics in ten nations, many tens of millions reported witnessing divine healing. What is more striking for this chapter, however, is that in this survey 39 percent of Christians who did not claim to be Pentecostal or charismatic claimed to have witnessed divine healing.

Granted, critics would not accept all of these claims as incontrovertible miracles, but we should not underestimate the many extraordinary works taking place. For the most part, the same *kinds* of miracles are experienced both among those who use the charismatic label and those who do not, although in some parts of the world they are prayed for and reported more frequently among Pentecostals and charismatics. I offer merely a handful of concrete examples; even in my thousand-page book on miracles, I could merely scratch the surface. It is impossible to keep up with all the firsthand reports.

For example, Flint McGlaughlin, director of Enterprise Research at the Transforming Business Institute, Cambridge University, prayed for a blind man in India in 2004. Both Flint and another witness present, Robin Shields, reported that instantly after prayer the man could see. His eyes had been clouded, presumably from cataracts, but the clouding had disappeared. He wandered around the site the rest of the day, gazing at trees and everything he could not see before. When he saw children's faces, he began to weep. "I have always heard their voices," he explained, "but now I can see them."

Bungishabaku Katho is president of Shalom University in the Democratic Republic of Congo, and an Evangelical Brethren minister. Even before the fighting had subsided in his region, he courageously returned there to work for reconciliation. We have been in contact for years, but during my research for the book on miracles I met with him both in my home and soon after at Wheaton College. When I asked him about miracles he quickly offered an example. Many years earlier he and friends were evangelizing in a village when a man brought his blind wife to them and asked them to pray. Neither medical help nor the local shaman had been able to cure her, but the man hoped that God might help her. The team had never been in such a situation before, but they decided that they had come for God's honor and would ask Him to heal her; certainly healings had glorified Him in the Gospels. After about two minutes she began shouting that she was healed, and her sight remained for the rest of her life.

I had heard the story of Thérèse before, secondhand, but finally was able to interview Thérèse's mother, Antoinette Malombé, in person in central Africa. This family belongs to the Evangelical Church of Congo (in the smaller Congo across the river from the Democratic Republic of Congo). One day Antoinette heard her two-year-old daughter cry out that a snake had bitten her. When Antoinette reached her, Thérèse was no longer breathing, and Antoinette was desperate. No medical help existed in the village and her husband was away on business. Unable to revive the child, she strapped her to her back and ran to a nearby village where Ngoma Moïse, an evangelist who was a family friend, was doing ministry. When she arrived, the child was still not breathing; the friend prayed, however, and Thérèse began breathing; the next day she was fine.

When I asked Antoinette how long Thérèse was not breathing, she had to calculate in her mind the distance between the villages, and after some thought concluded that it was about three hours. I had received accounts in which the revived person had been apparently dead for even longer than this, but what made this one special to me was that Antoinette is my mother-in-law; Thérèse is my sister-in-law. Thérèse suffered no brain damage, and she now holds a master's degree.

Missionaries often recount God's acts of favor in times of need. My wife grew close to Eugene and Sandy Thomas, missionaries planting churches in a less evangelized region of her country. Although Eugene was explicitly noncharismatic, he grew up in a Christian home because his parents were converted through the ministry of a Pentecostal woman evangelist. Eugene and Sandy shared with us many of their stories. In one case, they had to travel by river, and about 150 miles from home, the boat's motor burned. Sandy suggested that they pray. Normally Eugene was ready to pray, but this time he did not see much point. He opened the motor and showed her how it was burnt inside. "Honey, if you want to pray, you lead the prayer," he insisted. After she prayed, however, the motor worked until they reached their destination—and not a minute longer.

I do not see extraordinary miracles every day (I spend most of my day doing research, after all), but I have seen a few. For example, when I was in college I was involved with a Bible study in a nursing home. Every week Barbara, who was confined to a wheelchair, would complain repeatedly, "I wish I could walk." One day the Bible study leader, a charismatic seminarian named Don, stepped over to her and commanded her to rise and walk in Jesus's name. As he lifted her from her wheelchair, she looked as horrified as I felt. And yet she walked, appearing utterly bewildered as she did so. The healing was certainly not psychosomatic, since she did not believe it before she experienced it. After that, whenever I saw her she could walk—cautious at first, but gaining confidence as she continued to do it.

For another example, during my first year of Master's work, I twisted my ankle and probably broke it. It swelled and I had to be carried home. I did not have enough money to go to a doctor and the ankle never healed correctly. For the next two or three years if I tried to run the pain became so great that I could only limp. After one summer of personal evangelism in New York City I felt God inspire faith in my heart to pray for healing. The ankle was instantly healed and I began running again regularly.

MIRACLES ASSOCIATED WITH THE SPREADING OF THE GOSPEL

Signs reveal both God's character and His power, and God has often used them to draw attention to the gospel. The majority of conversions to Christianity in the third and fourth centuries were due to healings and exorcisms; the church fathers of the first few centuries regularly appealed to such healings as demonstrations of the truth of Christianity. In later history, such signs often accompanied the spreading of the gospel in new regions; missions histories often report, for example, stories about Columba in Scotland and Boniface in Germany.

Miracles and Evangelical Growth

Such signs are not limited only to the past. In *Kingdom Triangle*, J. P. Moreland reports the extraordinary growth of the evangelical movement worldwide in the past three decades, noting that up to 70 percent of that growth involves "signs and wonders."

Certainly the explosive growth of the church in China during the last two decades of the twentieth century included such influence. Some estimate that experiences of healing account for half or more of all new conversions during that period. These were not "gullible charismatics"; these were non-Christians so convinced by the experiences that they abandoned centuries of contrary tradition to follow Jesus. (What proportion of China's churches are charismatic depends partly on one's definition. For example, one statement produced by some of China's house church movements warns against demanding tongues yet affirms that all the gifts are for today.)

Such a pattern of miracles attracting the attention of non-Christians appears in many locations. A study three decades ago in Chennai, India, found that a tenth of non-Christians in that city had experienced healing through prayer to Jesus. Although clearly not all who were healed converted—in India some non-Christian movements also claim healings and vie for attention—the attention of many of those who do convert is first drawn to the gospel through healings. The church of one of my former students, a Baptist minister in north India, grew from a handful of members to over six hundred, most of them drawn to the gospel through answered prayers for healings.

Elsewhere, in a survey of Assemblies of God members in Ecuador, over one-fifth of respondents were converted in response to a healing. In one study in the Philippines, 83 percent of those interviewed reported healings, including from punctures, wounds, cancer and the like. Eyewitnesses I know have reported seeing goiters instantly disappear during prayer there.

Some hypercessationist critics question the genuine faith associated with this global movement of the Spirit, emphasizing biblical predictions of end-time apostasy. Signs of apostasy may be plentiful in a variety of movements, but what about the biblical promise of the good news spreading among the nations before the end?

Examples of Miracles and Evangelical Growth

My friend Douglass Norwood, then a charismatic minister in a noncharismatic denomination, was preaching in Nickerie, Suriname in 1994. Over the past two centuries the gospel had made relatively few inroads among an unreached people group there. Believers humbled themselves before God, however, and experienced an outpouring of the Spirit, which led them to begin sharing their faith. As a crowd gathered, Doug watched as an aged skeptic whose arm had been paralyzed since birth defied the Christians. Through God's grace and no faith of the skeptic, the man was immediately healed without anyone touching him. He was immediately converted, others were converted, and a people movement began in which tens of thousands were converted to faith in Christ over the next decade.

Albert Bissouessoue is a close friend of our family in Congo, a deacon in the Evangelical Church of Congo. Years ago he evangelized when he was inspecting schools in a less evangelized part of the country. One day people brought him a girl who had died about eight hours earlier; she was clearly dead, and the inquirers explained that they had gone to local shamans first. Albert demanded that they turn from the false gods and fetishes and recognize the true God. When he prayed, the child returned to life. Later, his wife Julienne had the same experience with another child in the same village. The restoration of these children had a remarkable effect. Through the witness of the Bissouessoues, many people came to Christ.

The Nigerian denomination Evangelical Church Winning All (ECWA) was started by SIM missionaries and is not charismatic—although I know from many personal conversations that there are ministers there who do believe in gifts of the Spirit. Many are critical of the false miracles and abuses in some independent Pentecostal churches, yet ECWA ministers also know stories of miracles in their own movement. My close friend Dr. Emmanuel Itapson, my colleague in Old Testament at the Baptist seminary where I used to teach, shared with me some of his childhood experiences. He grew up as the son of Nigerian missionary Anana Itap, who pioneered churches in northern and central Nigeria. I will recount just one story here.

One day Anana was getting ready his home in a new village. Rainy season was starting, and people were mocking him because he could not get a roof on his house quickly enough to protect his few possessions. In anger, he blurted out, "It will not rain for four days, until I have a roof on this house!" His critics walked away laughing, and he fell on his face, apologizing to God for what he had said. For the next four days, however, it rained all around the village, yet not a drop of rain fell in the village. At the end of those four days, only one person in the village remained a non-Christian, and to this day, the village recounts that as the experience that turned the village's attention to the gospel. These were not gullible people inclined to believe Christianity anyway; these were non-Christians who knew what was supposed to happen during rainy season. Some explain many cures as psychosomatic; such an explanation is difficult in the case of rain, however.

Watchman Nee had a similar experience in China. When he and others were evangelizing a village, people mocked them, noting that their local god was so powerful that for over two hundred years it had never rained on his festival day. "It will rain on that day this year!" one of the Christians insisted. When Watchman and the others heard what their friend had said, they chided him for staking the gospel on this matter. Then again, no one was listening to their message anyway, so they began to pray. On the appointed day, the rain was so severe that the festival had to be rescheduled, and this time the Christians boldly announced that it would rain on the newly scheduled day. When the downpour came on that day, faith in the local deity was decisively broken and many villagers were converted. Like Moses confronting Pharaoh's magicians, the Christians had displayed faith in the God whose power was greater than that of other gods.

I will share here just one of my own accounts, although it is much less dramatic than those recounted above. During summer break from college I was working at some retirement

apartments. I had been reading the Book of Acts and notic-
ing that while people were converted through the gospel, not
signs, the most common way of drawing people's attention to
the gospel was signs. I had led many people to Christ on the
streets (where I had also been beaten for my witness at times),
but I was delighted to discover an additional approach. One day
Mabel Cooper, one of the residents, was complaining about her
knee. With her permission, I prayed for it, and a few days later
she intercepted me.

"The doctors couldn't do anything for my knee," she exclaimed, "but it has been better ever since you prayed for it!
Now I need you to pray for my lungs. I've been coughing up
blood and the doctor thinks I have lung cancer."

"I'll pray for your healing," I promised, "but you really ought
to give up smoking."

"My doctor tells me that, too," she said, as if this were unusual
advice.

On my lunchbreak, I came by her apartment to pray for her.
"But first we need to take care of something more important.
Whether God heals you or not, someday you will die. You need
to be ready to meet him." She prayed with me to commit her life
to Christ, and then I prayed for her healing. She didn't cough up
blood anymore, and her doctor concluded that she didn't have
lung cancer after all. But of course the greatest miracle was that
she became a new creation in Christ.

TONGUES AND PROPHECY TODAY?

Many people allow that God still performs miracles but deny
what they call "sign" gifts or "revelatory" gifts for today, such

as prophecy or tongues. This distinction is of course arbitrary and extrabiblical, since no such distinction appears in Paul's lists of grace gifts. It also usually reflects a misunderstanding of the distinction between the purpose of the canon and the purpose of God communicating with us in other ways.

When Gifts Will Pass

Paul does not distinguish between short-term and long-term gifts for the church. For him, the entire present age until Jesus's return is the final era, living in God's power and on the edge of expectation. Paul in fact tells us quite clearly when to expect the cessation of gifts, which are partial: when we have complete knowledge at Christ's return (1 Corinthians 13:8-12).

Even as a young believer, when a Baptist elder whom I greatly respected tried to explain this passage as referring to the completion of the New Testament, I simply looked at the context and pointed out to him that this is clearly referring to when we see Jesus face to face—at His second coming. In the meantime, our tongues, prophecy, and knowledge are, like other gifts, partial and limited blessings to use for others until we know fully. Tongues and prophecy appear destined to pass away when present knowledge does—and if present knowledge had passed away, we might not be in a position to "know" it! Certainly we do not yet know fully as we are known (1 Corinthians 13:12). As Gordon Fee points out, Paul could not have expected any of his readers in Corinth to understand him as speaking about the completion of the canon. Instead the passage fits the expectation of Jesus's return elsewhere in 1 Corinthians.

The wrong, mostly modern idea that the passage refers to the completion of the New Testament may be partly behind the idea that God would not reveal anything once the New Testament was finished. It does seem strange, however, to think that God would reveal His voice to people throughout the Bible and then suddenly stop with the last verse of Revelation without any biblical advance notice. Because the Bible does not offer advance notice, the doctrine that God would not speak after the completion of the Bible is a postbiblical doctrine—the very sort of postbiblical "revelation" one would hope that people would avoid.

Some might derive the idea of no further communication from God from the warning against adding words to "this book" in Revelation 22:18. This verse refers plainly to the Book of Revelation, not the entire Bible, and earlier similar warnings appear in Deuteronomy (4:2; 12:32; cf. Proverbs 30:6) and even some other writings outside the Bible. But Scripture was never meant to be all of God's speaking; its function is a canon, a measuring stick by which we can evaluate all other claims. If it was all that God ever said, what are we to make of many prophets whose words are never recorded in Scripture (e.g., 1 Kings 18:4)? Or of the many prophecies in the early church that are not recorded in Scripture (1 Corinthians 14:29-31)? The rule Paul gives us is not to despise prophecies but to test them (1 Thessalonians 5:20-21). We may find that many prophecies fail the test (I would agree); but to discard all prophecies wholesale is despising them, is it not?

I do not look for new doctrinal revelations; but I certainly look for God to speak at times. At the very least this communication is the Spirit reassuring our hearts that we are God's children (Romans 8:16; and what is this, if not "experiential"?), and the Spirit declaring God's love to us through the cross (Romans 5:5-9).

Grounding in Scripture is meant to protect us from radical subjectivity, but Scripture itself repeatedly models for us and invites us to experience a subjective, personal relationship with God. That is true from the faith of Abraham to the emphasis of Paul that Christ lives in us. Emphasizing experience does not easily appeal to the intellectual, introverted side of my personality, but then, neither does love, which our Lord modeled to the death (John 13:34-35). If we can all hear God's Spirit within us on a basic level, why can we not allow that some are gifted to hear Him somewhat more fully than others? Such prophecies were not infallible even in the New Testament, where, even among believers, they had to be tested (1 Corinthians 14:29; 1 Thessalonians 5:20-21). But Paul certainly valued the gift, and invites his readers to do the same (1 Corinthians 14:1, 39).

Those who would rather throw out all prophecy than use discernment are usually inconsistent. They are also aware that false teaching exists, yet they do not for that reason reject all teaching or declare that the gift of teaching passed away. They use discernment. The same is necessary for prophecy, as in the Bible.

Many of the church fathers claimed the continuance of these gifts, and these gifts have sometimes occurred in subsequent history. Rather than rejecting prophecy because of false prophets, both Scripture and the church fathers invited discernment between the true and the false. The *Didache*, for example, one of the earliest post-New Testament Christian writings, urged discernment between true and false prophets (the latter being those who ask for money). Church fathers did not refute the Montanists by denying the continuance of prophecy, but by pointing to the superiority of their own circles' prophets.

Paul explicitly urges believers to prophesy and warns against forbidding tongues-speaking (1 Corinthians 14:1, 39, texts often skirted by the very people who accuse charismatics of biblical infidelity!) The body of Christ needs all the gifts to bring us to maturity, though some gifts are particularly strategic in equipping others (those listed in Ephesians 4:11-13 involve especially ministry of God's Word).

Examples of Prophecy and Tongues Today

Some critics charge that if these gifts were true, then they should happen today. Probably there are few prophetic people today like Samuel, who could be expected to tell people where their lost donkeys were (1 Samuel 9:6, 20). Then again, it is not clear that most true prophets in the Bible functioned this way, either; that was not their primary purpose. I personally appreciate more general prophetic words that echo the message of Scripture, as biblical prophecies often did, since that makes discernment easier.

Nevertheless, there are in fact plenty of examples of accurate, concrete prophecy today, and some of them we know first-hand. For example, when my wife was in Republic of Congo, in a setting with barely any white people, three people independently prophesied to her, without knowledge of each other, that she would marry a white man with a big ministry. One of those prophecies was given when she was a refugee in the forest. Another was given by a woman who was annoyed by what she felt led to say because she did not personally approve of interracial marriage! Later, Médine and I became engaged but I initially kept the matter secret at my Baptist seminary. At that time, a charismatic staffworker took me aside. "You have found your future wife," she explained; "Don't worry that you are from different cultures or continents." Others also gave similar unsolicited prophecies.

When Médine was hoping to get a valid passport so she could leave her country and we could be together, her country's passport office had no record that the passport had even been filed for. That in turn meant that her supporting documents needed to get a passport were also lost. We panicked, but Rosamund, a Ghanaian Baptist, said, "I feel that God is saying that the passport is done." I protested, but she remained insistent. The next day an official informed Médine that he had her passport. "It's been ready for a long time," he explained.

One brother from Ethiopia, who had not been informed that I was a writer, prophesied to me about two big books I was writing, the second of which would be larger than the first. At the time, I thought him only partly correct, because I could not imagine writing a larger book than the Acts commentary on which I was then working. I did not yet know myself that my large book on miracles, which was taken from a growing chapter in my Acts commentary, would come out first and the second book—the four-volume Acts commentary—would indeed be the larger one. I also think of a number of people over the years who have accurately and independently prophesied to me details of my calling that I have not shared (and continue not to share with anyone).

Not to belabor the point about prophecy, I should give a couple of examples regarding tongues. Del Tarr is a Pentecostal academician but also a scholar of linguistics; he has been present on occasions when people recognized the language being spoken by someone speaking in tongues, and not mere snippets.

One of my students told me how her mother was converted from a non-Christian background by hearing a Pentecostal worship at great length in the non-Christian's language, to which the Pentecostal had no exposure. (The Pentecostal did not even know that the non-Christian was present during that service.) Despite some more ambiguous reported cases, there are a number of other clear accounts like these. Of course, I realize that this is not how tongues always works (perhaps not even how it usually works), and that usually there is no one present who knows the language. But then, that also happened in only one of the five biblical passages about tongues.

As for whether someone has to know about tongues to speak in them, I have my own experience relevant to that question. I was converted from atheism from an unchurched background. I had very little knowledge of Christianity apart from the basic gospel message through which I had been converted; I had never heard of speaking in tongues. Two days after my conversion, I was so overwhelmed with a sense of God's majesty that I had to praise him, and God was so great that I felt that only he could inspire me with the words to praise him. Since it was obvious that God knows all languages, it made sense to me when I heard the worship coming out in another language. This is a gift that has remained dear to me in my private prayer life, one that has at times helped protect my faith in the God of the Bible when I faced many academic challenges to that faith.

Hard Cessationist Criticisms of African Christianity

One of the speakers at the Strange Fire conference lambasted most African evangelicals as following false teachings. Some of the concerns are valid and often noted (including by many African Pentecostals), but as a blanket judgment they too easily leave a false impression of African Christians. Such an approach allows hard cessationists to dismiss the value of miracle claims from Africa and much of the Majority World. Some of the less valid criticisms have even focused on Pentecostals' emphasis on prayer time or spiritual experience—emphases that most Christians historically would have found praiseworthy, not syncretistic.

Although I am from the U.S., I have spent much time in Africa learning from Africans, including living for months in African homes. More relevant are the range of African associates whose views have informed my thinking. In particular, my wife is African; she holds a PhD in history and is conversant with a wide range of African cultures and history.

Unlike me, my wife does not pray in tongues; nevertheless, like most African Christians, she recognizes that God continues to bless people with spiritual gifts. She comes from the Evangelical Church of Congo, the largest Protestant denomination in her country. Her circles often experienced Pentecostals as excessive yet recognized that gifts of the Spirit were biblical and, with discernment, to be welcomed. Many of the recently criticisms circulated I had already heard from her and others—except that they saw these as sad aberrations rather than the norm.

Welcoming African Perspectives

We may not always feel comfortable with the cultural forms in which God chooses to move, or with people who have not shared our Western academic backgrounds. But I wonder how many of us readily identify with Abraham, a seminomadic herder? Yet he is the spiritual ancestor of all those who walk in his steps of faith (Romans 4:11-12). So far as we know, none of Jesus's early disciples were scribes or members of the elite; they came from backgrounds closer to that of most of global Christianity today, not like most of us who could afford to attend Western seminaries.

I will treat below the question of syncretism (mixing the gospel with incompatible elements of other religions), but not all cultural relevance is syncretism. Communicating the gospel in culturally relevant ways is in fact helpful, so long as the gospel itself is not being watered down.

Christians in various parts of the world highlight some emphases lacking in the West, and African churches often exhibit distinctively African characteristics relevant to their communities. Yet some teachings in the Bible were first highlighted in the Bible when God's people were confronted with new questions in new cultural settings. Thus, for example, biblical doctrines of the resurrection and demonology began to be particularly emphasized when God's people were in Persia.

African and other Christians have a window on aspects of the biblical message that we have neglected in the West. In fact, it is Western blind spots that are sometimes unusual globally. For example, Western scholar Rudolf Bultmann took for granted that no one in the modern world believes in miracles. By contrast, Latin American scholar Justo González and Malaysian Methodist bishop Hwa Yung point out that Bultmann's worldview is inconsistent with the realities experienced by Latino and Asian Christians. When local Christians read the Bible on their own, they did not find cessationism, but expected the God of the Bible to continue to act the ways that he did in Scripture.

Although not all African Christians are "charismatic," only a small proportion are cessationist. Some "noncharismatic" Majority World Christians, trusting God to speak through dreams and other means, are far more charismatic in their faith than many Western charismatics. For some, the label "charismatic" carries negative connotations—yet they welcome and experience various spiritual gifts and miracles. Of those nonwestern charismatic Christians I know, most are theologically sound and far more committed to the Great Commission than most Western Christians I know. Both charismatics and noncharismatics I know from Africa are publicly critical of syncretistic movements and false claims, yet they would dismiss the recent unfair caricaturization of African Pentecostals and charismatics that has come from MacArthur's circle.

Most of the minority of African cessationists received their traditions from the West. Of course, earlier Western missionaries originally taught cessationism to most Protestant mission churches, and it was reading the Bible for themselves that brought African Christians to expect something different. (Similarly, in the early twentieth-century Korean revival, Western missionaries were the ones caught by surprise as healings and deliverances from spirits abounded.) In many places, traditional churches, such as the massive Anglican churches in Uganda and

Nigeria, provide biblical teaching without rejecting continuing gifts.

African Perspectives on Pentecostalism

Given Africa's vast size and diversity, that one could find some African pastors to denounce most African Pentecostals as not Christians is not surprising. There is a reason, however, to doubt whether these denunciations are representative, at least for the continent as a whole. Thus, for example, some non-Pentecostal researchers have surveyed Catholic and non-Pentecostal Protestant attitudes toward Pentecostals in Jos, Nigeria. (Most Protestants in Nigeria qualify as evangelical, regardless of denomination.)

Ninety-five percent of Catholics and 85 percent of non-Pentecostal Protestants viewed Pentecostals as genuine Christians. Seventy-six percent of Catholics and 75 percent of non-Pentecostal Protestants believed that the Bible is properly taught in Pentecostal churches. (Undoubtedly those of us who are Bible scholars would be more critical of most churches' Bible teaching, charismatic or not, but everyone agrees that there is work to be done.) Fifty-six percent of Catholics and 63 percent of Protestants affirmed that Pentecostals make the Bible relevant. These are the views of local Christians who know local Pentecostals.

The thousands of pastors I have taught in Africa included hundreds of Pentecostals and charismatics, including scores of ministers I taught in specifically Pentecostal and charismatic settings. In these settings I always found the Pentecostals hungry for Bible teaching, on some of these occasions willing even to sit and take copious notes for forty hours in a week. (Admittedly, MacArthur might be pleased to know that some of the students were slow to abandon the pretribulational eschatology they had received from Western Bible teachers.) Many were living sacrificial lives to bring the gospel to non-Christian people.

Some have suggested that most African Pentecostals are being funded by Western churches. It is unfortunately true that eager Western prosperity preachers have funded the spread of their teachings widely. Historically, however, the traditional mission churches were the ones with the most funding. Nor does it seem likely that the majority of African Pentecostals receive Western funding. The U.S. Assemblies of God, a Pentecostal denomination, partners with African Assemblies of God movements, but the African movements are expected to be mostly self-supporting. Other movements, such as Redeemed Christian Church of God and the holiness-oriented Deeper Life Bible Church directly originated in Africa.

The vast majority of new believers around the world—like the vast majority of people around the world—are not theologically trained. Sometimes the bottleneck in training does lead to belief systems incompatible with Christian faith; sound teaching is an urgent need. Incredible growth in many of the churches (often both Pentecostal and more traditional) makes it difficult to keep up with providing sufficient teaching. This is not least because of the rapid population increase in many areas. But what an opportunity for sound Bible teaching that is respectful of the churches!

I am aware of wide-scale examples of abuses, but also of widespread faithfulness. Most of the witnesses I interviewed regarding miracles, both charismatic and noncharismatic, acknowledged that God is sovereign and that God is the one who performs miracles. Are there false miracles? Many whom I have surveyed shared reports of these; we also read of these in some biblical accounts. Without exception, however, my informants noted that real miracles are occurring; most African Christian critics of fake miracles recognize that God is performing true miracles. Yet some noncharismatic missionaries working on the front lines told me that they were afraid to recount in U.S. churches miracles they had witnessed because of the hard cessationist bias in some supporting churches. They doubted that most Western hearers would believe what they had witnessed or heard from trustworthy sources.

Observations from an Experienced non-Pentecostal

I conclude my discussion of African Pentecostalism by citing the testimony of one of my closest friends, Danny McCain, who is not Pentecostal and has taught for thirty years in all sorts of churches and academic venues in Nigeria. He has a clear sense of the pulse on spiritual life in Nigeria, and has recently been involved in a major project studying Pentecostalism in Nigeria. This correspondence is from Oct. 28, 2013 and I share it with his permission.

"Although this was not a particular part of our research, it is my general observation that Pentecostals stress being 'born again' far more than the non-Pentecostals, particularly the original missionary churches. And the fact that many churches, like the Anglicans and Methodists are now stressing a personal relationship with Christ is directly due to Pentecostal influence.

"In every Pentecostal evangelistic service I have been in (and there have been a lot more of these than among non-Pentecostals) there has been a clear-cut presentation of the gospel and very clear statements about what it means to become a follower of Jesus.

"The Pentecostal and Charismatic movements have breathed real life into the non-Pentecostal churches in Africa. From my observations, it would be only a tiny percentage of non-Pentecostals who would deny that.

"It is argued by Matthews Ojo, probably the leading Pentecostal scholar in West Africa, that it is the Pentecostals and Charismatics that are driving missions in Nigeria and West Africa today. I have personally taught at two of these missionary schools and from my observations, the missionary candidates are very committed 'born again' believers who are reproducing converts after their own kind, including many Muslim converts.

"Of course there are charlatans and hypocrites among the Pentecostals and Charismatics and of course, some of their public teachings make me cringe at times and, in fact, even make me angry.

"However, speaking as a non-Pentecostal, if I had to choose the personal faith of the typical Pentecostal or the typical non-Pentecostal Christian in Nigeria, I would choose the Pentecostal every time. I think that as an average, Pentecostals exhibit greater personal commitment to Christ, are more open with their faith and practice more spiritual disciplines than the non-Pentecostals. In fact, in the university where I teach, which probably represents a good cross-section of the general population, by far the majority of the students who make up the campus ministries and have weekly Bible studies and serious prayer meetings are Pentecostals or have been Pentecostalized to some extent.

"I do not know whether this is different in other parts of the world. However, there was a Pentecostal revival that began in the 1970s that brought a level of intensity and seriousness to the body of Christ in Nigeria that has positively affected all parts of Christianity. This revival did not just introduce the Pentecostal phenomenon. It stressed being born again; it fanned the flames of evangelism and missions; it promoted prayer in a way that had not been done before; it brought energy and enthusiasm to praise and worship; it was initially characterized by a great stress on holiness but that has waned a bit. That movement still has lingering effects on the body of Christ here in Nigeria even to the point that 90 percent of the people who identify themselves as Christians today go to church on Sunday. Many if not most of these Pentecostal churches have all night prayer meetings once a month. Outreach programs are commonplace. Church discipline is taken far more seriously than in western churches.

"And to specifically answer your last question. From my very extensive experience of interacting with both Pentecostals and non-Pentecostals, I would think that nominalism is far more characteristic of the non-Pentecostal branch of Christianity than the Pentecostal and Charismatic branch.

"So, the bottom line, Craig: there has been almost a merging of Pentecostal and non-Pentecostal churches in Nigeria. However, if I had to chose [sic] the faith of one over the other, I would take the Pentecostal version. And I make this statement as a non-Pentecostal."

If emphasizing the experiential side of Christianity, such as the new birth, is a bad thing, then Pentecostals and charismatics are guilty. Yet these emphases have pervaded modern evangelical revivals, including in the United States. These included not only the more Arminian Second Great Awakening but also the more Calvinist First Great Awakening. It is moreover difficult to evade experiential language in the New Testament, such as the Spirit bearing witness to our spirit that we are God's children.

As a biblical scholar, I wholeheartedly affirm the importance of objective grounding in Scripture. But one cannot read Scripture very long before one notices that it everywhere invites us to a personal relationship with God, something that is experiential and not merely a matter of intellectual affirmation. The Psalms are full of emotion. The God of the Bible addresses the whole person, an approach that resonates with Christians around the world, many of whom will never have the opportunity for the elite education that many of us have had.

CHARGES OF CHARISMATIC SYNCRETISM?

At his conference, Dr. MacArthur claimed that the "vast majority" of charismatics are "in the dark." Already in answering a question in a church in 2001, he is quoted as saying that he believes that some Pentecostals are Christians, but that in his "conviction, the vast majority are not." Together with a claim at the Strange Fire conference that compared a large proportion of African pastors to witch doctors, these comments at the very least suggest a movement overrun by syncretism, the mixing of the gospel with spiritually foreign elements.

Although false claims do abound, they are hardly limited to some Pentecostals. Indeed, the caricature of the vast majority of African Pentecostals as not being Christian is also a false claim. In some places, in fact, Pentecostals and charismatics are the least syncretistic, and in at least some places they are the only people preaching the Christian message of salvation.

Pentecostal Critiques of Errors

If error is widespread, it is not because no one is speaking against it. The idea that Pentecostals and charismatics let error run rampant without speaking against abuses is not correct; many of us have spoken explicitly on these points. Unfortunately our critiques, like MacArthur's, have largely been read only by those who agree with us. Charismatics are not a movement in the organizational sense and no magisterium controls their beliefs. What defines charismatics is shared kinds of experience, which now appear in a variety of church movements.

Because we have had to confront the errors sooner than many outsiders, we have often been among the first to challenge such errors (e.g., Gordon Fee's *Disease of the Health and Wealth Gospel*). Julie Ma, a Korean missiologist at the Oxford Center for Mission Studies, has written extensively on Pentecostal church growth as a result of healing, but has also critiqued syncretistic sects. Without downplaying my charismatic experience, I was ordained a Baptist minister over two decades ago, but I earlier attended an Assemblies of God college and seminary. In these Pentecostal schools I heard many accurate critiques of charismatic excesses such as prosperity teaching. Indeed, I heard even some critiques of some charismatic beliefs and practices that I found unfair to those beliefs and practices.

Because my primary calling and gifting are in the Scriptures, I have spent much time over the years debunking charismatic use of verses out of context, though I believe that hard cessationists deploy a different repertoire of verses out of context (stretched with much theological extrapolation) to support their positions. In a recent article in a volume dedicated to Ron Sider I criticized the overshadowing of Scripture with experience in some charismatic circles, much as I think some parts of the church neglect forms of experience that the Bible leads us to expect. I have repeatedly challenged prosperity teaching, have acknowledged that healing often does not occur, and have critiqued abuses of "spiritual warfare" language. I argue that when miracles occur they are samples of the future kingdom, but that the deepest revelation of God's compassion toward us is the cross, which reveals (among other things) that even in the deepest tragedy, God is at work to bring about his purposes.

African Prosperity Teaching

Over a decade ago I even planned an entire book challenging prosperity teaching. The prospective publisher turned it down, shortsightedly complaining that no one believes in prosperity teaching anymore. I knew from wide experience that this death knell was premature, but the book would not likely have accomplished much anyway; I would have been preaching to the choir.

I would probably go further against prosperity teaching than most people. I am committed to living simply for the purpose of meeting others' needs. For many years when I was single lived as close to subsistence as possible, so that I could give away as much as possible. I have long believed that our nation's prosperity will eventually come to an end, and Christians need to learn to live simply and serve others.

Nevertheless, many who hold this teaching are genuine believers, and I find it ironic that for the first time ever I am forced to come to their defense! In some locations where I ministered, my primary colleagues in reaching nonbelievers with the gospel assumed prosperity teachings because they had been taught them. At the same time, these teachings were incidental to their faith that was also nourished by regular study of Scripture. More than their commitment to prosperity teachings, they firmly believed the saving gospel, lived sacrificially, and were leading people to Christ. Some in time did recognize errors on various points and left them behind. Surely the solution for their wrong teaching was loving dialogue rather than pronouncing them excluded from the kingdom. Indeed, excluding them from the kingdom would actually act on a false gospel, adding to faith in Christ's saving work other doctrinal conditions for salvation.

Meanwhile, not everyone accused of prosperity teaching is actually an advocate of it in the form in which we criticize it. Prosperity teaching is far too widespread, but preachers who genuinely read their Bible often begin to adjust their teachings in light of it. Granted, some conspicuously prosperous preachers, especially in particular countries, use prosperity teaching to exploit their flocks. Others, however, have begun moving in a more balanced direction. These others have begun emphasizing principles of economic development and encouraging a work ethic to transcend poverty. They may still overemphasize prosperity, but some of these mediating voices are merely telling their people things that most North American Christians, charismatic or not, have taken for granted for most of the past century.

In one survey, a majority of Africans—not just Pentecostals—affirmed that God can provide prosperity through faith. Western critics, however, have drawn mistaken conclusions from such surveys. Conversations with Africans from some of these locations leads me to believe that many Africans responded "Yes" to this question simply because they mean that they are depending on God to supply their desperate needs. This is something that Jesus tells us to do (Matthew 6:25-32), and can be antithetical to prosperity teaching.

Of course, many of these same Christians would buy exotic homes and fancy cars if they could. I do not personally find that desire consistent with Jesus's teaching. But they are no different than the majority of noncharismatic Western Christians who pursue the American dream. Everyone needs sound teaching on use of resources, whether faulty teaching has given them a theological justification for their consumerism or not.

Real Syncretism versus False Syncretism

The extreme charismatic paradigm that tries to control God or what He will do is genuinely and dangerously unbiblical. One of the most important patterns in the Book of Acts is that God often surprises us and accomplishes what is unexpected. That principle of course offers a challenge to hard cessationists and extreme charismatics alike. Yet the majority of charismatics I interviewed regarding healing experiences acknowledged that God is sovereign. Granted, most charismatics I interviewed were "mature" charismatics, but if some are not, our response should not be to disbar them from fellowship. The point of our teaching should be to bring everyone to maturity in Christ (Colossians 1:28).

Plenty of real syncretism exists, and some confusion exists because of the range of groups sometimes classified as "charismatic." Indigenous African churches, for example, span a range of beliefs; some are fully evangelical, whereas some others virtually deify their founder and are therefore not Christian. Lumping them all together is not fair. Statisticians who use the highest figures for "charismatics" do include movements that are not Christian by any historic definition of the term, for example, the current movement honoring Isaiah Shembe. Academic studies often must use sociological rather than theological categories, and some Pentecostal and charismatic scholars have already warned others against drawing the wrong conclusions from such statistics.

Nevertheless, African Pentecostals have often been among the Christian groups most hostile toward local pre-Christian religious traditions. As noted, some of the African indigenous churches are orthodox, whereas others draw heavily on African traditional religions. In contrast with the latter, the newer and now faster-growing Pentecostal and charismatic churches have sometimes provided the strongest front against the older beliefs. Indeed, less zealous outsiders often criticize Pentecostals for destroying fetishes that other African Christians deem part of their cultural heritage.

Such zeal can be taken too far and applied superstitiously, but the other extreme, zealously criticizing Pentecostals of witchcraft, also holds dangers. Some Pentecostals and evangelicals have too freely accused rival Pentecostal and evangelical groups of occult practices without proper examination. Comparisons with non-Christian belief systems are sometimes fair, and sometimes people do continue their culture's pre-Christian religious traditions with a Christian veneer (cf. even Acts 19:18). Nevertheless, occasions of false charges of witchcraft are widespread and should be denounced rather than encouraged.

Not all claims of syncretism are fair, and guilt by association can sometimes descend even into crass racism. Although my book about miracles noted claims from around the world, an interview with me in *Christianity Today* naturally highlighted some stories from my wife's country of Congo. Without bothering to read the book, one critic complained in various online venues (including Amazon's website) about me citing accounts from Congo. He noted that children are killed as witches in Congo.

This was a very conspicuous case of guilt by association, and involved several errors. First, there are two Congos in Africa, and he had the wrong one. Second, my wife and I knew the people that we were citing; like us, all of them would have firmly rejected groups that harm children (or anyone else). They were also not from a religious group that has ever been associated with that charge. Third, the critic was criticizing an entire people based on the deeds of some—essentially the sin of racism. If Congolese Christians reciprocated such attitudes, foreigners such as myself would become unwelcome there. They could cite the abortion rate in the U.S. or various scandals they have heard of here as grounds for condemning Christianity in our country.

Hypercessationist critics have also practiced guilt by association when criticizing, for example, Rolland and Heidi Baker. Anyone who wants to criticize someone can find points on which they disagree or find weaknesses. Undoubtedly many things could be done better with more insight; but then again, there is truth in a reply attributed to D. L. Moody: when someone not engaged in personal evangelism criticized the way he was doing it, he replied, "I like the way I'm doing it better than the way you're not doing it."

Heidi and Rolland highlight especially love, caring for thousands of orphans. Miracles in their ministry (alongside use of the Jesus Film) have brought thousands to faith in Christ. They neither preach nor model a prosperity gospel. They recognize that not everyone is miraculously healed. Nevertheless, visiting scholars, including some that I know, have witnessed the eyes and ears of blind and deaf nonbelievers opened and the resulting responses of villages to Christ—much like Philip's ministry in Acts 8, for example. They do preach Christ as the one true Lord and Savior, and through their movement some parts of Mozambique that were entirely unchurched are now officially classified as majority Christian.

Yet some critics complain that Heidi and Rolland received negative spiritual influences from being prayed for by someone who was prayed for by someone else who believed in prosperity teaching. I have long been an explicit critic of prosperity teaching, but the fear of spiritual contamination passed on by the prayers of one advocate of that teaching raises a serious theological question. Aside from the question of whether holding that teaching entails being demonized (and charismatics see demons everywhere?), is it possible that the critics have greater fear of spiritual contamination than they have trust in the gospel to purify? When Jesus touched the unclean, did He become impure, as people expected, or did He purify the unclean? If Rolland and Heidi effectively preach the saving gospel, are they really contaminated?

Those with such fear of spiritual contamination may be echoing the sort of belief system that many true African Christians have left behind. Enemies tried to curse my father-in-law, a first-generation African convert, even putting items cursed by local shamans into his office to harm him. My father-in-law had stronger faith in Christ than in his opponents' fetishes, and he simply ignored their attempts and kept preaching the gospel. I believe that my father-in-law was right: the gospel is more powerful than the darkness. My father-in-law, a member of the Evangelical Church of Congo, did not pray in tongues, but many people were healed when he prayed for them simply in the name of Jesus, including my wife. I believe that these were acts of God's kindness.

A Western Log in Our Own Eye?

None of us agree with everything that other Christian groups teach, and many of us do not even agree with everything usually taught in our own groups. Still more to the point here, in any culture, most genuine converts from a non-Christian background embrace the true gospel of Christ along with a mixture of other beliefs they have held or are being taught. Most of us have had to mature a long way since our conversions. I was converted from atheism over thirty years ago, and I carried with me a burden of antisupernaturalistic skepticism that it took me time to surmount—even despite some experiences that should have done so. Hearing believers' testimonies from around the world as I worked on the miracles book helped my own faith.

Yet this background of antisupernaturalism is what makes hard cessationism a plausible belief for many Western Christians. Like fear of spirits in some cultures, antisupernaturalism is in the air in our culture, especially in academic culture. Deism was a compromise with antisupernatural skepticism more popular several centuries ago. (Antisupernaturalism first advanced its case based on earlier forms of cessationism, which was an overreaction against false medieval claims, just as cessationists today often react against "hypercharismatics." But that is a different story.)

Hard cessationism allowed people to accept biblical miracles without having to fight the wider skepticism of the culture. At the same time, it also subverted part of the message of biblical miracles—trust that God can do anything and that he might well continue to do such things among us today. Again, that biblical message is something I have expounded elsewhere (especially in *Gift & Giver*), so I will not rehearse it here. Yet I am convinced enough that Scripture is clear on this point that I would view hard cessationism as a form of syncretism—with antisupernaturalism or deism. At the very least it sifts the biblical message unfairly through the grid of its postbiblical tradition.

I would not for that reason deny that most hard cessationists are my brothers and sisters in Christ. I would, however, urge them to lay aside the cultural and experiential prejudice they have against God's activity and hear Scripture more clearly.

CONCLUSION

Sometimes people with gifts for teaching and people with gifts for evangelism (or other gifts) oppose one another, perhaps because we have spiritual pride. Instead we could help one another much more by serving one another. Claims that have been widely circulated by some in MacArthur's circle—such as that most charismatics are not Christians or that the vast majority of African evangelicals are heretical—are not merely overstated. They are slander and they divide God's people. How does the Bible invite us to address such actions? We should not underestimate the tragedy of false charges that divide Christ's body, for our Lord prayed, "that they all may be one ... so the world may believe that you sent me" (John 17:21). For our Lord's honor, may we find in him the unity that transcends our differences.

Endnotes

[1] Editor's note: See now Dr. Keener's review of *Strange Fire* for Pneuma Review: http://pneumareview.com/john-macarthurs-strange-fire-reviewed-by-craig-s-keener/

Why NT Prophecy Does NOT Result in "Scripture-quality" Revelatory Words

(A Response to the Most Frequently Cited Cessationist Argument against the Contemporary Validity of Spiritual Gifts)[1]

Sam Storms

The single most oft-heard argument by cessationists in defense of their view that revelatory spiritual gifts such as prophecy and word of knowledge are no longer given by God to the church is that this would pose a threat to the finality and sufficiency of Scripture. How can we argue that the canon of Scripture is closed, asks the cessationist, if we believe that God is still "revealing" inspired truths to contemporary Christians?

This is a critically important question that we who are continuationists must answer. So, what reason is there to believe that NT prophecy does not result in "Scripture-quality" revelatory words? In other words, why do continuationists believe that the authority of NT prophecy is of a lesser order than that of OT prophecy?

Undoubtedly the most oft-heard objection of cessationists to the validity of prophecy today is their belief that any prophetic utterance that is decidedly from God must be infallible and

equal in authority with canonical Scripture. To embrace contemporary prophecy is therefore a fundamental denial of the
finality and sufficiency of canonical Scripture. Referring to the
NT gift of prophecy, Doug Wilson insists that "we must treat
such words as the Word of God, which means that we must treat
them as Scripture" (www.dougwils.com), August 11, 2011).
Why do I believe Wilson and like-minded cessationists are
wrong on this point? Here are ten reasons.

First, this view fails to reckon with what would undoubtedly
have been thousands of prophetic words circulating in
the first century, none of which are part of canonical
Scripture and thus none of which are binding on the conscience of Christians throughout history.

According to Acts 2, revelatory gifts like prophecy, together with revelatory dreams and visions, are said by Peter to be characteristic of the New Covenant during these
last days, spanning the time between the two comings of
Christ. In Acts 19 we read of disciples of John the Baptist who prophesied, yet Paul and Luke show no concern
for the need to preserve their words. In 1 Corinthians 14
Paul exhorts the church to desire spiritual gifts, especially
that we might prophesy. Assuming that the Corinthians,
and all other churches to which Paul ministered, obeyed
this command, there had to have been countless thousands of prophetic words forthcoming in the first century (prophecy is found in the churches in Jerusalem,
Antioch, Ephesus, Caesarea, Rome, Corinth, and Thessalonica; no doubt it was also present in Colossae, Philippi,
and other cities as well).

My question is this: If such words, each and every one
of them, were the very "Word of God" and thus equal
to Scripture in authority, *what happened to them*? Why
were the NT authors so lacking in concern for whether
or not other Christians heard them and obeyed them?
Why were they not preserved for subsequent generations
of the church? I'm *not* suggesting this *proves* that these
"revelatory gifts" operated at a lower level of authority,
but it certainly strikes me as odd that the NT would por-
tray the operation of the gift of prophecy in this manner
if in fact all such "words" were Scripture quality and essential to building the foundation for the universal body
of Christ.

In an unpublished paper Wayne Grudem similarly asks:

"Were thousands of 'prophets' actually speaking the very
words of God? Were God's people to be expected to
go around to the many hundreds or even thousands
of churches in the first century world and collect the
prophecies given week after week, and write them down,
and produce hundreds of volumes of 'words of the Lord'
which they were to obey as they obeyed Scripture? In fact,
we have no record of anything like this happening, nor
do we have any record anywhere in the New Testament
of churches recording or preserving these prophecies as
if they were 'words of the Lord.' Rather they preserve and
obey the writings and teachings of the apostles, not of the
prophets."

In his book *Strange Fire*, John MacArthur takes up the
cessationist argument in this regard. In one place he

asks: *"If the Spirit were still giving divine revelation, why wouldn't we collect and add those words to our Bibles?"* [emphasis mine] But this is a sword on which MacArthur himself (as well as Doug Wilson) must fall. After all, he himself believes that the Spirit was giving divine revelation to the men and women, young and old, on the Day of Pentecost (Acts 2:17-18). MacArthur believes that the Spirit was giving divine revelation to the four daughters of Philip, all of whom prophesied (Acts 21:8-9). MacArthur believes that the Spirit was giving divine revelation to the disciples of John the Baptist who prophesied (Acts 19:1-7). And MacArthur believes the Spirit was giving divine revelation to Christians in the churches in Rome (Rom. 12), Corinth (1 Cor. 12-14), Ephesus (Eph. 4:11ff.; 1 Tim. 1:18), and Thessalonica (1 Thess. 5:19-22), and undoubtedly in every other church throughout the ancient world. So why, may I ask, didn't Paul and Luke and John and others "collect and add those words" to canonical Scripture? Why is it that, aside from the two recorded prophecies of Agabus (Acts 11:27-30 and 21:10-12; have I overlooked any others?) we do not possess so much as a single, solitary syllable from all those alleged "Scripture-quality" and divinely inspired words?

If such prophetic words were, as MacArthur and Wilson contend, equal in authority to the Bible and thus ought to be included in and regarded as inerrant Scripture, where are they? Again, don't miss the point: typical cessationists such as MacArthur and Wilson believe that each time the Spirit imparted divine revelation, which in turn was communicated through a prophetic gift, in-errant, Scripture-quality words were spoken. If they believe this requires that such words be treated like Scripture and thus added to the Bible (and they do; see their statements above)those, then why wasn't this done in the first century when the gift of prophecy was, according to both men (and all other cessationists), still very much in operation? The simple fact is that cessationists like MacArthur and Wilson have created a concept of what NT prophecy entailed that simply does not correspond to how prophetic words were delivered and treated in the NT itself.

Second, a related point is found in Paul's exhortation to the Thessalonians that they not "quench the Spirit" by "despising prophecies" (1 Thess. 5:19-20). Rather, they are to "test everything," i.e., they are to weigh, judge, evaluate, or assess what purports to be a prophetic word and then "hold fast what is good" and "abstain from every form of evil" (vv. 21-22).

The Thessalonians held in high regard the Word of God, for Paul said of them, "when you received the word which you heard from us, you accepted it not as the word of men but as what it really is, the word of God, which is at work in you believers" (1 Thess. 2:13). If these Christians believed (as cessationists tell us they should have) that prophetic words in their church were equal to Scripture, they would have esteemed them highly and would never have "despised" them. If Paul had taught them (as cessationists tell us he did) that such "words" were revelation on a par with and possessing equal authority to the very Scripture that he is writing to communicate this concept (namely, the letter of 1 Thessalonians itself), would the Thessalonian Christians have been guilty of despising them?

Is it not more likely that these believers were tempted to "despise" prophetic utterances because they knew that such "words" were a mixture of divine revelation and fallible human interpretation and application and that, for whatever reason, people in their midst had in some way abused the gift or had used such words to manipulate others or promote themselves or had predicted some event(s) that had not come to pass?

If the prophetic utterances in Thessalonica were equal in authority to Scripture and altogether infallible, would not Paul have harshly rebuked the Thessalonians for *not* receiving them as such but for treating them as dispensable and unimportant? If such "words" were perfectly infallible revelation on a par with Scripture would he not have simply said, "Submit to them without hesitation and obey them" rather than "test" them to see what is in them that is good and what is in them that is bad?

Third, although I realize that cessationists have a different understanding of 1 Corinthians 14:29, I believe Paul is saying here much the same thing as he said in 1 Thessalonians 5:19-22. "Weigh" (*diakrino*) what is said by the prophets. That is to say, sift the word and identify what is of God and what is the human and thus fallible admixture. I find it difficult to believe that Paul would have commanded this sort of assessment if all prophetic words were by definition inerrant Scripture quality revelation from God.

Fourth, in 1 Corinthians 14:30-31 Paul writes: "If a revelation is made to another sitting there, let the first be silent. For you can all prophesy one by one, so that all may learn and all be encouraged." Paul appears to be indifferent toward the possibility that the first prophecy might be lost and never heard by the church.

Some object and say that the first prophetic word wouldn't necessarily be lost. The person could simply remain silent until the second had finished and then resume his speech. But as Wayne Grudem has pointed out, "if the first prophet was *expected* to resume speaking, why then would Paul command this *first* prophet to be silent at all? If the first prophet could retain his revelation and speak later, then so could the second prophet. And in that case it would make much more sense for the second prophet to wait, instead of rudely interrupting the first prophet and making him give his speech in two parts" (*The Gift of Prophecy in the New Testament and Today,* 63). Again, Paul's apparent lack of concern for the loss of such prophetic words seems incompatible with a belief that they were equal in authority with Scripture itself.

Fifth, yet another statement in 1 Corinthians 14 confirms this understanding of NT prophecy. In v. 36 Paul asks, "Or was it from you that the word of God came?" He doesn't say, "Did the word of God originate with (or "first go forth from") you," as some have suggested. Let's not forget that the "word of God" didn't originate with Paul either!

Rather, Paul's statement is designed to prevent them from making up guidelines for public worship, based on an alleged prophetic word, contrary to what he has just stated. His point is that a Scripture quality, authoritative "word of God" has not, in fact, been forthcoming from the Corinthian prophets. Paul does not deny that they have truly prophesied, but he denies that their "words" were equal in authority to his own. Such "words" were in fact of a lesser authority.

Sixth, related to the above is 1 Corinthians 14:37-38, where Paul writes: "If anyone thinks that he is a prophet or spiritual, he should acknowledge that the things I am writing to you are a command of the Lord. If anyone does not recognize this, he is not recognized." Paul is clearly claiming a divine authority for his words that he is just as obviously denying to the Corinthians. "According to Paul, the words of the prophets at Corinth were not and could not have been sufficiently authoritative to show Paul to be wrong" (Grudem, 68).

And yet Paul believed the prophecy at Corinth to be a good and helpful gift of God, for he immediately thereafter exhorts the Corinthians once again to "earnestly desire to prophesy" (v. 39)! Paul obviously believed that the spiritual gift of congregational prophecy that operated at

a lower level of authority than did the apostolic, canonical, expression of it was still extremely valuable to the
church.

Seventh, although I don't have space to provide an extensive
exegetical explanation of Acts 21, I believe we see in this
narrative a perfect example of how people (the disciples
at Tyre) could prophesy by the Spirit and yet not do so
infallibly or at a level equal to Scripture. Their misguided,
but sincere, *application* of this revelation was to tell Paul
("through the Spirit," v. 4) not to go to Jerusalem, counsel
which he directly disobeyed (cf. Acts 20:22).

Now, if Paul believed that NT prophetic "words" were always inerrant and equal in authority to Scripture, why
did he disobey this prophetic exhortation? Paul clearly
resisted their "word" and went to Jerusalem in spite of
the fact that following the word from Tyre and following
the word from Agabus and following the "urging" of all
concerned, including Luke, he was persuaded that they
had not spoken the infallible "word of God" to him (see
Acts 20:22-23).

Grudem correctly points out that "the expression
'through the Spirit' (in Greek, dia tou pneumatos) mod-
ifies the verb 'they were telling in the Greek text (it mod-
ifies the imperfect verb, elegon). That is why the verse is
translated, 'And through the Spirit they were telling Paul
not to go on to Jerusalem' . . . . So here is speech given
'through the Spirit' that Paul disobeys! This fits well with
a view of prophecy that includes revelation given by the

Holy Spirit and an interpretation and report of that revelation that is given in merely human words, words that
the Holy Spirit does not superintend or claim as his own,
words that can have a mixture of truth and error in them.
This is why the prophecies have to be tested, and this is
why Paul feels free to disobey in this case" (unpublished
paper).

Eighth, in conjunction with the previous point, I should also
mention that the prophetic warning of Agabus, though
correct in speaking of the persecution Paul would endure
should he go to Jerusalem, was wrong on two points: (a)
it was the Romans who bound Paul, not the Jews (Acts
21:33; 22:29); and (b) far from the Jews delivering Paul
into the hands of the Gentiles, he had to be forcibly rescued from them (Acts 21:31-36). Those who insist that
the NT gift is no less infallible than its OT counterpart
are faced with accounting for this mixture of truth and
error. To this point I have only heard that we continua-
tionsts are being "overly pedantic" or are guilty of "pre-
cisionism." Yet it appears that the strict standards applied
under the OT are now conveniently stretched in the NT
under the pressure of a passage that doesn't fit the cessationist theory. Might it not rather be that NT prophecy is
occasionally fallible, and therefore to be carefully judged
(1 Cor. 14:29; 1 Thess. 5:19-22)?

Some have objected to this reading and insist that Paul's
report in Acts 28:17 of what took place in Acts 21 is essentially the same as prophesied by Agabus. But Paul's

point in 28:17 is simply that he was transferred from Roman custody in Jerusalem into Roman custody in Caesarea. In other words, Acts 28:17 is his description of his transfer "out of" Jerusalem into the Roman judicial system at Caesarea (as found in Acts 23:12-35), and is *not* a description of the events associated with the mob scene in Acts 21:27-36. Agabus cannot so easily be let off the hook.

Ninth, yet another reason why I believe the cessationist is wrong on this point is the failure to recognize different ways or senses in which God might "reveal" something to us. In Philippians 3:15 he tells the church that "if in anything you think otherwise, God will *reveal* that also to you." And in Ephesians 1:17 Paul prays that a "spirit of wisdom and *revelation*" would be granted to believers. "Once more," notes Grudem, "it would not be possible to think that every time a believer gained new insight into his privileges as a Christian and reported it to a friend, the actual words of that speech would have been thought to be God's very words. It would be the *report* of something God had 'revealed' to the Christian, but the report would only come in merely human words" (Grudem, 65). We see two other similar uses of the verb or noun form of "reveal/revelation" in Matthew 11:27 and Romans 1:18.

The point is simply that not all "revelatory" activity of God comes to us as Scripture quality, divinely authoritative, canonical truth. Thus, as D. A. Carson points out, "when Paul presupposes in 1 Corinthians 14:30 that the gift of prophecy depends on a revelation, we are not limited to a form of authoritative revelation that threatens the finality of the canon. To argue in such a way is to confuse the terminology of Protestant systematic theology with the terminology of the Scripture writers" (*Showing the Spirit,* 163).

My tenth and final argument comes from an implication regarding Paul's permission that women can prophesy but his prohibition of them from teaching men or participating in the public evaluation of prophetic utterances.

Clearly women can prophesy (see Acts 2:17-18; 21:9; 1 Cor. 11:5). But if that is true, what does he mean in 1 Cor. 14:34 when he says, "Let the women keep silent in the church; for they are not permitted to speak"? The likely answer is that Paul is prohibiting women from participating in the passing of judgment upon or the public evaluation of the prophets (14:29). Evidently he believed that this entailed an exercise of authority restricted to men only (see 1 Tim. 2:12:15).

If one should ask why Paul would allow women to prophesy but not evaluate the prophecies of others, the answer is in the nature of prophecy itself. Prophecy, unlike teaching, does not entail the exercise of an authoritative position within the local church. The prophet was but an instrument through whom revelation is reported to the congregation. "Those who prophesied did not tell the church how to interpret and apply Scripture to life. They did not proclaim the doctrinal and ethical standards by which the church was guided, nor did they exercise governing authority in the church" (Grudem, 121-22).

But to publicly evaluate or criticize or judge prophetic utterances is another matter. In this activity one could hardly avoid explicit theological and ethical instruction of other believers. If we assume that in 1 Timothy 2 Paul prohibits women from teaching or exercising authority over men, it's understandable why he would allow women to prophesy in 1 Cor. 11:5 but forbid them from judging the prophetic utterances of others (especially men) in 14:34.

Answering a few Objections

In the book, **Are Miraculous Gifts for Today? Four Views** (Zondervan), I interacted at length with some objections to the contemporary validity of prophecy articulated by Richard Gaffin (whose view differs little, if at all, from that of MacArthur, Wilson, and other cessationsts).

Gaffin objects to the possibility of post-canonical revelation on the grounds that we would be "bound to attend and submit to" it no less than to Scripture. Aside from the fact that this wrongly presupposes that contemporary prophecy yields infallible, Scripture-quality words from God, the problem is one Gaffin himself must face. For were not the Thessalonian Christians, for example, "bound to attend and submit to" (lit., "hold fast"; 1 Thessalonians 5:21) the prophetic words they received, no less than to the Scripture in which this very instruction is found? Evidently Paul did not fear that their response to the spoken, prophetic word would undermine the ultimate authority or sufficiency of the written revelation (Scripture) that he was in process of sending them. The point is this: non-canonical revelation was not inconsistent with the authority of Scripture then, so why should it be now? This is especially true if contemporary prophecy does not necessarily yield infallible words of God.

Someone might ask, "But how should we in the twenty-first-century, in a closed-canonical world, respond to non-canonical revelation?" The answer is, "In the same way Christians responded to it in their first-century, open-canonical world, namely, by evaluating it in light of Scripture" (which was emerging, and therefore partial, for them, but is complete for us). Such revelation would carry for us today the same authority it carried then for them. Furthermore, we are in a much better position today than the early church, for we have the final form of the canon by which to evaluate claims to prophetic revelation. If they were capable of assessing prophetic revelation then (and Paul believed they were; witness his instruction in 1 Corinthians 14:29ff. and 1 Thessalonians 5:19-22 to do precisely that), how much more are we today! If anything, contemporary claims of prophetic revelation should be easier to evaluate and respond to than such claims in the first century.

Therefore, if non-canonical revelation was not a threat to the ultimate authority of Scripture in its emerging form, why would it be a threat to Scripture in the latter's final form? If first-century Christians were obligated to believe and obey Scripture in the open-canonical period, simultaneous with and in the presence of non-canonical prophetic revelation, why would non-canonical revelation in the closed-canonical period of church history pose any more of a threat?

Gaffin argues that contemporary prophecy cannot, in fact, be evaluated by Scripture because of its purported specificity. But this is no more a problem for us today than it would have been for Christians in the first century. Did not they evaluate prophetic revelation in spite of the latter's specificity and individuality? If they were obedient to Paul's instruction they certainly did (1 Corinthians 14:29; 1 Thessalonians 5:21-22). Why, then, can't we? And are we not, in fact, better equipped than they to do so insofar as we, unlike them, hold in hand the final form of canonical revelation whereby to make that assessment?

Gaffin also believes that to admit the possibility of revelation beyond Scripture unavoidably implies a certain *insufficiency* in Scripture that needs to be compensated for. But one must ask, "What is Scripture sufficient for?" Certainly it is sufficient to tell us every theological truth and ethical principle necessary to a life of godliness. Yet Gaffin himself concedes that God reveals himself to individuals in a variety of personal, highly intimate ways. But why would he need to, if Scripture is as exhaustively sufficient as Gaffin elsewhere insists? That God should find it important and helpful to reveal himself to his children in personal and intimate ways bears witness to the fact that the sufficiency of the Bible is not meant to suggest that we need no longer hear from our Heavenly Father or receive particular guidance in areas on which the Bible is silent.

Scripture never claims to supply us with all possible information necessary to make every conceivable decision. For example, Scripture may tell us to preach the gospel to all people, but it does not tell a new missionary in 2013 that God desires his service in Albania rather than Australia. The potential for

God speaking beyond Scripture, whether for guidance, exhortation, encouragement, or conviction of sin, poses no threat to the sufficiency that Scripture claims for itself.

Although much more could be said, I hope this brief exposition helps us in the understanding of this remarkable spiritual gift and also fuels our passion to obey Paul's injunction: "Earnestly desire to prophesy, and do not forbid speaking in tongues" (1 Cor. 14:39).

Endnotes

[1] Originally posted November 4, 2013.
http://www.samstorms.com/enjoying-god-blog/post/why-nt-prophecy-does-not-result-in–scripture-quality–revelatory-words–a-response-to-the-most-frequently-cited-cessationist-argument-against-the-contemporary-validity-of-spiritual-gifts

Did the Authentic Fire Cease in the First Century?

A Response to Tom Pennington's, "A Case for Cessationism"

Steven S. Alt

In the opening session of the Strange Fire conference, John MacArthur makes the statement: "The Charismatic Movement *as such* has made no contribution to biblical clarity, no contribution to interpretation, no contribution to sound doctrine."[1] Of course, the only reason he can say this is because everything the Charismatic Movement contributes to our understanding of Scripture he rejects as heresy. He does this because he is a cessationist. Cessationists deny the gifts of the Spirit are for today, but these are the very gifts the Pentecostal/Charismatic Movement has restored to the church.

Does the Charismatic Movement contribute anything good to the church. That question cannot be answered without answering whether cessationism is a biblical doctrine. Tom Pennington's presentation at the Strange Fire conference, "A Case for Cessationism," lays out the Scriptural support for cessationism. What follows is a description of the main points of Pennington's argument, followed by a reasoned, Scriptural response.[2]

Argument 1: The Unique Role of Miracles

Pennington first argues that the "primary purpose of miracles has always been to confirm the credentials of a divinely appointed messenger—to establish the credibility of one who speaks for God." He cites three periods of history of about 65-70 years during which, he claims, most of the miracles of the Bible took place: the time of Moses and Joshua, the time of Elijah and Elisha, and the time of Jesus and the apostles. He then goes on to demonstrate that in each of these cases the primary purpose of the miracles was to validate the messenger, and thus a heavy concentration of miracles was only needed in these rare times of rich revelation from God.

First, a clarification: Pennington is not denying that miracles and healings ever occur. His point is that the gifts of the Spirit as listed in 1 Corinthians 12:8-10 are no longer offered to the church. Charismatics, on the other hand, argue that all nine gifts in this list are just as valid today as they were when Paul wrote 1 Corinthians.

Pennington makes a sound case for miracles as validation of prophets who speak God's words. However, he seems to lump all the miracles performed in these distinct periods of history into this category when it seems that many of them do not serve that purpose. Responding to Pennington in his blog, Andrew Wilson points out that some of the miracles of Moses and Joshua, not to mention Jesus and the apostles, were not primarily to authenticate the prophet, but to serve another purpose.[3] The exodus (Exodus 7-14), the sun standing still for Joshua (Joshua 10:14), Hezekiah's healing (Isaiah 38), and the prophecies of Samuel, David, and all the writing prophets would all qualify, under Pennington's definition, as exercises of miraculous gifts, but they do not seem to serve the primary purpose of authenticating the prophet.

Two New Testament passages break down Pennington's argument. In John 14:12 Jesus says, "whoever believes in me will do the works I have been doing." This would presumably include those works that Pennington calls validation miracles. In Matthew 28:19 Jesus tells the disciples to teach "all nations" to "obey everything I have commanded you." In Matthew 10:8, Jesus taught them to heal the sick, raise the dead, cleanse lepers, and cast out demons. I can see no reason why the disciples would think that this teaching was not included in "everything I have commanded you." Even if they are not for validation, the same miracles that were used for validation seem to be available for all believers to perform.

Even if the primary purpose of every miracle was validation, it still would prove nothing for cessationism. That is because, authentication is not the only purpose of miracles, and it is not purpose of the charismatic gifts listed in 1 Corinthians 12:8-10. Pennington admits that validation is not the only purpose of miracles when he refers to it as "primary," not exclusive, and he even mentions times when Jesus healed out of compassion and not for validation. But he never mentions why these non-validation miracles should cease. Yet these are the very types of miracles that the charismatic tradition argues are continuing today.

Continuation gifts are not validation miracles. Validation miracles are only needed when God's messengers speak God's word before unbelievers. All the examples Pennington gives fit this category: Moses before Pharaoh, Elijah before the prophets of Baal, Jesus before Jews who did not believe, Peter before Jews whom he called to repentance. But continuation gifts do not function primarily for unbelievers, but for believers. The entire discussion of the gifts in 1 Corinthians 12-14 is in the context of ministry within the body of Christ during Christian gatherings. It is gifted ministry of believers to believers. There is no need for validation miracles among believers.

Pennington is guilty of a category error, arguing for the cessation of validation miracles, when the continuation miracles that charismatics believe in and practice are of a different type and serve a different purpose. If Pennington means to argue that the cessation of validation miracles also means the cessation of all other types of miracles, that would be a *non sequitur*. If God has ceased to perform validation miracles, it does not necessarily follow that He has ceased performing all miracles. That would have to be proven from Scripture, but there is no Scripture that asserts such a thing, which Pennington admits, as we shall see.

Argument 2: The End of the Gift of Apostleship

Pennington rehashes a common cessationist argument, claiming that all charismatics are cessationists to a degree because they admit that, "there are no more apostles like the Twelve or like Paul." He then argues that since this gift ceased without a clear statement in Scripture that it would, then other gifts might cease without a clear statement in Scripture indicating it.

Pennington misuses the term "cessationist" here to try to make continuationists appear inconsistent. Acknowledging that the unique ministry of the twelve apostles and Paul is over does not make charismatics "cessationist to a degree" any more than believing in the continuation of the ministry of pastor, teacher, and evangelist makes cessationists into part-time charismatics. As Pennington himself defined the term, cessationism refers to the belief that the nine gifts of the Spirit outlined in 1 Corinthians 12:8-10 have ceased functioning in the church. Other gifts listed in other parts of the Bible are not included under the term, so what one believes about the cessation of any gifts in Ephesians 4:11 has nothing to do with whether or not a person is cessationist.

That means this argument is ancillary to the main point, but because this is a point frequently made by cessationists, a few words of response are in order. Pennington would likely argue that even though the apostolic gift does not fit under the cessationist label, the point is that if this gift ceases, why not others, too? And since this gift involves people who are responsible for a great many of the miracles found in the New Testament, their cessation would suggest a major decrease in the gifts of the Spirit would have occurred when the apostles died.

Pennington has already argued that the miracles of the apostles should be categorized as validation gifts. So by his own definition, apostolic miracles do not fit the category of gifts of the Spirit in 1 Corinthians 12:8-10. So the problem of category error arises again. The gifts of the Spirit are distributed not only to apostles, but to all believers. Paul said, "when you come together, each of you has a hymn, or a word of instruction, a revelation, a tongue or an interpretation" (1 Cor 14:26). These gifts have no necessary connection to the apostolic ministry, so even if the gift of apostleship ended with the death of the Twelve (which it did not),[4] it does not affect the continuation of these gifts.

But the bigger issue Pennington raises concerns the lack of a statement in the New Testament that a gift given to the church will cease. If this is true concerning the apostles of Ephesians 4:11, argues Pennington, then it may also be true concerning the gifts of 1 Corinthians 12:8-10. This argument is important to cessationists because it is well known that their doctrine has no clear statement in Scripture to support it. Unfortunately for Pennington, this argument does not work, because in 1 Corinthians 15:8 Paul explicitly states that the last resurrection appearance of Jesus was made to Paul. This plainly states that the unique ministry of the twelve apostles and Paul would end with their deaths. Wilson shows the significance of this for cessationists:

> The resurrection appearances of Christ are explicitly said to have ended with Paul (1 Cor 15:8),whereas there is no such statement concerning the miraculous gifts, despite the obvious relevance this would have for Christian communities within a few years of the epistles. There is a huge gulf between saying "eyewitnesses of Christ have ceased, because the NT says so" and "all miraculous gifts have ceased, despite the fact that the NT doesn't say so".[5]

Pennington might argue that 1 Corinthians 15:8 does not qualify as a plain statement, but even without this verse, Pennington's argument does not work because the need to tell the church that the eyewitness apostolic ministry will cease does not stand on the same ground as the need to tell the church that the gifts of the Spirit will cease. As Wilson noted, within a few years of the writing of the epistles, it would have been crucial for the church to know that the gifts of the Spirit would cease - so important, in fact, that it would be highly unusual for the New Testament not to mention it. But the church already knew that the special role of the twelve apostles would be temporary on the simple basis that it required that they be eyewitnesses of the resurrection. It was so obvious, in fact, that it would be highly unusual for the New Testament to mention it. To make the inference Pennington does from this alleged silence in the New Testament amounts to special pleading.

Argument 3: The Foundational Nature of the New Testament Apostles and Prophets

Ephesians 2:20 says the apostles and prophets were the foundation of the church, and once the foundation is laid, they are no longer needed. Pennington concludes: "we should not expect any more apostles, prophets, or revelation."

Pennington's argument is dependent upon the supposition that all apostles and prophets serve a foundational role in the church. But Romans 12:6 and especially 1 Corinthians 12-14 describe a role of prophecy in the church that is not foundational. The apostles and prophets of Ephesians 2:20 have unquestionable authority, so much so that their writings were included in the canon. Peter O'Brien says the prophets of Ephesians 2:20 are unique in that they "are linked with apostles and enjoy a role with them not found elsewhere in the Pauline letters."[6] That means the prophets of 1 Corinthians 12-14 are not foundational and have less authority than those of Ephesians 2:20

Frank Thielmann says the apostles and prophets of Ephesians 2:20 form a single foundation "because they first proclaimed the gospel to the gentiles."[7] The prophets referred to in 1 Corinthians 12-14 were not involved in the initial outreach to the Gentiles, further proving their inferior status. The words of the Corinthian prophets are to be judged by previous revelation (1 Cor 14:29), that is, they are judged according to the teachings of the apostles and prophets of Ephesians 2:20, but not vice-versa. Since not all prophets are foundational, we should still expect to see prophets.

Argument 4: The Nature of the Miraculous Gifts

If the gifts of the Spirit operating among charismatics today, especially tongues, prophecy, and healing, are the same as those described in 1 Corinthians, then they should be very similar to the manifestations found in the New Testament. But Pennington argues this is not the case: "The charismatic gifts claimed today bear almost no resemblance to their New Testament counterparts."

Pennington argues from Acts that tongues are always a known human language, but most tongues today are a private prayer language. However, In 1 Corinthians 12-14 Paul's argument about tongues is based on the fact that the hearers do not understand what is being said. This is noticeably different from Acts 2, where everyone understands at least one of the languages being spoken. Pennington seems to be aware that this argument is greatly weakened when 1 Corinthians is considered, so he claims that Luke considered 1 Corinthians and still defined tongues speech as known languages. But there is no evidence in Acts that Luke is interpreting Paul when he refers to tongues speech.

Pennington argues for New Testament prophecy being the same as it was in the Old Testament. This has been ably refuted by Wayne Grudem, who shows that much New Testament prophecy is of a lower level of authority than Old Testament prophecy.[8] For example, Old Testament prophets were the highest spiritual authority in Israel, but in the New Testament they are lower than apostles (1 Cor 12:28). Also, the inferiority of the prophets of 1 Corinthians to those of Ephesians 2:20, mentioned above, demonstrates that at least these prophets were inferior to Old Testament prophets.

Pennington is right when he says much that is called prophecy in the Charismatic Movement has little or nothing to do with biblical prophecy, but it is a mistake to require modern prophecy to be as authoritative as biblical prophecy. No man alive today has the kind of authority that Moses and Peter and Paul had, and the prophecies of such people today reflect that lesser authority. That does not justify the myriad false prophecies being announced seemingly on a daily basis or the failure of the church to rein them in. Charismatics should do a much better job of policing the exercise of this gift. But that does not mean there is no true prophecy within the movement, or that the true prophecies bear no resemblance to biblical prophecy.

Many healings claimed in the Charismatic Movement are exaggerated and unverified, so it is difficult to assess their quality. Pennington seems comfortable saying that charismatic healings are the "antithesis" of healings in the New Testament. But many charismatics can testify from personal experience of instantaneous, permanent healing, and Craig Keener's book, *Miracles*, is a scholarly account of verified miracles occurring all over the world. No discussion of the quality of charismatic healings is complete without interaction with this book.

Tongues, healings, and prophecy are not closely supervised in the Charismatic Movement. But cessationists make a recurring error when they measure *all* charismatic gifts by the way they are used by well known television preachers. Most of the genuine miracles happening today are not occurring on television, but in huts and villages all over the world. That is why Keener travelled the world to gather the data for his book. If Pennington and other cessationists at the Strange Fire conference had done the same, they might have a different opinion of the Charismatic Movement.

Argument 5: The Testimony of Church History

This is a three-fold argument: a) The gifts in the church waned during Paul's own lifetime as seen in his letters, b) the gifts waned during the New Testament period as evidenced in Hebrews 2:3-4, and c) the gifts ceased after the apostolic period as attested by church leaders throughout history.

The waning of the gifts in Paul's letters

Pennington makes a bold statement when he claims the gifts actually declined during Paul's own lifetime. He claims the later epistles have nothing to say about tongues, which are discussed in the earlier documents. For example, Paul wrote nine letters after writing to the Corinthians, but never mentions tongues in any of them.

This is probably Pennington's weakest argument. He acknowledges that speaking in tongues is only discussed in Acts and 1 Corinthians. The lack of discussion of tongues in later epistles does not represent a waning of the gift any more than its lack of mention in the previous epistles signifies an increase of the gift.

There is a reason tongues are rarely mentioned in the epistles. Epistles are not systematic theology nooks. Everything discussed in an epistle represents an issue or controversy that the author needs to address. The contents of any epistle is determined not by the normal activities taking place in the church, such as tongues speech, healings, and prophecy, but by abnormal or controversial activities that demand the apostle's attention or require his correction, such as an abuse of tongues or the acceptance of circumcision.

The only reason Paul ever mentions tongues at all is because there was a controversy over them at Corinth. The reason Paul does not mention tongues in his later epistles is because there is no controversy, not because there is no tongues speech. If not for the controversy in Corinth, cessationists would be able to deny that Paul even believed in speaking in tongues.

It is also noteworthy that Pennington restricts his discussion to evidence that he can use to support his thesis. Why only refer to epistles? The last canonical book written was probably Revelation. That book is more full of charismatic occurrences than any other book of the New Testament. John sees visions, is visited by angels, receives prophecies, witnesses miracles, and even meets Jesus himself, not to mention the (out-of-body?) experience of making a trip to heaven. Speaking in tongues is only one of many charismatic manifestations of the Holy Spirit. There is no historical evidence in the New Testament to support the theory that the gifts waned during the apostolic period.

The waning of the gifts in Hebrews 2:3-4

The argument from Hebrews 2:3-4 is probably Pennington's strongest argument because at least there is serious exegesis taking place in defense of his thesis. Of this text he states: "The writer of Hebrews is putting himself in a third generation: 'Us.' And he said of the 2nd generation, the Apostles, 'God also testifying with *them*', not with us, 'by signs, wonders, and gifts of the spirit.' Already, before AD 70, the writer of Hebrews is saying, 'That was then and this is now. That's something the Lord and the Apostles did and we witnessed.'"

In response, let us look at verses 3b-4 in full.

> This salvation, which was first announced by the Lord, was confirmed to us by those who heard him. God also testified to it by signs, wonders, and various miracles, and by the gifts of the Holy Spirit distributed according to his will.

This passage describes two categories of supernatural activity and also two categories of people. In the first category of gifts are the "signs, wonders, and various miracles," and in the second are the "gifts of the Holy Spirit."[9] The first category of people is the apostles, whom Pennington calls the 2nd generation, who were eyewitnesses to the resurrection and proclaimed the message to the second category of people, the "3rd generation": the believers who witnessed the apostolic signs and subsequently received the gospel. Pennington argues that only the 2nd generation operated in the validation gifts of signs and wonders, proving that they had ceased by the time of the third generation.

But here the category error arises again. In response to Pennington's first argument I differentiated between validation gifts and gifts of the Spirit. Arguing for the cessation of the former to prove that the latter have ceased represents a category error. Even if it is granted that the gifts that validate the proclamation of the message ceased, that does not mean the gifts of the Spirit have ceased. To prove his point, Pennington has to prove that the second category of signs, the gifts of the Spirit, have ceased, but he seems to lump the gifts of the Spirit with validation gifts as if they are the same thing, but they are not.

Donald Guthrie says, "the *gifts of the Holy Spirit* are in a rather different category" from the signs and wonders, though they are "closely allied." Bruce identifies these "gifts of the Holy Spirit" with the gifts mentioned in Galatians 3:5.[10] There Paul refers to God who, "works miracles among you" in the present tense. Paul is not in Galatia at the time, so these are not miracles Paul worked. O'Brien concurs with Bruce, saying, these gifts are "probably to be understood of the spiritual gifts of the Holy Spirit, which God has graciously distributed to his people."[11] So these gifts are given not just to the apostles, but to "his people."

That means the signs, wonders, and miracles of Hebrews 2:4a were given to the apostles, Pennington's 2nd generation, but the gifts of the Holy Spirit were given to the rest of the people, Pennington's 3rd generation, showing them to be a different type of gift than the apostolic validation gifts.

Pennington is not the first to argue cessationism from Hebrews 2:4. Daniel Wallace gives one of the best exegetical presentations of this argument. Using Galatians 3:5 as a contrast, he says Hebrews 2:4 makes no mention of a current manifestation of these "sign gifts, " which is inexplicable unless they were no longer occurring: "The author of Hebrews, who is so articulate a defender of his position, lost a perfect opportunity to remind his audience of the reality of their salvation by not mentioning the current manifestation of the sign gifts."[12]

It is unlikely that the original readers would have understood Hebrews 2:3-4 to mean that the gifts had ceased. This conclusion only seems to be drawn by cessationist interpreters. That the initial presentation of the gospel was attended by signs and wonders does not infer that such miracles are no longer happening any more than the mention of persecution as occurring in the past in Hebrews 10:32-34 infers that they were no longer suffering persecution. In fact, we know they were (Heb 12:4). Just because the author refers to what was "then" does not mean "now" is nay different. It only means his argument is dependent upon what happened "then," not on what is happening "now."

Furthermore, what is happening "now" is that the gifts are still present. Wallace fails to notice the difference between the "sign gifts" and the distributed gifts of the Spirit. He also does not interact with the argument of the author, who is using an *a fortiori* argument to compare the initiation of the Mosaic covenant to the initial proclamation of the gospel message. For this reason the author necessarily restricted his comments to the supernatural phenomena that occurred when the gospel was first preached to him and his audience. That is why the emphasis is on the distribution of the gifts and not on the gifts themselves. But the distribution implies the ongoing experience of the gifts. Of these gifts, William Lane comments: "It is presumably the perpetuation of the charismata in the life of the community (cf. 6:4-5) that provides indisputable evidence of God's seal upon the word received by the congregation."[13]

This is not a "that was then, this is now" situation. It is more like, "that was then and it still is now." There is no reason to derive an implication that gifts of the Spirit were no longer occurring in the churches to whom Hebrews was written.

The waning of the gifts in church history

Pennington goes on to cite numerous cessationists throughout history to demonstrate that the gifts ceased after the apostolic age. Then he cites Sinclair Ferguson, who gives a classic historical argument against the continuation of the gifts: "Continuationism provides no consistent theological explanation for the disappearance of gifts in church history."

Wilson exposes the attendant danger of cessationists using this argument: "this sort of argument - that, since something gradually disappeared from the church over the course of the first two or three centuries, it must therefore be invalid - should strike any five *sola* Protestant as providing several hostages to fortune."[14]

Moreover, to cite cessationist authors throughout history in order to prove cessationism begs the question and hardly deserves a response. But I will at least note that the gifts did not cease at the end of the apostolic period. One of the oldest documents of the Christian church, the *Didache*, was written after the death of the apostles, but included in it are instructions for how to treat travelling apostles and prophets. This demonstrates that a dew decades after the apostles died the church was not cessationist. They believed the apostolic and prophetic ministries were still being carried out. Also, in the second century a group called the Montanists arose, and prophecy was one of their specialties. They were declared a heretical group, but not because the church believed prophecy had ceased. Throughout the history of the church there have been groups who believed in and practiced gifts of the Spirit.[15] The practice of these gifts was pushed to the fringe by the established church, but they could still be seen in every era of the church's existence.

But there is no doubt that the gifts waned. How can this be explained? Actually, several factors contributed to it. The structure of the church changed very soon after the apostolic age ended. Bishops were added to control orthodoxy in each city, and the clergy was separated from the laity. Suddenly, some 98% of the church was no longer expected to contribute to the church service, virtually eliminating the opportunity to exercise spiritual gifts where they are most likely to occur. There was also a stigma attached to the gifts because they were associated with heretical groups like the Montanists. Christian apologists found it easier to separate the church from the gifts than to separate the gifts from the heretics. Also, the Roman Catholic church, evolving into an authoritarian regime, had no room for people speaking with equal or greater authority than the pope.

These factors combine to make it easy to understand how the gifts waned. Nevertheless, they did not die out. In spite of these many obstacles, Spiritual gifts and miracles continued to occur throughout the church age, as Hyatt demonstrates.[16]

But one need only look at the cessationist churches in the world today to see how the gifts can cease. They cease wherever people believe they have ceased. And they believe this despite being surrounded by untold millions of people who claim to speak in tongues and to have witnessed healings. It is really not difficult to explain why the gifts waned. What we need to ask is how we can restore them.

Argument 6: *The Sufficiency of Scripture*

The cessationist view of Scripture is briefly illustrated by the following statements made by Pennington: "The Spirit speaks only in and through the inspired Word...The man of God needs no additional revelation from God. He has it all right here (pointing to the Bible)...The result of a completed canon is an all-sufficient Scripture...We don't have to wonder if that message in our mind is from God or not." In giving advice to his listeners, he also said, "Don't ever talk about feeling something from God."

The question we need to ask is this: does Scripture actually teach what cessationists say about it? The only verse quoted by Pennington in defense of his view of Scripture was 2 Timothy 3:16, which teaches the inspiration of Scripture, and states that it makes the servant of God "thoroughly equipped for every good work." after citing this verse, Pennington said, "there's nothing left." Actually there was something left: the New Testament. When Paul wrote 2 Timothy 3:16 the New Testament canon had not yet been established. When Paul refers to "Scripture" in this verse, he is referring exclusively to the Hebrew Scriptures. All Scripture is inspired, and that also applies to the New Testament, and it does equip believers for every good work, but the concept, "there's nothing left" is absent from this verse. In fact, nowhere in Scripture is it ever taught that Scripture is the only way God communicates with man. What does the Bible reveal about the way God speaks to man?

Of course, Scripture gives abundant testimony to God speaking directly to men, from Abraham to Moses to David and the prophets, God has spoken to men directly or through angels to communicate his will. In the New Testament, some of the most important revelations ever given to man came independent of the Scriptures. For example, God revealed his plan for the Incarnation to Mary and Joseph through an angelic visitation, and He revealed His will to take the gospel to the Gentiles to Peter through a vision. God called Paul to minister to the Gentiles through a prophet (Acts 9:15), sent him on a trip to Jerusalem "in response to a revelation" (Gal 2:2), redirected his ministry through a vision (Acts 16:7-10), and gave him a personal word of encouragement through a vision during one of the lowest points of his life (Acts 18:9-10). Paul also said he received revelation from God that he was not permitted to tell anyone (2 Cor 12:4). This revelation was not given to help complete the canon. It was just between him and God.

Cessationists often respond by saying God's communication was necessary until the canon was closed. Once the canon closed, no more direct communication from God to man exists, except through Scripture. This argument is unconvincing. First, it must be proved that the apostolic community believed that the canon was still open. If they did not, then they would have been cessationists, too.

Second, the closing of the canon is not sufficient for the needs that were met by God's personal communication with his people. Where in Scripture would Paul have learned that he should go to Macedonia or to Jerusalem? If God has a specific will for our lives, why would he not reveal that to us? Why would he impose a rule forbidding him from communicating to the objects of his love except through the written words of the Bible? No human relationship of any depth could survive with such a restriction. There is no reasonable explanation why God would so restrict himself.

The doctrine of the cessationists denies that God ever speaks personally to any of his children. The reason he did to Peter, Paul, and Mary was because he was unfolding his salvation plan and all these communications were going to be included in the canon of Scripture. In other words, every time in the Bible God speaks to man, it is an exception to the rule that God does not speak to man. The problem is, there are dozens and dozens of examples of God speaking to man, but there is not a single place in Scripture that states this so-called rule. It is putting it mildly to say the exceptions outweigh the rule. It is indeed ironic that the bibliocentric doctrine that God only speaks to man objectively through Scripture itself an unbiblical doctrine.

The completed Scriptures give us general teachings that equip every believer and they are sufficient for that. But they do not give any personal instructions on matters of individual import. God loves each one of us, and he is not content only speaking to us objectively and collectively. He wants us to feel something from him. Surely Paul felt something from God when by the Spirit of sonship he cried out, "Abba, Father" (Rom 8:15), and when he groaned inwardly, waiting for his adoption (v. 23). These are evidences of a personal relationship.

When Peter confessed that Jesus was messiah and son of God, Jesus pronounced him blessed for one reason: because the revelation he received did not come from man but from the Father. This is what Jesus declared to be the foundation of the church (Matthew 16:16-18). In other words, Peter is the pattern of all believers after him. If the church of Jesus Christ is founded upon a confession that comes from a revelation given independent of Scripture, we should be very cautious about declaring such a thing unbiblical.

Conclusion

When the Pentecostal/ Charismatic Movement began in 1906, one of its major contributions to the church was a restoration of the gifts of the Spirit. Over 500 million souls have been saved through Pentecostal/charismatic missions in just the last 100 years. If Satan is behind this movement, then his kingdom is about to fall, because he is divided against himself. My prayer is that the church will not be so divided over this issue or any other, but will come together in open, honest dialogue, respecting each other, and learning from each other. This article was written in the hopes of moving in that direction.

Endnotes

[1] John MacArthur, "Strange Fire Session 1, Strange Fire Conference (Southern California: October 16-18) http://www.gty.org/resources/sermons /TM13-1/strange-fire-john-macarthur. For a written summary of the session, see Mike Riccardi, "Strange Fire-Session 1-John MacArthur," October 16, 2013. http://thecripplegate.com/strange-fire-session-one-john-macarthur/.

[2] References to Pennington's session will be taken from Mike Riccardi, Strange Fire-A Case for Cessationism-Tom Pennington, on line transcription of Tom Pennington, "A Case for Cessationism," session 6, Strange Fire Conference (Southern California: October 16-18), http://thecripplegate.com/strange-fire-a-case-for-cessationism-tom-pennington/. For the video of Pennington's session, see http://www.youtube.com/watch?v=A3Gb9ApstX4. For links to all the sessions at the conference, see http://www.tmstrangefire.org/.

[3] Andrew Wilson, "Cessationism and Strange Fire," on line blog page, Oct 18, 2013. http://thinktheology.co.uk/blog/article/cessationism_and_strange_fire. Last accessed Oct 29, 2013.

[4] It is beyond the scope of this article to prove this point, but the *Didache*, an early 2nd century document, gives instructions on how to treat apostles and prophets, proving that these gifts continued in the early church after the death of the Twelve.

[5] Andrew Wilson, "Cessationism and Strange Fire," on line blog page, Oct 18, 2013. http://thinktheology.co.uk/blog/article/cessationism_and_strange_fire. Last accessed Oct 29, 2013.

[6] Peter T. O'Brien, *The Letter to the Ephesians* (Pillar New Testament Commentary; Grand Rapids: Eerdmans, 1999), 216.

[7] Frank Theilman, *Ephesians* (Baker Exegetical Commentary on the New Testament; Grand Rapids: Baker, 2010), 180.

[8] Wayne Grudem, *The Gift of Prophecy in 1 Corinthians* (Washington D.C.: University Press of America, 1982), 82-105, cited in O'Brien, *Ephesians*, 214-15.

[9] Donald Guthrie, *Hebrews* (Tyndale New Testament Commentaries; Leicester: IVP; Grand Rapids: Eerdmans, 1983, reprint, 1999), 83, italics in original.

[10] F.F. Bruce, *The Epistle to the Hebrews* (New International Commentary on the New Testament; rev. ed.; Grand Rapids: Eerdmans, 1990), 69.

[11] Peter T. O'Brien, *The Letter to the Hebrews* (Pillar New Testament Commentary; Grand Rapids: Eerdmans, 2010), 90.

[12] Daniel B. Wallace, "Hebrews 2:3-4 and the Sign Gifts," Bible.org., June 30, 2004. https://bible.org/article/hebrews-23-4-and-sign-gifts. Last accessed November 13, 2013.

[13] William Lane *Hebrews 1-8* (Word Biblical Commentary; Nashville: Nelson, 1991), 40.

[14] Wilson, *Cessationism and Strange Fire.*

[15] Eddie Hyatt briefly traces the practice of the gifts through history in *2,000 Years of Charismatic Christianity: A 21st Century Look at Church history from A Pentecostal/Charismatic Perspective* (Dallas: Hyatt International Ministries: 1998).

[16]Hyatt, *2,000 Years.*

A Missions Perspective on Charismatics and Cessationists

David Shibley[1]

I t has been my privilege to witness the beauty of the diversity of the Church across decades and across continents. One year I was humbled to receive the ordinance of the Lord's Supper with fellow believers on five continents. Interacting with thousands of conservative evangelicals, Pentecostals, and charismatics in over sixty nations over the last thirty years, I can testify that the global Pentecostal and charismatic expressions of the Church are anything but monolithic. Charismatic Anglicans in many nations are, in fact, the main defenders of evangelical doctrine. Mission outreaches by classical Pentecostal denominations have accounted for much of the advance of the gospel in our lifetime. Independent charismatic churches can be found in venues ranging from brush arbors and storefronts to imposing *avant garde* buildings at the hubs of many cities' commerce.

To make broad brush denunciations of all Pentecostal and charismatic expressions of the Church is unwise because the movement is simply too diverse and too large to pigeonhole. Such unqualified castigations invite shoddy research and incomplete analysis. Further, the indictors themselves run the risk of employing the very practices of hermeneutics they would typically disdain: contextualization can easily surrender to proof texting and serious exegesis is sometimes dismissed for weak, even embarrassing eisegesis.

Just as Jesus taught in Matthew 13, there are both wheat and tares within the Pentecostal / charismatic movement. I saw this vividly in conversing with a respected mission leader from Nigeria during the Third Lausanne Congress on World Evangelization at Cape Town in 2010. This man described himself as a charismatic believer. He had suffered much for the gospel. He served as president of an indigenous missionary sending agency that has sent hundreds of Nigerians to many parts of the world to plant churches. As we discussed the state of the Church in Nigeria, this charismatic Christian lamented the negative impact the prosperity message has had on the missions impulse among Nigerians. He told me that, in his opinion, the way the prosperity message had been preached and the way it had been received and perceived by many Nigerians had blunted missions zeal and the call to sacrifice for Christ. Remember, this critique was coming from a charismatic who said he frequently prays and worships God employing a private prayer language.

I honor this brother and his desire to simply be a biblical Christian who lives under Christ's lordship and seeks to obey His commission. Some charismatics would do well to stop pacifying some hyper-prosperity proponents who equate gain with godliness (which Paul explicitly condemns). Instead of teaching that faith invariably produces wealth, let's teach God's Word: "Did not God choose the poor of this world to be rich in faith . . .?" (James 2:5, NASB).

As a charismatic evangelical (the adjective further describes the noun), it is, in fact, my belief in the inerrancy of Scripture that prevents me from considering cessationism as viable.

When it comes to a rationale for cessationism, Bible scholars who otherwise are conservative can sound quite liberal. After all, the essence of liberal biblical interpretation is to either downplay or disregard the obvious intent of Scripture. This is what cessationism does.

I readily acknowledge the right of cessationists to believe as they do. At the same time, they have thrown down the gauntlet on this issue and their accusations beg a response. Most cessationists will always consider both charismatic doctrine and experience somehow "sub-biblical." But it is cessationists who have constructed a convoluted hermeneutic. In seminary I was often reminded that we show honor to the Scriptures by careful exegesis. Cessationism simply fails to do this.

Whether some like it or not, the enemies of the gospel lump all Bible believers together. As never before, the energies of all who trust solely in the finished work of Christ on the cross are needed to respond redemptively to a rapidly darkening culture. What a serious accounting awaits us all if we cannot work together to get the gospel to every person and make disciples of all the nations.

Endnotes

[1]David Shibley founded Global Advance in 1990 to help train and resource indigenous leaders in the Majority World to become catalysts for the discipling of their nations. The author of over twenty books, he is a graduate of John Brown University and Southwestern Baptist Theological Seminary. He also received an honorary doctorate from Oral Roberts University.